FURTHER

ASPECTS

OF

BELFORD

A HISTORY OF WAYS OF LIFE, PEOPLE AND BUILDINGS IN BELFORD

Written and compiled by members of the
Belford & District Local History Society

Edited by Jane Bowen

First published in Great Britain 2011 by Belford Bowen Publishing, Belford, NE70 7DA

Printed by Martins the Printers, Berwick-upon-Tweed.

ISBN: 978-0-9569909-1-4

Designed by Janet Ward

> *Front Cover*: Early postcard of the Blue Bell Hotel, Belford reproduced by permission of Berwick-upon-Tweed Record Office.
> Early postcard of St. Mary's Parish Church, Belford.
> Detail of the Market Cross, Belford, from an early postcard.
> *Back Cover*: Belford Hall from Squire's Pond.

CONTENTS

INTRODUCTION

Further Aspects of Belford is the outcome of three further years of research by members of the Belford and District Local History Project Group. We have been encouraged by the enthusiasm with which our first volume was received and the willingness of Belfordians, past and present, to contribute their recollections and mementoes to our records. Without their help, and that of other friends of Belford, this book could not have been written. Hopefully their help has been appropriately acknowledged in the individual chapters, but should anyone have been inadvertently omitted, on behalf of the group I now offer both our apologies and our grateful thanks. The annual village summer History Exhibition, also, has provided a good opportunity to present aspects of our work, and to benefit from the resultant feedback.

During the time we have been working on the book, a number of documents relating to Belford in the eighteenth and early nineteenth century have been sold at auction. That we have been able to access many of these is due both to the generosity of individual members of the History Society, and to that of other purchasers, at home and abroad, who have passed on documents or copies of documents to us. Thanks are also due to the *Community Foundation*, and in particular its *David & Susan Ratliff Fund*, for assisting us with publication.

As editor, it has been my privilege to pull together the different chapters into the book. One of the fascinations of the task has been to see how information and names, apparently the preserve of one subject, suddenly pop up again in another:

- the importance of Waren as a harbour;
- the working of the postal service;
- the quarries supplying stone for different building projects; and
- pupils of the National School becoming the soldiers of the First World War.

Often one thinks of history as a series of parallel lines, each reflecting a particular theme such as education, transport, war etc. The reality, as became clear in the making of this book, is that it is much more a mesh of interconnecting strands.

We hope you enjoy reading our book, that it enriches your appreciation of Belford and its surroundings, and that every so often you will remember those whose lives we have recorded, and possibly sense their presence in some of their old haunts.

Jane Bowen

NOTES ON CURRENCY AND WEIGHTS

In weights there were:

- 16 ounces (oz) to 1 pound (lb);
- 1 ounce is approximately 25 grams;
- 2.2 pounds, 1 kilogram;
- 112 pounds is 1 hundredweight (cwt).

In pre-decimal coinage, there were:

- 12 pennies (d) to the shilling;
- 20 shillings (s) to the pound (£).

Throughout the book, payments and prices are given in the pre-decimal currency in which they were levied, although thcy need to be taken in the context of wages earned and prices paid. The following chart of approximate wages and prices may help provide this context.

	1750	1850
Cost of 1lb beef	3d	5½d
Cost of 1lb tallow candles	6½d	5½d
Cost of 1lb oatmeal	1d	1¾d
Farm Labourer's daily wage	10½d	1s 6d
Craft Labourer's daily wage	1s 6d	3s 8d

OF ROADS AND POSTS AND COACHES
Belford's role as a Post Town 1573 to 1851
by Jane Bowen

As you enter Belford, you are greeted by the sign which describes the village as a *Historic Coaching Town.* That it was so, is due to its particular location on the Great North Road, for until 1983 the A1 ran directly through the centre of Belford, a route which had been used to link London with Edinburgh since at least the early middle ages. In those days, since the majority of the population did not move far from home, the main users of the road were merchants and the Kings' messengers, carrying the dispatches of royal officials to important people and places along the route, and to the Scottish Court at Edinburgh. To facilitate their work, in 1481, Edward IV established a system of horse relays at post stations approximately 20 miles apart - the distance it was calculated a strong horse could travel at speed before it would need to be exchanged. Although not twenty miles distant from either Alnwick or Berwick, Belford was well placed to become such a staging post. Having spent the night at Alnwick, Margaret Tudor, the future wife of James IV of Scotland, is recorded as stopping to eat in Belford on her journey north in 1503:

> *Syr Thomas D'Arcy, Capittyne of the said Barrwyk, had maid rady hyr*
> *dynner at the said place very well and honestly.*

It is a reasonable assumption that by then the town was already regarded as a post station.

Early Records

In Queen Elizabeth I's reign, the situation becomes clearer. In 1573, Belford is listed as the 26th of the 27 stages between London and Berwick-upon-Tweed. The following year new regulations were issued. At each stage the Postmaster was to have at least three horses constantly ready for hire. When he heard the sound of the rider's post horn, indicating that the mail bag was about to arrive, he was to prepare his own post-boy to continue the journey, so that the mail was delayed no more than 15 minutes before continuing its journey. This at least was the theory. In 1582, however, Robert Gascoigne complained to the Queen's Secretary, Francis Walsingham, about delays in the post from Berwick. A letter sent by the Warden of the East March (the eastern section of the Border), Sir Henry Wodrington, at 5.00p.m. on August 25th, was not received at Belford until midnight, and did not reach Alnwick until 10.00a.m. the following morning. It is not clear from the letter, however whether the delays were due to the inefficiencies of the postmasters or the dreadful state of the roads. The complaint resulted in a new regulation requiring postmasters to attach a label to the mail packet, which each postmaster would sign, recording the day and time he received the packet. He would also maintain a mail book recording the same data. It also reiterated that postmasters should keep two or three good horses in their stables (so time was not lost bringing them in from the field), and stated the expectation that the post-boys would maintain an average speed of six miles an hour. To judge by a marginal note on the order, however, the reality was known to be very different:

> *Few or none have any horses in their stable, but all at grass, and very many ill horses.*

Perhaps this was the situation in Belford, for in 1589, charges *over negligence with the post* were preferred, referring to delays of seven hours between Berwick and Belford and ten between Belford and Alnwick. This may be a recurrence of an old problem, but as the times are the same as in the 1582 letter, the case may refer to that complaint and be an indication that justice was as slow as the mail!

Under the Stuarts, Belford emerges a little further from the shadows, as does the way the system worked. In 1609, the carrying of post on the designated Post Roads, became a Royal monopoly, and in 1657 this was extended to include the hiring of horses, so that only the designated postmaster was permitted to do this. In 1635 the hire of horses for post-boys and other travellers was fixed at 2½d. a mile, to be paid in advance. This was increased to 3d. a mile in 1657, with a further stipulation that a guide for the post-boy should be provided at a cost of 4d. a mile. Meanwhile it was no longer only royal letters which were being carried. In 1642, charges for carrying private mail were introduced:

- 2d. for any letter travelling on a post road up to 80 miles from London;
- 4d. for letters travelling between 80 and 140 miles;
- 6d. for any further distance in England; and
- 8d. for those going to Scotland.

There were no cross-country mails. If anyone sent a package, say from Belford to Holyhead, the recipient would have to pay both the cost of sending it to London and then from London to Holyhead.

When, in 1633, Charles I decided to make a visit to Scotland, it is recorded that Belford was provided with extra post horses for His Majesty's journey, both on the outward journey on June 8th, and for his return on July 17th. Clearly, however good the normal posting arrangements in Belford were, they were not sufficient to deal with the royal retinue. Four years later, when postal responsibilities were reviewed by the Court of Star Chamber, the postmaster at Belford was to receive 2s. 2d. per day for his responsibilities (This was the standard daily wage of a craftsman builder at the time). It was not a bad salary, given that most postmasters were able to carry out some other occupation, most commonly innkeeping, but there could be problems in getting it.   In 1643, it is recorded that the Belford postmaster, Thomas Armorer, was owed £28.17s. 6d!

In 1685, Sir John Cochrane was arrested, following an attempted coup against James II. He was tried, sentenced to death and imprisoned in Edinburgh, pending the arrival from London of the duly signed death warrant. Somewhere between Belford and the border, it is said that his daughter Grizzel, dressed as a highwayman, robbed the post-boy who was carrying the warrant, thus creating sufficient delay to enable others to obtain a pardon for her father. Exactly where the robbery took place is the subject of some dispute, but some accounts state that the night before the robbery Grizzel spent the night at the Angel Inn (where Well House now is) in Belford. Shortly afterwards, in 1687, the postmaster is recorded as Thomas Car or Carr. He continued in post until 1703, when he was succeeded by Grace Carr, possibly his daughter, who held the post for a further 10 years, Belford's first recorded postmistress. Their salary for the post was £24 per annum.

The Eighteenth Century
In the eighteenth century, as businesses grew, there was an increased demand for communication, and indeed for transport, both for people and goods. The roads, however, were very poor, despite a number of regulations requiring each parish to maintain the section within its boundaries. Nor did the heavy goods wagons improve the situation, often churning the already poor surfaces into a quagmire in bad weather.
The routes were not well marked, and the need to avoid bad areas often resulted in a number of apparent ways, with no clear indication of how to go. Perhaps this was the difficulty which faced the post-boy who left Berwick on 20th November 1725, but never arrived in Belford.

> *A most diligent search has been made, but neither the boy, the horse nor*
> *the packet has yet been heard of. The boy, after passing Goswick, having*
> *a part of the sands to ride which divide the Holy Island from the mainland,*
> *it is supposed he has missed his way, and rode towards the sea, where he*
> *and his horse have both perished.*

The working of the post system is well recorded in a surviving way-bill of 1762 recording the time of arrival and departure from each stage on an express journey from Edinburgh to London. It left Edinburgh at 1.30 p.m. on July 21st, and after changes at the three Scottish changes it reached Berwick.

> *Received at Berwick July 21st, 1762 at ½ past Eleven at night, and Sent*
> *   away at Twelve at midnight by JAMES GRIEVE.*
> *Recd. At Belford July 22, at three in the morning and sent away ½ past by*
> *   WM. BUGG..*

> *Recd. At Alnwick at ½ past six in ye morning and sent away (time and*
> *signature illegible).*
> *Recd. At Morpeth at ½ past nine in the day and sent away Immediately.*
>   *p. T. J. Sarle*
> *July 22nd Recd. At N'Castle at ¼ past Twelve Noon and sent away ½ past*
>   *ditto. p. H. Bell.*

It finally arrived at Greys Inn, London on July 24th at 7.10p.m. The journey, travelling night and day had taken 77½ hours and averaged just over five miles per hour.

The Cow Causey to Buckton Burn Turnpike Trust

Although the use of stage coaches is recorded from the mid seventeenth century, the slowness and discomfort of the ride and the tendency for coaches to literally become bogged down in bad weather conditions, meant that the majority of travellers preferred to go on horseback, if they could. Even in 1763, the return stage coach service between London and Edinburgh was monthly, with each single journey taking a fortnight, during which passengers spent the middle Sunday at Boroughbridge. By then however, matters were beginning to improve. In particular, the work of talented engineers such as John Metcalf (Blind Jack o' Knaresborough) was resulting in new and more durable approaches to road building. All that remained was to find a means of paying for their implementation. The answer to this was the creation of bodies known as Turnpike Trusts. These trusts were established by Act of Parliament which empowered a group of local landowners to take control of a stretch of road, repair and maintain it, if necessary buying adjacent land to re-route it. Some of this work would be carried out by the parishes as previously, but the majority of money was raised by the positioning of gates (Turnpikes) at intervals across the road and charging a fee or toll to all traffic wishing to pass through.

In 1747, Parliament passed an Act for
> *Repairing the High-Road leading from the North End of the Cow-Cawsey*
> *(near the Town of NEWCASTLE upon TYNE), to the Town of BELFORD,*
> *and from thence to BUCKTON-BURN, in the County of*
> *NORTHUMBERLAND.*

This was necessary, the Act said, because
> *The high post-road from London to Edinburgh, is, in divers places, by*
> *reason of the many heavy carriages passing thereon, become so deep and*
> *ruinous, that travellers cannot pass thereon, without great danger; and the*
> *said road cannot.....be effectually amended, and kept in good repair,*
> *unless some provision be made for raising money to be applied for that*
> *purpose.*

Among the just over 300 Trustees appointed to the trust were Abraham Dixon (IV) and William Smart of Belford; other local landowners included George Carr of Bowsden, William Carr of Etal and three Thomas Forsters, of Lucker, Adderstone and Warenford respectively. Toll gates were erected at Gosforth, Morpeth South, Morpeth North, Alnwick, Heckley and Belford. The trustees could also set up check gates at the points where other roads joined the Great North Road, to prevent travellers accessing the road without paying the toll.

Belford Toll House
Courtesy of A. Gilhome

The initial tolls for travelling on the road were set as follows:

- Carriages and waggons were charged according to the number of horses or draught animals pulling them – a shilling per animal to a maximum of 6 shillings for six or more horses or draught animals;
- every beast of burden - sixpence;
- every drove of oxen or cattle – 1s. 3d. per 20; and
- every drove of calves, hogs, sheep lambs or goats – 7½ d per 20.

Ten years later a further Act of Parliament increased the charges by one third. The only significant later alteration in the tolls came in 1838 when it was decided to reduce the charges for horses drawing coaches or wagons to 5d. per horse.

Detailed accounts for the Trust do not survive, but they obtained their revenue by letting or subsequently auctioning the toll gates, initially for three year terms, and then annually. Figures for some of these survive.

Toll Gate	1793	1799	1832	1836	1838	1845	1850	1857	1869	1873
Gosforth	£511	£597	£1403	£1160	£1585	£1144	£520	£591	£805	£810
Morpeth S.	£398	£446	£704	£888	£1045	£768	£219	£180	£177	£155
Morpeth N.	£336	£360	£625	£646	£800	£686	£210	£180	£195	£165
Alnwick	£345	£360	£440	£478	£610	£487	£115	£134	£270	£160
Heckley	£161	£192	£264	£225	£350	£282	£144	£130	£115	£100
Belford	£86	£101	£141	£125	£300	£206	£62	£57	£170	£225

In 1796, the Belford Toll Keeper is recorded as John Gilroy. The Belford Toll was, in the early years, the least profitable. Probably this was because, despite Abraham Dixon (IV)'s best efforts, the town was significantly smaller than Alnwick and Morpeth, and so attracted fewer visitors. Also, for those continuing north, many left the road either at Morpeth or Alnwick to take the westerly route to Scotland through Wooler and Coldstream. Its change in fortunes in the latter years, is probably due to a decision to introduce check gates at the junctions of the Adderstone road and the Spindlestone/Outchester road with the Great North Road in 1868. The *Newcastle Courant* of 3rd April carried the notice for a meeting to discuss the matter, but though not the decision taken, but it is hard to think of any other event or development which could have so greatly increased the worth of the tolls. The slump in all the tolls in the mid nineteenth century reflects the impact of the arrival of the railway. The *Newcastle Courant* records a motion to discuss *the continuance or abolition* of the Trust in 1871, signed, amongst others, by R. Burdon Sanderson of Budle Hall but since the tolls continued to be auctioned until at least 1873, clearly the Trust continued. It was finally closed in 1875, when the roads were handed over to the County Council.

Kitchin map c.1764

With the setting up of the Turnpike Trust, came some local changes to the roads. The most significant of these was an alteration to the route just north of Belford. Seventeenth and early eighteenth century maps show the road running very much as the village road does now, entering from South Road, passing the Market Place, and continuing up North Bank, along the west side of the Hall grounds, and continuing down the hill, passing immediately to the west of Buckton before resuming the line of the present A1. This last stretch, however, was notoriously wet and marshy, and the Trustees used their powers to divert the road at Detchant, taking it on through Kettleburn and Fenwick, before joining the present route.

Abraham Dixon (IV) also used the opportunity to divert another local road, enclosing the existing road to Easington which the 1755 report of the formal inquiry into the change describes as:

> Beginning at the South West corner of a certain
> dwelling house situate in Belford aforesaid, now in
> the tenure of Thomas Bell Gent., and extending
> eastwards over the lands of the said Abraham
> Dixon, to the east side of a certain Rock or Scar in
> a certain parcel of ground called Hollow Hope
> Scar.

This was replaced by a road which left the Great North Road, north of Belford at the north corner of Abraham Dixon's plantation and ran due east in a straight line until it rejoined the original road to the east of Hollow Hope Scar. From the description, this would seem to be Quarry Bank Road. We know from the account of the Agriculturalist, Arthur Young, who visited Abraham Dixon in 1771, that the Belford stretch of road was regarded as particularly well maintained.

> Mr. Dickson(sic) applied himself with great spirit
> to rendering the road to Belford, north and south,
> as good as possible; this he effected as far as his
> influence extended, and would not have left a mile
> of bad road in the whole country, had others been
> as solicitous as himself about so important an
> object.

Paterson map 1796

Milepost in Lowick village

In 1792, a new Turnpike Trust was set up to cover the road from Belford to Ford Bridge, the milestones for which are still clearly visible along the Lowick-Ford road. In 1805, there was an attempt to bring a further new Turnpike road through Belford. By now the country was at war with Napoleon, and corn was fetching premium prices in the south. Following the success of the Corn Road from

Rothbury to Alnmouth, there was a move to build a similar road from Wooler through Chatton to North Sunderland Harbour, with branches off to Belford.and via Doddington to join the Great North Road at Bowsden Burn. A public meeting was held at the *Blue Bell* on November 5th to discuss the matter. It was agreed that the Wooler to North Sunderland Road and the two branches should be under separate trusts. The expenses for making the roads, excluding the cost of having the necessary legislation put through Parliament, were given as:

Wooler to North Sunderland Harbour   £4,500

Belford branch   £500

Wooler to Bowsden Burn branch   £1500

This money was to be raised by public subscription, with subscribers given the opportunity to specify to which part of the project they wished their money to be applied.

AT a meeting holden at the house of Mrs. McDonald, in Belford, on Tuesday the fifth day of November 1805, in pursuance of an advertisement, to take into consideration the propriety of applying to Parliament for an act for making and maintaining a turnpike road from the town of Wooler, in the county of Northumberland, to Chatton, and from thence to North-Sunderland harbour, in the said county: and also a branch from the said road to Belford: and also a road from Wooler by Doddington to join the Berwick turnpike at Bowsden Burn.

RESOLVED,

THAT it appears expedient and that it will be attended with great public advantage to have not only a road from Wooler to North-Sunderland harbour, according to a plan thereof which has been prepared and laid before the meeting, but also to have a branch to lead therefrom to Belford, and a road from Wooler to join the Berwick turnpike at Bowsden Burn, in order to open out a communication with the sea coast, for the purpose of exporting corn and other things, and for the purpose of importing merchandize and other goods.

RESOLVED ALSO,

THAT the road from Wooler to Sunderland, and the two branches shall be under seperate trusts, and that persons subscribing to the said roads shall be at liberty to specify to which of the said roads their subscriptions shall be applicable.

RESOLVED ALSO,

THAT the expences of making the estimate and of passing the act of parliament and other contingent expences, shall be paid out of the subscriptions to the said road and branches, in such proportion as the expence of making the said road and branches shall bear to each other.

Wooler Turnpike meeting 1805

In the event, the project was stillborn. When the local landowners were asked to subscribe, there were few positive responses. For the Wooler/ North Sunderland route, the Duke of Northumberland offered £1000, always providing there were subscriptions to cover the whole sum needed; the Lord Crewe Trustees offered £500 on the same condition; John Dinning of Newlands and Thomas Graham offered £100 each without conditions and the Vicar of Chatton offered £30. The Earl of Tankerville would provide £400 for the Bowsden Burn branch provided the rest of the money could be raised, but there were no subscribers at all for the Belford branch. Since Wooler offered many of the same facilities as Belford, it is perhaps understandable that there was little interest in a Belford route. It is less clear why the plan to use North Sunderland Harbour as an export port for local produce, attracted so little interest. A letter which Robert Thorpe, the Alnwick lawyer, wrote to his father on November 24th, shortly after the meeting in Belford, mentions two possible concerns, firstly that the Greenwich Hospital Commissioners who, then as now, held estates in the area, would oppose the project as it would provide competition for their harbour (presumably Budle), and secondly that North Sunderland Harbour was not presently a free port, and ships using it had to pay an additional 5 shillings customs duty. Whatever the reason, the Bill was not enacted by parliament. In 1825, however, a lesser version of the scheme was put into practice when an Act was passed to create the Adderstone to Wooler Turnpike, with gates at Bellshill and Chatton.

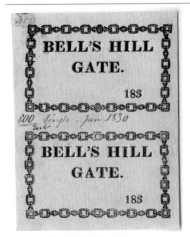

BELL'S HILL GATE.

183

800 *Single - Jan 1830*

BELL'S HILL GATE.

183

Bellshill Toll tickets
Courtesy of the
Northumbrian Collections
NZMD-178-10-9

The new section of the Great North Road Turnpike had avoided the marshy ground, but proved to have its own problems. In October 1821, the Berwick Advertiser comments in reference to a report that it is intended to increase the speed of the mail coaches to nine miles an hour from the previous seven, *up here the longer stages may prove difficult because of the winding roads etc.* In September 1827, a race between two local coaches, the *Defence* and the *Despatch*, resulted in what was nearly a very nasty accident. *Both coaches on their way from Belford to Berwick, were passing through the village of Detchant, the* Despatch *being first, and that the defendant (*Alexander Falconer, driver of the Defence*) attempted to pass the* Despatch *on the* wrong side, *just while the latter was taking the sharp bend at the north end of the village, where the road is very narrow and has a considerable declivity. In doing this he drove so close to the other coach, that he locked the wheels of the two together, and would in all probability have overturned one or both coaches, if there had not happened to be a cart on the other side of the* Despatch, *in such a position that by the shock the wheels of the coach were forced against and locked with one of those of the cart, which prevented any injury except the breaking and damaging the harness of the* Despatch.

Berwick Advertiser 6 October 1827

In 1843, the *Berwick Advertiser* reported another accident, which took place on December 5th, this time at Kettleburn, when one of the leading horses of the mail coach north, went into a cart belonging to a Henry Elder of Coldstream. The horse was badly injured and the driving pole of the coach broken. Elder was convicted both of careless driving and of driving an unnamed cart. He was fined £2 on each of the counts, together with costs, which were probably substantial as an official of the General Post Office London had attended the hearing. As Elder could not pay, he was sent to Morpeth Gaol for a month.

In 1835, the engineer, Thomas Telford, was appointed to resurvey the Northumberland section of the Great North Road, with the actual groundwork being done by Henry Welch, later County Architect for Northumberland. As a result of this, at some time in the 1840s, the road was once more realigned, and more or less resumed its original straighter route.

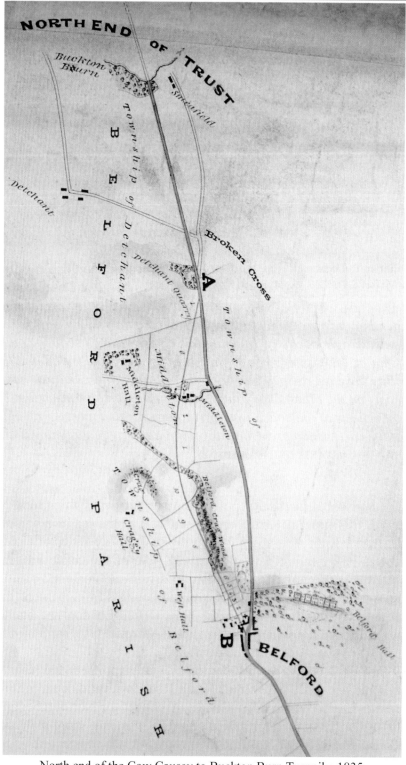

North end of the Cow Causey to Buckton Burn Turnpike 1835
QRUP32.1 (detail) Courtesy of Northumbrian Collections

The Coming of the Mail Coaches

The transport of mail by post-boys continued until the 1780s. There were, however, problems. Most post-boys were young, and despite horn, gun and guide, vulnerable to attack, particularly as they were required to ride through the night. Also accounts suggest that, like many young men, some were prone to distractions – there are accounts of the mail bag left at the side of road, while the rider played football with the locals, others were found simply relaxing on the journey. John Palmer, the Bath theatre manager and entrepreneur, who suggested using stage coaches as an alternative, painted a very damning picture of them in the 1780s:

The mails are generally entrusted to some idle boy, without character, mounted on a worn-out hack, and who, so far from being able to defend himself or escape from a robber, is much more likely to be in league with him.

But then he would. Nevertheless, while many objections were raised to Palmer's plans, little effort seems to have been made to defend the character of post-boys. In 1785, with considerable reluctance, it was agreed to trial Palmer's scheme for using special stage coaches to deliver mail on the London Bath route. So successful was it, that by the end of 1786 the scheme had been introduced on all seven Post Routes (London to Dover, Exeter, Bristol, Holyhead, Carlisle, Edinburgh and Great Yarmouth).

1827 Royal Mail Coach
Courtesy of the Science Museum,
London/SSPL. Image Ref. 10439258

The first red, black and maroon mail coach to reach Newcastle arrived on November 7th, 1786, at the Cock Inn at the head of the Side. Its landlord, Matthew Hall, was the only Newcastle innkeeper prepared to accept the Mail contract, others feeling that the required 7 miles per hour speed was too damaging for the horses. In that they were perhaps not entirely wrong - 18 horses are recorded as having dropped dead in their shafts on the Great North Road. Nevertheless the new system was here to stay, and the mail coaches cut 22 hours off the London - Edinburgh journey, reducing it to 60 hours. The cost to the Post Office was the leasing of 10 coaches, 620 horses and a subsidy for more than 200 inns on the Great North Road alone. So successful was the mail coach north that by 1793, the letter box on the rear of the coach was no longer adequate for all the mail it was to carry.

Ask Mr. Hasker if a large leather covering cannot be fixed to one side of the Edinburgh Coach, and wrapt over the Edin[h.] Bag which Mr. Hasker

*represents now to go to the top of the Coach for want of room and to be
liable to be cut off, but the P.M.G. thinks that might be prevented if such a
leather covering as is above described was fastened with a portmanteau
Chain and Padlock, as it can hardly be worth while to establish a second
Mail Coach to go a long the same road at the same time, at a great Expence
and to the injury of the Turnpike, for the sake of a simple Bag if it could be
avoided.* (POST 42/10)

Such a complicated arrangement was avoided by separating the newspapers
from the letters, and merely placing the wrapped newspapers on the top of the
coach. This solution to the problem, by which two outside seats on the coach
were reserved for the newspapers remained in place until 1837 (when it cost
£52 a quarter) when the Edinburgh mail was re-routed via Birmingham.

The system, as it affected Berwick, is described in Good's 1806 directory.

*The South Coach comes in at nine o'clock in the evening, Stops half an hour
for supper, and sets out for the North immediately. The North Coach comes
in at half past ten, or eleven o'clock at night. Stops half an hour for supper,
and sets out for the South immediately. This coach is well protected with a
Guard, well armed, who changes here; and an able Driver who changes
every stage. The coach is allowed to take only four passengers, and none on
the top. Every passenger when he takes his seat must pay his fare so far as he
rides. They always stop at the* King's Arms. *Letters and News-papers every
day in the week, Wednesday excepted. Edinburgh News-papers, twice a-
week. Newcastle News-papers, twice a-week. Kelso News-papers, twice a-
week.*

Remarkably, a description of the first mail coach driver to drive between
Belford and Berwick still survives. He was Walter Wright, and having driven
from the start of the service, and survived six or seven changes in the holders of
that stage contract, was still in post when, at the beginning of January 1824, he
was presented with *a superfine scarlet frock coat, a blue waistcoat, and a fine
black hat, with gold lace band, and a black cockade* as a mark of the esteem in
which he was held. The *Berwick Advertiser* described him thus:

*Those who have been accustomed to travel by this conveyance cannot but
have noticed Walter's unaffected and modest civility and attentiveness to his
passengers; and also, what is of most essential importance in a coach
driver's character, his habitual sobriety. To his temperate habits indeed, we
think must be mainly attributed that, though for about thirty five years he
drove the coach, at the rate of thirty miles a day, in the night time; viz, from
seven o'clock in the evening till two o'clock in the morning, he is now at an
advanced age, still a hale man, and may, in all probability be able to do the
duties of his situation for many years to come.*

The competence of the driver was a key component of a safe journey, but then as now the weather also played a part. The mail coaches were no less susceptible to snow than any other vehicle, with the additional problem for travellers that the first duty of the driver and guard was to the safety of the mail and not the passengers. It was a requirement that if necessary the driver and guard would go on by foot to get the mail to its next post. Once, in Dumfriesshire, they perished in the attempt. A record of the impact of the snow on the Great North Road in 1814 survives in the *Reminiscences* of the great Georgian actor-manager, William Macready.

> *The snow was falling fast, and had already drifted so high between the Ross Inn and Berwick-on-Tweed that it had been necessary to cut a passage for carriages for some miles. We did not reach Newcastle until nearly two hours after midnight...the next day the mails were stopped; nor for more than six weeks was there any conveyance by carriage between Edinburgh and Newcastle. After some weeks a passage was cut through the snow for the guards to carry the mail on horseback, but for a length of time the communication every way was very irregular.*

The more cynical amongst us might feel that little has changed in 200 years!

In 1825, the original mail coach service was revised. There were now two London-Edinburgh services a day; one went via Wooler, but the other, the 'quick mail', left London at 8.01 a.m. arriving in Edinburgh 46 hours later, after a 40 minute stop at Belford. On the return journey the coach left Edinburgh at 4.10 p.m. and the passengers had a 30 minute break at Belford. The break at Belford provided a doubtless much needed refreshment stop for the passengers, but also an opportunity to sort the mail for the stages ahead. This change in timetable was not appreciated by the folk of Berwick, who lost both the letter sorting and the custom of the coach passengers.

> *If, as has been stated, the reason for removing the sorting of the mail from Berwick to Belford was for the accommodation of the passengers, it being too great a distance to travel from Weatherby (sic) to Berwick to breakfast, how does it happen that the sorting office has not been fixed for Alnwick, a much more convenient stage for breakfast, and also a town of four times the population of Belford, and of considerable commercial importance, particularly in the corn trade, whereas Belford is of no commercial importance whatever?*
>
> Berwick Advertiser, 2nd July 1825

To add insult to injury, £30 was deducted from the Berwick postmaster's salary and given to John McDonald, the Belford Postmaster, for the extra responsibility of sorting the mail. By now, the mail coach service was entering its final years. With the coming of the railways, there was a swifter and more secure means of conveying the mail, with the added advantage that it could be sorted en route. On June 12th 1847, a minute was sent to the Postmaster General in London, alerting him to the fact that the railway between Newcastle and Berwick was due to open on the 18th of the month, and proposing arrangements to transfer the mail to the railway immediately after 14th July, when the current Day Mail Coach contract expired. As far as Belford was concerned, it was proposed that the cheapest arrangement possible should be made to convey the Belford mail bags by omnibus between the Post Office and the Station. In the event the change to the railway was made nine days early on July 5th, and a £40 annual contract was negotiated to carry the mail bags between the Post Office and the Station.

Other Coaches

Although the romance of the mail coaches as portrayed on innumerable Christmas Cards, is what captures popular imagination, unless a journey was exceptionally urgent, travel by mail coach was not particularly popular. For many people the speed and the poor suspension gave rise to travel sickness. Rushed meals, often at inconvenient times, did not help, always assuming one got the food at all; there are several accounts of Inns taking the payment, but failing to deliver the meal before the departure of the mail coach which had to maintain a strict timetable. Nor was travelling through the night on unlit roads a comfortable or reassuring experience. Consider driving from Fenwick to Detchant via Kettleburn today in the darkness with no headlights! For the most of the period, the lack of outside seats on the mail coaches, made them a particularly expensive form of travel. Slower, and more affordable was the Stage, or Heavy Coach. With the improvement in the roads, a number of such services called at Belford. In 1822, Pigot's Directory lists the following:

- The *Union* Coach ran a daily service between Newcastle and Edinburgh, going north, calling at John McDonald's in the Market place at 12.45 p.m., and, going south, at 4.00 p.m. The cost of fares on the Union in 1806 was 6d. per mile inside, and 4d. outside.
- The *Defence* ran daily between Berwick and Alnwick, going south, calling at John McDonald's in the Market place at 8.00 a.m. and, going north, at 6.00 p.m.
- The *Dispatch* ran daily between Berwick and Alnwick, going south, calling at the *Black Swan* at 10.00 a.m.. and, going north, at 6.00 p.m.

By 1837, the *Defence* and *Dispatch* had gone, but two new coaches were calling at Belford on a Berwick - Newcastle run, the *Royal William* and the *Wonder*. The *Royal William* called at the *Bell Inn*, and the *Wonder* at the *Black Swan*. Although apparently separate companies, they worked their timetable together so that they alternated between arriving at Belford from Berwick at 8.00 a.m.

and 10.00 a.m., and from Newcastle at 5.00 p.m. and 7.00 p.m.

A fine advertisement poster survives for the *Royal William*, but there are few accounts of travelling on these coaches. In November, 1829, however, the *Berwick Advertiser* records that the *Union* overturned two and a half miles north of Belford, when the horses were frightened by a group of gypsies on the grass verge. Fortunately none of the passengers were injured, although the coachman sprained his foot. Snow was a problem for the coaches in February 1831, when the roads were closed for eight days. Lady Haggerston provided hospitality for the passenger and guard of the Union Coach at Haggerston Castle. The proprietors of the Alnwick to Berwick Coach applied to have the tax payable on the journeys refunded as they could not afford the expense if they were unable to carry passengers, and were eventually allowed £3. 12s. 6d. (£179.40 in today's money). These coach services were complimented by other locally based arrangements, such as Christopher Jobson's Gig which ran a passenger and parcel service taking in Berwick, Belford and Alnwick, departing Mondays and Thursdays for Berwick from Alnwick at 8.00 a.m., and making the reverse journey on Tuesdays and Fridays.

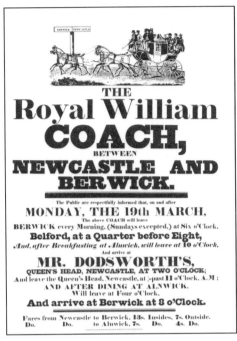

Courtesy of Jim Walker

Impact on Belford

The exact impact of turnpike roads and coaches on the people of Belford is hard to gauge. For most ordinary people travel on the Great North Road would have been the exception, rather than the rule, although the tolls on farm animals would have affected those bringing them to the town market, and particularly the spring Lamb Fair. On the other hand, both the improved road and the coaches generally brought more trade to the town. It also in a very real sense lessened the isolation of Belford and similar communities in relation to what was happening in the rest of Britain and even in Europe. The availability of daily newspapers on the mail coach brought detailed accounts of events to the middle classes, even if they were only read within an Inn, and from there they would filter down to the rest of the population. But the coach drivers and guards themselves were great broadcasters of news. When, in 1887, Jane Ward, a 93 year old inmate of the Belford workhouse died, the *Berwick Advertiser* recorded how she remembered the news of the victory at Waterloo being brought to the North by the coach arriving decorated with flags. (1st April, 1887).

Oct. 24	To Geo. Dickenson for carriage of a Box of Drugs from Belford	£00. 00s. 06d
Oct. 28	To Mr. Robert Air for 56lb of Hoggs Lard at 4d.	£00. 18s. 08d
	Carriage of do. From Belford	£00. 00s. 06d
Novr 21	To Alexander Wilson for carriage of 4 boxes of Drugs from Newcastle to Belford	£00. 03s. 08d
	To John Henderson for carriage of two boxes drugs from Belford	£00. 01s. 00d
Novr 27	To Thos Dickenson for carriage of 4 parcels from Belford	£00. 01s. 06d
Decr 5	To Geo. Dickenson for carriage of two parcels Drugs from Belford	£00. 01s. 06d

The coaches not only brought passengers, but also parcels. This made Belford a minor hub for goods distribution across the locality. This is well demonstrated by extracts from a page of the Lord Crewe Trustees Account Book for 1772.

The 1834 Pigot's Directory identifies five different carriers working out of Belford, John Moffat, Philip Wake, John Joures, Frances Wilkinson, all from their houses in West Street, and Mary Graham, from the *Nag's Head*.

The range of coaches going and coming through Belford on the Great North Road, also enabled urgent business messages to be sent locally For example, in October 1832, the *Wellington* Coach, brought the Grocer, George Macdonald, his patent medicine license. In fact the regularity and efficiency of such communication enabled a sub tax or Stamp Office to be based in Belford from approximately 1808 until December 1835. Stamps in this case were the taxes levied on a wide range of documents written on vellum, parchment and paper, including property sales, apprentice indentures, newspapers, playing cards, insurance policies, patent medicines and receipted bills for any sum over £5. In addition the office issued licenses for coaches and wagons, dealers in silver plate, sellers of patent medicines and racehorses. The need for such stamps was almost a daily necessity for those running businesses in Belford, and the ability to obtain them locally rather than travel to Alnwick must have been a tremendous boon. Until 1822, the office was run in Belford by John Rogers, a Draper, although the records suggest not very successfully. Robert Thorpe, who was in charge of the main office in Alnwick, consistently complained of the late arrival of the quarterly returns, and of stamps too dirty or damaged to be used. In 1817, he wrote, one feels with a sense of exasperation, *You know (I am convinced) regularity is absolutely necessary to the carrying on of a business with success and comfort.* Matters came to a head in March 1821, when after long delays in Rogers settling his accounts, and Thorpe having to threaten to contact his sureties to secure payment, the contract was ended and given instead to Robert Bromfield, described as a shopkeeper and merchant. In fact, Bromfield too ran a Drapery and Grocery store. He continued the business successfully until his death in December 1834, when it was taken over by his son George Alexander. An overall reorganisation of the Stamp Office in 1835, however, resulted in the Alnwick office being downgraded to a sub-distribution centre, and the Belford office closed.

Another business, which directly benefited from the through traffic, was that of the Blacksmith. Like other towns of its size, Belford had a number of Blacksmiths. The 1822 Pigot's *Directory* lists five - William Dickinson, Aaron Lisle, David Rodgers, (sic) James Scott and George Whittle. Of these the most significant was David Rogers, who, an article in the Berwick Advertiser says *was generally regarded as one of the best horse-shoers between Newcastle and Edinburgh.* (August 13th, 1887) . It was probably a measure of the respect in which Rogers was held which prompted William Clark, in 1836, to grant him and his son Thomas, a lease for three lives on the substantial property in the Neuk, a very unusual arrangement for the estate.

The Blue Bell
The greatest beneficiaries of the better roads, the coaches and most especially the mail coaches, were the inns in Belford, and most especially the inn which held the mail contract. The contract was particularly important as, until 1779, holding the contract gave the landlord the benefit of the monopoly on the hire of all horses for posting. Hence any traveller seeking to continue his journey on a hired horse must needs use the designated inn. When Abraham Dixon(IV) took over the Belford Hall Estate in 1746, he is credited with building a good inn by both Arthur Young and the Reverend Thomas Randal, who named it as the *Bell.* As part of the *Blue Bell* building dates no later than the early eighteenth century, it is possible that Dixon renewed or extended an existing building rather than erected a new one. It was the *Blue Bell* at which firstly the post-boys and then the mail coaches stopped to change horses and, in the latter case, drivers, and where everyone else also hired their horses. A relic of that time is the area on the south side of West Street between Williams Way and the High

Street, which on old maps was named Post Horse Close. It was as the *Blue Bell* too that the mail bags for the Belford area were off-loaded, and the outgoing mail taken on board, all in the few minutes allocated for changing horses. Although not certain, it is probable that for much of the eighteenth century, the mail was also sorted there.

> *There was an evident convenience in this, owing to the innkeeper being the postmaster in the other and original sense of the provider of horses to ride post, when it was common to send on expresses, by means of these agents, from stage to stage. But the innkeepers, being often farmers besides, had business more important than that of the post to look after, and consequently the work was delegated to others. The duty of receiving and dispatching the mails was frequently left to waiters or chambermaids, with the undesirable but inevitable result that the work was badly done. Often there was no separate place set apart for Post-office business; letters were sorted in the bar or in one of the public rooms, where any one could see them, thereby excluding all possibility of secrecy in dealing with the correspondence.*
>   J. W. Hyde (Superintendent of the General Post Office, Edinburgh) - The Royal Mail, 1889

In about 1778-9, Abraham Dixon had a change of mind. Instead of supporting the Blue Bell, he decided to develop another inn at the southern end of the village, the *Turk's Head* and divide the *Blue Bell* into two houses one for his wife's relative, William Bugg, who was also the postmaster, and the other for one of the town's doctors, Dr. Pringle. Exactly why is not clear, and still puzzled his friend and solicitor, Thomas Adams, when he tried to explain the situation to Lord Onslow, the grandfather of Dixon's heir, after Abraham Dixon's death. Adams suggested that Dixon was providing a business for two family retainers, and it may be that, with the end of the post horse monopoly, he saw an opportunity to develop a second flourishing inn. Whatever the reason, the project was not a success. One of the retainers, Mr. Wealens, died shortly before Abraham Dixon, leaving the inn badly in debt to the brewery and other suppliers, and with only a borrowed post-chaise available for hire. Despite the best endeavours of the other partner, Lancelot Turner, to repay the debts, the situation was beyond his powers, and eventually he had to surrender the inn. Meanwhile Lord Onslow's son, Thomas Onslow, M.P. for Guildford, wrote to Thomas Adams regarding the current poor provision for travellers at Belford:

> *At the requisition of several very respectable Gentlemen, who constantly travel the Northern road, and who in doing so, always pass thro' the town of Belford, I take the liberty of troubling you with this, to express their sentiments relative to the permanent establishment of a creditable Inn in that town. They assure me that the having one there, would be as materially beneficial to my son's estate as it wou'd be pleasant and convenient to themselves; and that whatever tenant might be put into it, he would be certain of success in his undertaking.*

In replying, Adams agreed that the complaints of the travellers had some foundation, and later he was to describe the *Turk's Head* as more like a Beer House. With the factor, Henry Barber, he planned to restore the *Blue Bell* to its former use, as soon as alternative accommodation could be provided for Bugg and Pringle. By the end of 1785, this had been done and the *Blue Bell* was once more in business, with an Aberdonian, Charles McDonald, as the Landlord. Over the next ten years, the business thrived so that, in 1799, Adams could again write to Lord Onslow about the *Blue Bell*:

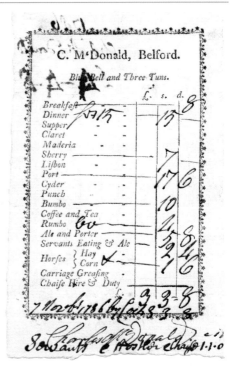

Blue Bell Inn bill for Rent Day dinner for 15 people 7th November 1786 showing dinner was one shilling each and also costs for fodder, servant, ostler and chaise.

> *It has the whole Business upon the great Main Road between London and Edinburgh, and no person, publican or other keeps a carriage in Belford....This house is of great consequence being the only place between Alnwick and Berwick for the Nobility of both Kingdoms to stop at for changing Horses or general accommodation (and to do the man and his Wife justice it is an excellent Eating house).*

The only problem, Adams noted, was that Charles McDonald was inclined to get drunk, but he had given him a severe lecture on the matter, and had made the Inn's lease an annual one subject to six months' notice in the hope of keeping him sober. Possibly Adams' actions had been left too late. Later that year, Charles McDonald was dead and the tenancy had passed to his wife.

Being the main inn in the village brought its share of problems as well as excitements and profits; for the McDonalds probably never more so than on July 24, 1797. According to the account Thomas Adams wrote later to Lord Onslow, about 4 o'clock in the afternoon, a lady and gentleman from Scotland came into the Blue Bell, having driven in his carriage, pulled by post horses, which needed to be changed. Ten minutes later a post chaise appeared, in which were the parents and sister of the lady, who, it transpired, was eloping. There was a great to-do in the inn, in the midst of which the young man went to his carriage, took out a pair of pistols, and going into the back yard, blew his brains out. The young man was later identified as a Dutchman, Alexander Van Dyke, who, it was said, had first seduced the young lady, a Miss Cunningham, while her father was commanding a Scots Brigade in the Low Countries. As if that was not bad enough, McDonald had then to deal with the inquest, and found himself left with Van Dyke's various possessions, which, six months later, he was still trying to get passed over to the Administrator of the dead man's estate!

During the nineteenth century, the *Blue Bell* remained the pre-eminent Inn in the village. It continued to provide horses for travellers, and, after the coming of the Railway, for some years it held the contract to carry the post between the Station and the Post Office. Its last link with its coaching heyday came in 1889, when the last Ostler, James Menzies, died in Belford aged 84. He had first come to the *Blue Bell* to take charge of the horses in 1830, and had remained there for 50 years, until he retired in 1881. His obituary in the *Berwick Advertiser* of May 3rd comments:

> *During this long period it fell to his lot to drive many illustrious visitors to the mansions of the great, as well as others of less noble descent, and many a poor, foot-sore traveller has blessed him for a kind lift in the empty coach.*

Although the *Blue Bell* remained important, once it had lost its monopoly of all posting, the way was open for other establishments to compete. The *Black Swan*, in particular, developed its own posting arrangements, providing horses for private travellers, and some commercial enterprises. Christopher Jobson for example collected his passengers and parcels from the *Black Swan*, and it was the boarding point for the *Dispatch* coach.

The Post Office comes into its own

The speed and regularity of the mail coaches brought with it a significant increase in the mail, which, in most places, began to be reckoned in bags rather than letters. By now, established post offices had authority to send mail directly to a limited number of places on the main route. This was the *Bye Mail*. Belford could dispatch mail directly to Alnwick, Morpeth, Newcastle and Berwick.

Post Office record of towns to which Belford could send letters directly. POST 14/418

As letters were not yet delivered, but had to be collected from the post office, this also resulted in the development of local rituals. Those likely to be in receipt of letters, as well as those with leisure to spare, would gather at the post office in the hope of correspondence, but in the certainty of news and gossip. Where the post office was located at the end of the eighteenth century, is not clear, but probably still in the Blue Bell, as a letter in the Postal Archives refers to the publican being accommodated. In November 1809, however, postal arrangements in the town changed, when the Postmaster General[1] approved an application from Belford, forwarded by the Secretary, Francis Freeling, that the townspeople should have their letters delivered.

My Lords,
I have the Honor to enclose a report from Mr Hodgson on an application from the Town of Belford to be relieved from any extra payments on the delivery of their Letters. It having been decided in a court of Law, that the Public may insist on the Delivery of their Letters for Postage only, within the Limits of a Post Town, your Lordships must of course comply with this application.
I am of opinion with Mr Hodgson that an allowance of £10 per ann to the postm[r] to pay a L.C. (Letter Carrier) is necessary and with your Lordships approbation it shall be included in the report preparing for Treasury.

(George Hodgson was the Riding Surveyor, or man in charge of postal arrangements for the North East).

19th November, 1838 Belford Penny post
Courtesy of Wilf Newton

This situation changed again in the 1830s, when, in common with many other market towns, it was agreed that Belford post could be delivered locally for one penny.

Of the early Post Masters, not a lot is known. Grace Alder (who may have been Grace Carr by another name) was postmistress from 1714 to 1720, and succeeded by Thomas Alder who was still in post in 1752. Sometime during the 50s, he was succeeded by Sarah Alder, who resigned in favour of William Bugg in 1760. William Bugg was the nephew of Ann Dixon, and the first postmaster who is more than a name. In January 1779, Thomas Adams wrote to Abraham Dixon, that he had given Bugg *some friendly advice* about the need to give more attention to the care of the letters, stressing that neglecting a letter could have ill consequences. The Postmaster General was always ready to summon an erring official to London, and deprive him of his position in order to provide for his own dependents. What Bugg had done to deserve this is not explained, but thirteen years later, in 1792, there is a formal minute to the Postmaster General that Bugg had been warned *'to attend personally to his duties'*. The Postal Archives holds the clue to this rebuke. (POST 40/6), in a letter to London from George Hodgson:

Belford
15 & 17 September   There is an intelligent Deputy but his attention in ingross[d] by his Farm 3 miles from the office his Clerk I found ignorant and

---

[1] For much if the 18th and 19th Centuries the Postmaster Generalship was held jointly by two men

had to give him much Instruction. The Deputy talks of retiring to his Farm
and only keeping a couple of Rooms or a small House in Belford for his Clerk
and himself occasionally, which I think should be resisted when he apply's
for leave so to do.
Letters from London to Belford often missent to this office.

In London, it was decided that they could not force Bugg to keep a house in the town, but he did have to do the job he was paid for. (POST 42/12)

Tho' the Postmaster of Belford may have Rooms and no House, he must
attend in person at the office hours.
October 11 1792

William Bugg may not have been the most efficient of postmasters, but it did not stop him feeling he was underpaid. In 1784, he approached his aunt, the now widowed Ann Dixon, who in turn asked Thomas Adams to raise the matter with Lord Onslow, as a man of influence in government circles. Bugg's complaint, apparently, was that his salary was not on a par with that of the postmaster of Alnwick. The application was successful. Thomas Adams records in December of 1784 that Bugg had received a letter from Secretary Mr. Todd, augmenting his salary, though whether it brought him to a par with Alnwick is not known. The other development of note during Bugg's tenure was that, in 1792, Belford post office was given the right to deal in money orders, which must have been a great help to many of the local people.

William Bugg died, still postmaster, in 1806. There was then a move to appoint a Mrs. Barbara Home or Hume from Wooler to the post. She had friends in the General Post Office who moved very swiftly to have her nominated, getting in ahead of Lord Onslow who wished one of his protégés, James Johnson, to get the job. The plan however unravelled. Mrs. Home visited Belford and went through the Post Office books. She was unimpressed and wrote to Mr. Hodgson declining the position. (POST 40 /102)

Wooler Feby 6th 1806
Sir,

I received both your kind and friendly letters, for which I return you my
sincere thanks, I went to Belford on Monday to meet with Mr Dinning, and in
Viewing Mr Buggs Books, I was greatly Surprised to See what a Small
income he had for doing the Duty of the office, I am Sorry my friends should
have had so much Trouble about it, as it is not worth my acceptance I have
therefore returned you the paper that I was to give my oath on, I am sorry to
hear that your Health is so indefferint. (sic) I Sincerely wish it soon to be
Restored,   I am Sir,

Yours Sincerely   B. Home

With Mrs. Home out of the way, the post was given to James Johnson, whose candidature was also supported by John Dinning, now the Estate factor:

a civil, steady, modest Man, and from my own knowledge well qualified to discharge the Duties required

He seems to have operated successfully until May, 1810, when a combination of circumstances proved his undoing. Unusually, two express mails arrived one day after the other, and Johnson, who was not used to this form of post, sent them on to Edinburgh, but without the necessary payments to take them through the barriers at the Press and Dunbar. Mr. Hodgson wrote to him to enquire what had happened. Johnson sent the belated payments to the Scottish postmasters, but did not reply to Hodgson. He then ignored a further letter, later claiming he was too embarrassed to write. Hodgson's son, William, who had succeeded his father as Riding Surveyor, wrote a further three letters to Johnson, but received no reply. He then formally complained to London. (POST 40/146)

Auckland Feby 17th

1811

Dear Sir,
I am extremely sorry to be under the necessity of representing to you the conduct of Mr. Johnson the Postm^r. of Belford, who seems to treat the official letters I have lately written to him with perfect indifference - I have addressed him <u>three</u> times on the subject of an <u>Express</u> irregularly forwarded and cannot get from him any answer - My Father wrote to him <u>twice</u> on the same subject, previous to my doing so, with no better success.
Perhaps you will have the goodness to give him a letter of admonition which may put him upon his guard and will greatly oblige.

Francis Freeling, the Secretary in London was instructed to write to Johnson, and it was then that the postmaster made his greatest mistake, for he replied that he had answered all three of the new Riding Surveyor's letters, and that they must have miscarried, a claim which no-one believed. The decision was taken to dismiss him, for lying, and for ignoring the letters, although it was also stated that he had on occasions been guilty of arrears and inattention to duty. As the Secretary wrote to their Lordships, the Postmaster General:

I am afraid however that where there had been so much neglect & so little truth & ingenuousness shewn even at the last, your Lordships can entertain little prospect of a right attention to the public business hereafter.

(POST 42/102)

Despite letters in mitigation by both John Dinning and Mr. Hodgson Senior, and a Petition from Johnson himself, Johnson was sacked, officially for *contumacious silence!*

First page of Johnson's petition
POST 40/146

Following the unexpected departure of Johnson in 1811, there was no-one waiting in the wings, seeking the post. In the end London asked the Hodgsons for their recommendations. George Hodgson wrote to Francis Freeling:

As you have very kindly given my Son leave to recommend to you a fit Person for the appointment to the Belford Office, and neither he nor I have knowledge of any such Person living in Belford, my attention has rested *upon a young Woman of the Neighbourhood, a Protege of my late Brother's, and to whom he gave a very good Education and £500. She is conversant in accounts, writes extremely well, is well-disposed, and in my opinion would make an excellent Postmistress;...... if however you have no better recommendation, I shall feel much obliged by your attention to this and your Int^{n.} with my Lords the Postmaster General in behalf of Isabella Forrest, spinster of North Sunderland near Belford.*

In 1814, Isabella Forrest resigned, though we do not know why. Possibly she was to be married, and married women could not hold the position in their own right, as, in those days, they had no independent legal existence, being merely their husband's property.

The nineteenth century trade directories suggest that, by then, the postmasters operated from their individual houses, although, by 1860, Belford Post Office was certainly located in the current and adjacent building.

In December of 1814, John McDonald, a local hardware dealer, and coach proprietor, was nominated as postmaster by the Northumberland M.P., Colonel Beaumont, and then appointed. McDonald remained postmaster until 1848, when he resigned in August, presumably due to ill health, as he died within three months. He ran the post office from his house on the east side of the High Street, close to the Market Place. The Account books from the end of his time in office, give an interesting picture of the operation. The rent for the Post Office was £10, with £20 for his living accommodation. He was allocated £8. 10s. 0d. for heating and lighting. He received an annual salary of £107. 14s. 0d., made up of a basic salary of £72, a further £3 for dealing with late letters, six guineas for handling private bags or pouches for the local gentry and nobility, £1. 8s. 0d. profits from the sale of postage stamps and envelope, and £25 for the employment of assistants. He employed two assistants, but only paid one; the other was presumably his wife, who succeeded him briefly on his death. By the time the various expenses were paid, his net salary was £59. 19s. 2d. One letter carrier was directly employed by the Post Office, and two deliveries were made daily.

John McDonald saw two massive changes to the way in which the post was dealt with, and ones which turned the office of postmaster from a side line into a full time job. First, the introduction in 1840 of the pre-paid penny post and the introduction of letter delivery, at first only to the most populated parts of the area, but gradually extending until everyone was covered. This originally included the dispatch of the letters for Belford to Wooler and oversight of a foot round from Belford to North Sunderland. Then, in 1847, came the change from mail coach delivery to railway. There were now two collections per day by omnibus and one night collection by horse from the station, for which the contractor was paid £40 per annum, although who that contractor was is not clear. When the contract was renewed in 1853, it went to the then landlord of the *Blue Bell*, Mr. Custance, although at only half the previous rate. Clearly, as the new system settled in, the costs of letter delivery were being looked at keenly. When John McDonald was succeeded by his wife, her annual salary was reduced from £72 per annum to £61, although she was given an allowance of £25 *for assistance*. The reason given for the reduction was that the previous salary was more than that paid to other postmasters with a similar amount of business. Perhaps it had taken till then for someone to question the salary increase given to William Bugg seventy years previously. In contrast, the post messenger delivering letters to North Sunderland, had his salary raised from 14 to 16 shillings a week, presumably a measure of the increased loads he was delivering. Whether because of the pay reduction or for some other reason, Mrs McDonald gave up by 1851, to be succeeded by the wonderfully named William Septimus Hindmarsh, who remained postmaster until his death in 1887.

Postscript

By the middle of the nineteenth century, the great days of Belford's importance as a post town were gone. With the departure of the mail coaches and the arrival of the railway, the town had effectively been by-passed as a commercial centre. Nevertheless it retained its own post and sorting office until well into the twentieth century, opened a savings bank in 1861 and a telegraph office in 1870. A new purpose built post office was opened on the Church Street site in 1893. It now provided a large general office with a mahogany counter and telegraph facilities, a large well lit sorting room, desks for the convenience of customers outside the counter, and a house for the Postmaster and his family. At that time the deliveries were carried out by 9 postmen, two of whom *had conveyances for their journeys*. The Postmaster now was David Rogers, the grandson of that David Rogers who had been famed as a blacksmith for the mail coaches.

Acknowledgments:
Particular thanks are due to the staff of the Postal Archive at Freeling House, London, for their patience and persistence in helping us locate relevant materials, and to the Science Museum, London, for permission to use the picture of the Royal Mail Coach.

Sources:
Croall, Thomas A., *Travelling Past and Present* Wm. P. Nimmo London & Edinburgh 1877
Davis, Sally, *John Palmer and the Mailcoach Era* Postal Museum Bath
Hyde, James Wilson, *The Royal Mail* Simpkin, Marshall and Co. London 1889
Jameson, Michael, *Coaching in the North Country* Frank Graham, Newcastle-upon-Tyne 1969
Moorhouse, Sydney, *Companion into Northumberland* Methuen 1953
Mountfield, David, *Stage and Mail Coaches* Shire Publications Ltd. 2003
Stray, Julian, *Moving the Mail by Road* The British Postal Museum & Archive
Wilkinson, Frederick, *Royal Mail Coaches* Tempus Publishing Ltd. 2007
Wright, Geoffrey N., *Turnpike Roads* Shire Publications Ltd. 1992

The *Berwick Advertiser*
The *Newcastle Courant*
Good's 1806 Directory for Berwick upon Tweed
Pigot's Northumberland Directories for 1822 and 1834
Thomas Adams Correspondence 1772 - 1800
Stamp Office Letter Books for Alnwick

2

"ANXIOUSLY DESIROUS TO SHEW THEIR ABHORRENCE OF THIS ABOMINABLE TRADE"
...a petition from Belford in 1792
by Valerie Glass

The transatlantic slave trade from Africa to the Americas began with European exploration of West Africa at the start of the 16th century. Slaves, captured or purchased, were shipped to the Atlantic colonies in the Caribbean, South and North America and put to work in the profitable sugar cane fields. At least an estimated 12 million African men, women and children were transported to the New World before 1850, the largest forced migration in history.

The north-east of England had links with slavery through a number of merchants, not only on Tyneside, but throughout Northumberland and the Borders. Such families as the Trevelyans of Wallington (sugar plantations in Grenada), the Graham Clarkes of Newcastle (plantations on Jamaica and sugar refineries in Newcastle), Ninian Home of Paxton House (plantations in Grenada) and the Cadogans of Brinkburn (plantations in Barbados), to name but a few, made fortunes through slave labour. Some people unwittingly acquired or inherited slaves through marriage or the will of a debtor.

Although not on the scale of some other cities such as Bristol, Liverpool or London, some of the North East's industrial wealth also derived from the Slave Trade. John Charlton, in his book *Hidden Chains*, shows how Ambrose Crowley's ironworks in Swalwell, County Durham contributed to the trade.

> *Over 2000 artisans and labourers used cottage forges to produce a breathtaking variety of metal goods. Among those listed in an inventory compiled in 1739 are candlesticks... frying pans... latches... bolts... shovels... knitting needles. Such items would be in great demand in the new territories across the Atlantic and in West Africa, where they were exchanged for Africans.*

In addition, the warehouse inventories show that the ironworks produced locks for Negroes' necks, branding irons and tools for slaves working on plantations in the Caribbean. The keelmen on Tyneside loaded coal on to ships bound for the boiling houses of Caribbean islands and north-east seamen provided crews for vessels carrying captured slaves from West Africa to the Caribbean.

Meanwhile those from the nobility and the newly developing merchant families of the area enjoyed the new products now available to those with money – beautiful furniture made from mahogany, tobacco, cocoa, coffee, spices and silver tableware for use with sugar.

FREE SUGAR.
BENJAMIN TRAVERS, Sugar Refiner, with a view to encourage the Importation of Sugar, produced by the labour of Free Men, and for the accommodation of that part of the community, who, from confcientious motives, abftain from the ufe of Sugar, which is cultivated by Slaves, has commenced the regular refining of Free Sugar, imported by the Eaft-India Company, which he is determined to fell upon the very loweft terms.
London, 19th November, 1791.

Newcastle Courant 11th February 1792

In Britain, by 1788, encouraged by articles in *The Times*, public opinion was beginning to turn against the Slave Trade. On March 5th 1788, *The Times* declared itself totally against slavery: *Though the world be for Slavery, THE TIMES are for freedom. The struggle to emancipate the negroes from chains, cruelty and base subordination, even though it should fail, would reflect honour on this country.*

Despite the role slavery played in the development of the north-east, the area is more notable for its part in abolition, well documented by John Charlton. Dissenting religion – Presbyterianism, Methodism, Unitarianism and Quakerism – expressed their opposition to slavery, the first such record being that of the Quakers in the 1730s.

In 1791, Thomas Clarkson, one of the leading abolitionists, presented his report inquiring into the Slave Trade to the House of Commons. This was published and widely circulated by *The Committee for Effecting the Abolition of the African Slave Trade*, formed in 1787. Another of the members of the Committee was Granville Sharp, the brother of Dr John Sharp who administered the Lord Crewe Charity in Bamburgh. So its work would be well known in this area. Also the first Newcastle anti-slavery society was founded in late 1791.

Granville Sharp

Courtesy of Newcastle City Library

The Committee encouraged:
- the boycott of slave-grown produce;
- used innovatory methods to promote the cause such as badges and icons; and
- organised hundreds of petitions calling for the abolition of the Slave Trade which were delivered to the House of Commons.

Over 500 petitions came from all over the country, with more than 400,000 signatories. It was clear that opposition was growing rapidly. Belford, then a village of no more than 700 inhabitants, many of whom were farm workers without formal education, sent one such petition signed by over 400 persons, more than half of the population.

The earliest mention of the petition from Belford appeared in the *Newcastle Courant* dated 25th February 1792

Northumberland Petitions. We hear that Petitions for the Abolition of the Slave Trade are now signing by great numbers of people in Alnwick, Belford, Wooler, Warkworth, Rothbury, and Hexham; there is little doubt, that every market-town in the North of England will express their abhorrence of a Trade so directly violating every religious and humane principle – vide advertisements for the Alnwick and Belford resolutions.

It also listed the resolutions which the Belford inhabitants passed:

Belford Meeting

At a Meeting of the Inhabitants of the Market town of Belford and Neighbourhood thereof in Northumberland, February 1792, RESOLVED unanimously,

THAT it is their opinion, that many thousand Africans are annually, by the Slave –Trade forcibly dragged from their native country, and the common blessings of Providence, into the most intolerable bondage and misery; and also, that thousands annually expire in the bloody conflicts excited by this Trade, and under the merciless and atrocious conduct of commercial tyrants.

THAT it is their opinion, that it is disgraceful to any country to encourage, to connive at, or any way tolerate such enormities; and that it is more particularly incumbent on a people, who enjoy the blessings of freedom and just government themselves, to forbear to lift the hands

The Belford Resolutions
Newcastle Courant 25th February, 1792

of oppression and tyranny against any class whatever of their fellow-creatures.

THAT it is their opinion that no national grievance would arise out of the suppression of this abominable commerce; and that the interest of a small part of the community, ought, without, hesitation, to be sacrificed to the justice and character of the nation, and the demands of religion and humanity.

THAT they are anxious to express the utmost horror at a continuance of these evils, miseries, and bloodshed, which are occasioned by this trade, to a race of men who never offended against the British nation from the generous temper of whose government, they rather expect protection and freedom, than slavery and destruction.

THAT for these powerful and irresistible reasons, they are earnestly desirous that the practice of transporting the natives of Africa to the British plantations be discontinued and suppressed, and they have signed a petition for that purpose, to the Honourable House of Commons in Parliament assembled, and intend to apply to the County Representatives to present the same, and to define, that when an opportunity offers, they may support, with their votes, a more equitable and effectual code of laws, than those which now exist for the protection and happiness of the Slaves already in the plantations.

Frustratingly, no names of persons, venue of meetings, or collection points for signatures are given in the newspaper account. The following week, on March 3rd, the Courant reported that the Petition had been sent to London.

We hear that the petitions from Alnwick and Belford, for the Abolition of the Slave Trade, were forwarded to London on Wednesday night to be presented to Parliament, the former signed by near 600 persons, and the one from Belford and its vicinity by 433 persons, some of the 433 are Ladies, who were anxiously desirous to shew their abhorrence of this abominable trade.

> We hear that the petitions from Alnwick and Belford, for the Abolition of the Slave Trade, were forwarded to London on Wednesday night to be presented to Parliament, the former signed by near 600 persons, and the one from Belford and its vicinity by 433 persons, some of the 433 are Ladies, who were anxiously desirous to shew their abhorrence of this abominable trade.

Newcastle Courant 3rd March, 1792

Unfortunately, the petition itself has not survived, all the petitions having been destroyed in a fire at the House of Parliament in 1834, so we cannot examine the truth of this statement nor can we examine the social status of the signatories. The involvement of women, however, was a matter of note, and attracted comment both at the time and from modern writers on the subject of Abolition. Indeed, in its report of the petition, *The Courant* had emphasised the part played by women. Adam Hochschild, talking specifically about the Belford Petition, in his book *Bury the Chains* states:

Women were supposed to keep demurely silent about politics but once again the moment was drawing them into public life;

whilst Clare Midgley, in her book *Women against Slavery*, comments on the Belford Petition thus:

Provincial abolition and local press seem to have been less hostile than the London Committee to feminine signatories, a reflection perhaps of their greater radicalism.

Clearly, it was not usual in 1792 for women to sign. There was even a commonly held belief that women's signatures were invalid, as indicated by the comments of the Quaker abolitionist, William Dickson who complained that in the case of the Dundee Petition *by a mistaken zeal some boys and 3 women have been allowed to sign.*

It is not merely the involvement of women, but the readiness of small market towns across the country to become involved in the Anti- Slavery campaign which has attracted attention. In his book, *Popular Politics and British Anti-Slavery: the Mobilisation of Public Opinion against the Slave Trade*, John Oldfield comments specifically on the situation in Northumberland.

In all some 400,000 people may have put their names to petitions in 1792 but just as important as the size of the campaign was its range and diversity. In Northumberland, for instance, even market towns like Belford (400 signatures), Wooler (400 signatures) and Alnick (600 signatures) organise petitions lending their voices to the gentlemen and ship owners of North and South Shields.

He goes on to suggest that, to understand why this was, there is a need to look at:

the mental outlooks of those men (and women) who shaped the movement at the grassroots level, mainly the middling sort, merchants, professionals, manufacturers and shopkeepers.

By 1792, the village of Belford had undergone substantial change under the Lord of the Manor, Abraham Dixon IV. Belford Hall, a Palladian mansion, had been built for his own use. Roads had been improved, new farmhouses built, a coaching inn, woollen mill, tannery and collieries established. Dixon became High Sheriff of Northumberland in 1759. Not only did his improvements increase employment opportunities, they attracted new people into the village, many coming from the Borders. The number of tradesmen grew. Belford was growing prosperous.

It is likely that Belford belonged to a network of informal contacts about the abolition movement in Newcastle. It had excellent transport communication with Alnwick, Newcastle and Berwick, being a staging post on the Great North Road. No doubt travellers alighting from the stagecoach to partake of breakfast at The Blue Bell Hotel would share local and national news. The subject may well have come up for discussion.

At the time of this first phase of public opposition to the Slave Trade, Dr Thomas Trotter was practising in nearby Wooler. At the age of just 23, he had spent some time as a ship's surgeon responsible for a cargo of slaves on board the notorious *Brookes*, which, built to carry 451 people, had taken a cargo of over 600 slaves to the Americas. Shocked at what he saw, Trotter had challenged the captain about conditions on board, but his views were ignored for reasons of cost. He later gave accounts of his experience to Thomas Clarkson who used these in his representations to Parliament in 1792. Trotter's presence so near to Belford may have had some influence on local views on the subject.

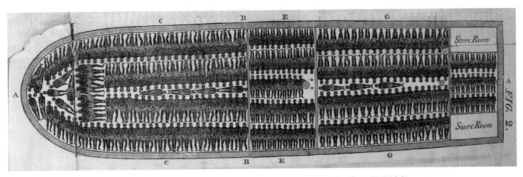

The lower deck of the slave ship *Brookes* Ref: DX449/1
By permission of the Chief Archivist, Tyne and Wear Archives and Museums

Amongst Belford families of that time, it is not possible to identify any definite contenders for the position of petition organiser. There is no evidence, for example, that the Rev. William Armstrong, vicar of Belford St Mary's from 1775 to 1797 was involved. Indeed, he looks an unlikely candidate, as he was not known for his love of Presbyterians, who formed the majority of residents in the village. It is far more likely that the Presbyterian minister had some responsibility for organising the petition or at least taking some supporting role.

The village of Lowick, a few miles from Belford, had one of the oldest dissenting congregations in the country, dating back to 1662. A Meeting House for Presbyterians was established at Warenford in 1771, followed by two more in Belford - West St. and Nursery Row, replacing earlier informal meeting places. So there was a well established Presbyterian following in the area. A document from the Minutes Book of the North Northumberland Presbytery, or group of Presbyterian Churches may offer some insight into the origins of the Belford petition. Of particular interest are the minutes from May to September 1788.

The minutes of 7th May 1788 record the following:
A meeting of Class was holden at Lowick. Mr Nicholls, Mr Wood, Mr Young, Mr Murray and Mr Wallace resolved that a petition be sent from the members of Class to the Honourable House of Commons praying an abolition of the African Slave Trade and that Mr Nicholl as Moderator should transmit the same to the Honourable Mr Grey representative of the County in Parliament requesting him in the name of the Class to lay the petition before the Honourable House of Commons.

Mr Grey was Charles Grey, the local MP who was attracted to the reforming views of Charles James Fox and the Whigs. On receipt of the Petition, Mr Grey replied to the petitioners in a letter dated 29th May and sent to Rev. Nicholls of Warenford that the Petition could not be presented to the House of Commons unless signed by all the petitioners, not just the Moderator. He declared his support:
I will do everything in my power to second the wishes of a body of men for whom I entertain so high a respect in effecting the abolition of that inhuman traffic.

A subsequent meeting on 6th August 1788 reported:
A meeting of Class was holden at Lowick. Present, Mr Nicholls, Mr Aitchison, Mr Young, [Mr Shellock] Mr T Murray, Mr J Murray, Mr Landels and Mr Wallace. A petition respecting the African Slave Trade to be presented to the Honourable House of Commons was subscribed at this meeting.

The Petition signed at the August meeting:
To the honourable the Commons of Great Britain in parliament assembled. The petition of the protestant dissenting ministers of Northumberland humbly sheweth that your petitioners have seriously reflected on the slave trade, consider that trade, the mode of conducting it, and the cruel treatment which the slaves receive from their masters in the British plantations, as disgraceful

to a polished nation, inconsistent with every idea of justice, shocking to the feelings of human nature, and opposite to the spirit of Christian religion which breathes universal benevolence.

Persuaded that the oppressed may expect all possible relief from the British parliament so long distinguished by the love of liberty, your petitioners earnestly pray that this honourable House would consider the pitiable situation of those who are in a state of Slavery and adopt the measures which shall appear most proper to relieve the distresses of that unhappy and helpless part of the human species.

Such an act of Humanity will ...... the approbation of Heaven, command the respect of surrounding nations and adorn the age and country with unfading honours till time shall be no more.

It can be assumed that all those present at the meeting signed the Petition, as no abstentions are recorded. None of those names, however, can be attributed individually to Ministry at Belford. At the same meeting, however, a request for the supply of sermons was received from the Belford dissenters, and for the name of a person recommended to replace a Mr Waters, to preach at Belford. Robert McEwen was recommended and was ordained at the next meeting on 30th September at Belford. It is possible that it was his influence which drove the Belford Petition.

The Minute Book does not refer to a resubmission of the petition with all signatories. A search in *The Times Digital Archive* however, reveals that Mr Grey presented the petition from *dissenting ministers of Northumberland* to the Commons on 6th February, when it was ordered to *lye on the table.* (*The Times*, Saturday, 7th February, 1789).

For the present, lacking other evidence, it seems likely that it was these men who were instrumental in organising the petition from Belford in 1792. Sadly, their endeavours and those of the ordinary people of Belford who signed the petition, did not have immediate success in persuading parliament to end the Slave Trade. The House of Commons agreed to do so, but the House of Lords refused. It took another 15 years until the act for the Abolition of the Slave Trade was passed in 1807.

A subsequent petition from Belford calling for the end of slavery in the British Empire was presented to Parliament in 1824, but even less is known about this petition which is listed in the British Colonial Weekly Register along with many others. Its aim was finally achieved with the passage of the Emancipation Act in 1833.

212   **British and Colonial Weekly Register.**   [July 3, 1824

sions, such contempt of the law will meet with due reprehension and punishment. The conduct of such masters shall be particularly reported, and duly commented on, to the Court of Directors, who have required by the 34th article of the same laws, that all proceedings concerning slaves shall be recorded and sent home to them.

The Governor and Council being resolved, as far as lies in their power, to accomplish the instruction of the slaves in the Christian religion, and in the principles of morality, hereby give

A LIST OF THE PLACES
From whence Petitions have been presented to Parliament during the late Session, praying for the mitigation and gradual abolition of Slavery in the Colonies.

The letter p denotes those Petitions which are printed.

BEDFORDSHIRE. | Gillingham.   HEREFORDS...

Wigston Magna, Oad- p Whitchurch
by and Countisthorpe. | SOMERSETSHIRE. | YORKSHIRE.
LINCOLNSHIRE. | Bath | Askrigg and ... bridge.
p Boston. | p Bridgewater | Banbridge (?)
p Brighouse, &c. (?) | p Chard | p Beverley.
Crowle. | Frome Selwood | p Bowes.
p Donington. | Milborne Port | p Barlington.
Epworth. | p Milverton | p Clerk Heaton.
p Fulbeck ...aden- | p Ne... ...wey and

A LIST OF THE PLACES

From whence Petitions have been presented to Parliament during the late Session, praying for the mitigation and gradual abolition of Slavery in the Colonies.

The letter p denotes those Petitions which are printed.

Sutton Vallance, Chart Sutton, and East Sutton.	Kislingbury.	Woodbridge	Beith.
	p Middleton Cheney.	Woolpit	Borrow
	p Northampton.	SURREY.	Brechi...
Tunbridge.	p Rowell Desborough.	Chertsey	Buckh...
West Malling.	p Peterborough.	Chobham	p Dalkei...
Whitstable & Herne	p Rushden	p Croydon	Denny
› Wye.	Thrapston.	Dorking	Dubbi...
LANCASHIRE.	p Wellingborough.	Farnham	p Dunde
› Accrington.	Wilbarston.	p Guildford	Dunfer
› Ashton under line	p Wollaston.	Reigate	East C
› Barton upon Irwel	NORTHUMBERLAND.	SUSSEX.	Edinb...
› Blackrod.	Alnwick.	p Chichester	Falkir...
Blackley and Har- purhey.	p Belford.	Cuckfield	p Forga...
	p Hexham.	Ditcheling	p Freuch
› Borwick & Hutto...	p Morpeth.	p Horsham	p Glasg...
Botusfleming.	Newcastle (3 pet.)	Hustperpoint	Haddi...
Bury.	p Ovingham.	p Lewes	p Inverk
› Farnworth and Kearsley.	Walls' End.	Lindfield	Jedbu...
	Wooler.	WESTMORLAND.	p Johns...
Gorton.	NO......	Appleby	p Kelso.
› Haslingden.	p Bosford and Bull- well	Bicker (?)	p Lanar...
Hawkshead.		Brough	Leslie.
› Heaton Mersey.	Beckingham	Kendal	Linlith
Heywood.	p Beeston and Chil- well	Kirkby Stephen	Meth...
Holcome.		Kirkby Thorr,	Monte
› Leigh.	Blyth and Hartley	Long Martin and	&c.
› Manchester.	p Calverton and Ep- perstone	Dufton	Montr
Middleton.		Milthorp	Moreb
› Newton and Fails- worth.	p East Retford	Morland	Newb...
	p Gedling and Carl- ton	Shap	New
› Oldham.		WARWICKSHIRE.	North
› Over Hutton and Westhoughton.	p Great Gringley	Atherstone	Peebl...
	Mansfield	Birmingham	p Perth.
Pilkington.	p Misterton	WILTSHIRE.	p Polloc
p Rochdale.	p North and South	Aldeburgh	p Ross.

British and Colonial Weekly Register - 3rd July, 1824
Courtesy of the British Library

It is heartening to know that the petition from Belford succeeded in establis
the principle of women's support in such campaigns, at a time when this ....
almost unknown elsewhere. By 1815, women in Hawick were collecting
signatures for similar petitions, and before 1833, Ladies' Societies organised
their own petitions - over 6000 women from Gateshead and Newcastle signed
the Ladies' petition for the immediate abolition of Slavery, one of 800 women's
petitions. In 1833, of the 300,000 signatures collected in favour of
Emancipation, more than half came from campaigns organised by women.

Sources:
Charlton, John *Hidden Chains, the Slavery Business and North-East England
    1600-1865* Tyne Bridge Publishing 2008
Clarkson, Thomas *An Abstract of the Evidence delivered before a Select
    Committe of the House of Commons in the years 1790 and 1791, on the part
    of the petitioners for the Abolition of the Slave Trade* James Phillips 1792
Dickson, William *Diary of a visit to Scotland on behalf of the London Abolition
    Committee* Temp. MSS 10/14 Friends House Library, London
Hochschild, Adam *Bury the Chains: The British Struggle to Abolish Slavery*
    Macmillan 2005
Midgley, Clare *Women against Slavery: The British Campaigns 1780-1870*
    Routledge 1992
Oldfield, John R *Popular Politics and British Anti-Slavery: The Mobilisation of
    Public Opinion against the Slave Trade 1787-1807* Routledge 1998
Newcastle Courant, Newcastle Central Library
The Times Digital Archive
BUR P 11/1 *Minutes of the Northumberland Class and Presbytery from 17 May
    1785 to 11 Sept 1826* Berwick Record Office

3

THE STORY OF ELEANOR'S DIARY
by Joan Wright

Introduction

A typed copy of a diary originally written in 1804 came to light in Belford in 2004. It had come from Cynthia Sanderson who once farmed at Newlands, just south of Belford. She in turn had been given it many years earlier by another farmer, Anthony Barber of Newham. His ancestors figured largely in the diary, as did some former tenants of Newlands. The journal had been written by Eleanor Weatherly, a twenty year old farmer's daughter from Outchester.

The Weatherly family were mainly tenant farmers, scattered throughout Berwickshire. Eleanor's father, John, was baptised in Coldingham in 1754. He became a Flour merchant and established a Bakery business in Berwick, where his four children were born in the 1780s - James, followed by Eleanor, their sister Susan and finally Nicholas. Their mother died just days after her last child was born.

Despite having a young family to rear John Weatherly did not marry again. After the death of his young wife, he gave up his Berwick business and returned to his farming roots, taking a lease from the Royal Greenwich Hospital for Outchester farm. His daughter Eleanor had been well educated, and

Outchester showing later addition of bay windows
Courtesy of John Sutherland

competently schooled in the domestic skills of spinning, sewing and cooking. At the age of twenty she was confidently running the family household.

It is evident from the diary that this family was well established there by 1804, and Eleanor and her sister had become good friends with Mary and Barbara, the daughters of John Dinning, the tenant at nearby Newlands.

Newlands
Courtesy of the late Cynthia Sanderson

Written just before the novels of Jane Austen were published, it is easy to identify with the period, but there the similarity ends. These words were not about fictional characters living in grand houses somewhere in 'Middle England', but about real families who had lived in, and around Belford. Here was an undiscovered piece of social history about the north of Northumberland, which had languished in a drawer for decades.

Surely it deserved a wider audience.

The following edited extracts are intended to give a glimpse into life at the very beginning of the 19th century, bearing in mind that these families and their acquaintances were of very comfortable means.

The Weatherly family were Presbyterians and normally worshipped at the Meeting House at nearby Warenford. However, when it suited, the young siblings were not averse to making use of the pew of their friends in the parish church in Belford.

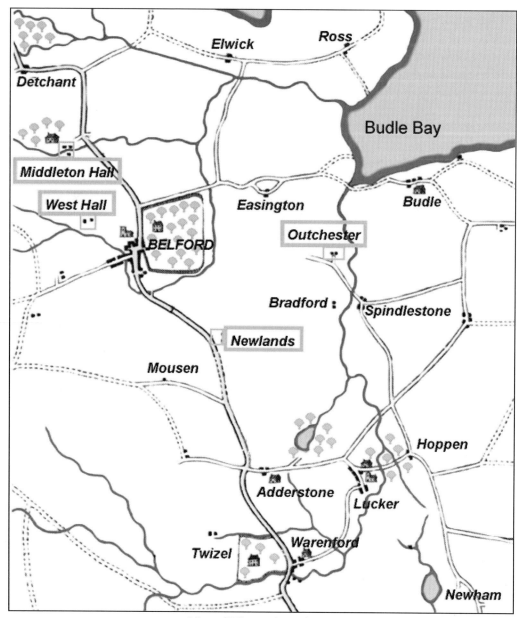

Map of 'Eleanor's territory'

During the winter months, when there were no balls or outdoor activities for entertainment, they and their friends played cards nightly, and always for money. They loved to gamble, and would place bets on just about anything. The favoured 'stake' for these bets, was always a pair, or pairs of gloves - which must have been music to the ears of the glove makers.

The diary begins - *'should curiosity induce anyone to read this book I hope they will forgive repetitions'......*

January 1804

2ⁿᵈ   *Mrs Hall and apprentice were here making our lace muslin gowns for the Belford dance. Miss Margaret Younghusband sent me a rye loaf as a New Year gift.*

4ᵗʰ   *I made a pair of shoe bows, went to Newlands for tea and from there to the Belford Ball. I danced the first two dances with Ensign Barber, two with John Younghusband, four with William Mole and the last two with Henry Dinning. The Ball broke up at 2 o'clock, we returned to Newlands for supper.*

5ᵗʰ   *Miss Bab Dinning, Susan and myself took a walk to Belford West Hall this morning, escorted by Capt'n Sanderson and the Reverend Mr Dawson - Sarah Redpath did not look so well this morning, but Miss Bawtrie looked interestingly lovely. We came back to dinner at Newlands with additions to the party, Mr Sandy Thompson of Scremerston and his sister Betsy and Mr Trotter of Middleton.*
William Mole and my father came to Newlands in the afternoon, we had a charming dance after tea. Mr Dawson is a very lame dancer. Miss Dinning did not dance with much spirit, having lost her heart the night before at the Ball. Miss B. D. sported some new steps, which I vainly tried to imitate but did not succeed. William Mole would have accompanied us home to Outchester, had my father not wished him goodnight at the road that takes off to Chesterhill. I was so vexed, I went to bed without my supper

7ᵗʰ   *Susan and I had a quarrel today because she would not give me a piece of clout[1] to mend my Morning gown. We exchanged a few blows - I came off victorious. I had a letter from Miss Dinning enclosing the fashions for 1804. One of our servants drawn for the Militia won 3d.*

8ᵗʰ   *There has been a very great fall of snow last night, I cannot get to Warenford, had to have a fire on in our room. Nichol had his usual search for his Catechism, but could not find it, nor never can.*

10ᵗʰ *This day has been replete with disappointments and hopes. My father*

---

[1] Piece of cloth or patch used for mending

says we are not to go to West Hall on Thursday to dine - I lost my dinner with the hare pudding being too salt - lost 1/6d at cards, and last of all lost my temper.

16th Mr Sanderson of Swinhoe called, we had roast pig to dinner, James came home from the Drill very ill, has got a severe cold. I have got such trouble in my eyes, can hardly see to write. The weather continues rainy.

17th I was dressed rather comical today. I had on a buff gown, green checked handkerchief, purple stock, black velvet round my head, with a large green shade - had to go to bed after tea as I was so ill.

21st Had a present of a turkey from Miss Young, Mr Barber of Doddington dined here, had Chatto Watson to tea.

25th There has been a great fall of rain last night - the waters are all up - not one in the neighbourhood is fordable. Mr Yellowly called. Susan and I had a dispute about making the tea - neither of us would do it, so my father did it himself. Lost 1/6d at cards.

28th I wrote a letter for one of our servants to her husband, then went to Newlands to tea, arrived before they sat down to dinner. Barbara, Harry and I took a ride to Belford - Harry treat us with sweetmeats.

February

2nd We were all much alarmed this morning by a report that the French are landed in Scotland. The Glendale Cavalry[1] are gone to Alnwick to join the Percy Tenantry. Lost 1/6d at cards, but got it back again.

3rd The report was false. The beacons were lighted by seeing some whins on fire. James came home from Alnwick, much mortified that he had not seen some of the French dogs. The Miss Dinnings spent the day with us, we took a walk to Waren and Spindleston, Chatto and John Watson called. We amused ourselves tonight with blacking each other's faces.

4th The Miss Dinnings stayed here last night, we did not go to bed until 1 o'clock talking about a dance my father has promised us. James wrote a card to Mr Fenwick Compton enclosing a ticket for the Belford dance. I have been busy today making marmalade.

---

[1] Volunteer militia raised locally

7ᵗʰ We went to Newlands to tea, from there to Mr Calvert's 2ⁿᵈ subscription ball. I danced with Harry Dinning, William Barber of Boomer and William Mole. The ball was honored by the presence of Sir Carnaby and Lady Haggerston, Sir Thomas Stanley and Miss Haggerston - the room was crowded as there were near 100 people in it - broke up at 4 o'clock.

Blue Bell Hotel, Belford scene of the Subscription Ball

11ᵗʰ Miss Younghusband and Miss Werges of Horton drank tea here. Margaret stopt all night as it was so dark she durst not drive the gig home. James had to be charioteer to Miss Werges.

15ᵗʰ Had a card from Mr Richardson this morning before I was out of mon lit. We went to Belford church and sat in the Younghusbands seat. Mr Cook treat us with Ratafie, took very ill after I came home. Read 3 sermons.

16ᵗʰ We had a large party here to tea and supper and a dance - the Younghusbands, Woods, Dinnings, Watsons and Moles. We danced till 4 o'clock, Misses Y.H and Dinnings stayed all night. James was very civil to the ladies.

18ᵗʰ Susan and I were at wars this morning - I beat her until she wept. I have had a very busy day cleaning out the closets - have been contriving a dress to have on at Elwick next week as I hear we are to have a dance. I could not get a game at cards tonight as I was short of cash.

26ᵗʰ This morning I did not know what I was about, as I sugared all the teacups twice.- but I always commit a multiplicity of mistakes *after seeing* <u>John Y.</u>

27th I expected to have gone today to see Lord Ossulton's Corps[1] inspected, but alas I am disappointed.

29th I had a pig merchant here this morning, but we could not agree a price, so did no business. I spun a clip of yarn before 4 o'clock. My father and cousin William Weatherly from Dunbar, Susan and James all went to Newham Newhouses to dinner. Susan came home in a sore temper having lost all her money at cards. I have been busy reeling my yarn tonight.

March

3th Mr Walton came to tea - we had a hand at cards before the candle was brought in - I lost nine pence. Showers of snow.

5th I have been six times dressed in my ball gown which I am to have on tomorrow night. Won nine pence at Whist and three pence at 'Watch the Ten'. This day has been very stormy with showers of sleet.

6th Susan and I dressed to go to the ball at Belford, I was the last that came into the room. Danced with Mr Thomas Smith, Mr Archbold and Cornet Grieve Smith. Mr Pringle was very civil to Miss Wilson. Went home with the Newlands party.

8th Quite alone today, began to spin the coarse lint

13th Susan and my father are gone to Scotland. I took a walk to Spindleston to see Mrs Crisp. Nichol and I went to Mr Forster's of Glororum to tea. A fine day.

17th Quite alone today, I expected Miss Forster and Mr Richardson, but suppose the weather has prevented them, it has rained incessantly this whole day. I have spun a quarter of a pound of Lint - altered a Habit skirt and hemmed 4 coarse towels today.

19th The kitchen maid and I spun half a spignol[2] of yarn today. My father and uncle David came from Scotland.

---

[1] Captain of the Glendale Cavalry, son of the Earl of Tankerville
[2] In spinning terms four hanks make a spinnle, and twelve cuts are a hank or slip. These terms are now unknown save to old people. (R.O Heslop, Northumberland Words 1892)

30th This being Good Friday I went to Belford church - from there to Wandylaw with Barbara Dinning for dinner - saw a great number of officers at Belford. Remarkably fine day, James was sowing wheat late.

31st Had a walk with James through the fields seeing the lambs. John Younghusband was here to tea, got my Ball Gown home from Edinburgh, all over silver trimming with velvet sleeves. Badly off for pens

April

3rd Rode up to Newlands at 3 o'clock, had my hair dressed by Mr Cousins at 4, drank tea at 5 - finished dressing by 7 o'clock. Was led into the Ball by Mr Dinning, this is Calverts last subscription Ball. Returned to Newlands at half past 3 o'clock, supped and went to bed.

4th Newlands - rose at 10 o'clock, quite refreshed. Had 4 slices of tongue, 3 of ham, an egg and three cups of tea to my breakfast.

8th Was at Warenford Meeting, took very ill after I came home and went to bed after dinner. Miss Dinning wrote a card for me to come up to Newlands - I grew immediately better and went there for tea.

Warenford Meeting House (now demolished)
Courtesy of George Nairn

11th My cousin W Weatherly, Mr Rankin of Berwick and the Miss Dinnings drank tea here. We went as far as the turnpike with the Miss D's - I without hat or shawl had to walk home on dirty roads, had on my best morocco shoes. Lost 1/6d at cards.

14th I expected to have gone to Newlands today, but was disappointed as my Father would not allow me to go - I had been so lately there. James has been at home this whole day. Finished spinning the doze of coarse lint begun on March 8th.

17th Went to Warren House to tea, after tea I went in the carriage with Mrs and Miss Watson to Belford to the Silver Miner's concert - the house was crowded.

24th Wrote to Susan, went up to Newlands to tea, was home before sunset. Spun nine cutts of yarn, read a novel, William Weatherly came to supper - did not get to bed until half past 12 o'clock.

28th Been remarkably busy today cleaning out my room. I have got a severe headache with working so hard. I have been very dull all this week, having seen the Miss Dinnings so seldom. The weather is beginning to settle, this has been a very fine day.

May

3rd Was up this morning at 6 o'clock to spin - I spun until seven in the evening and had two slips of yarn.

5th Had a letter from Mr Robert Younghusband in Dublin. My cousin John Weatherly of Butterdean Mains came to spend a few days. I have been uncommonly restless today - I first began to red[1] up my drawers - next to spin - then read, about half an hour after that began to make a watch chain, but did not finish a job today. At last I found some amusement in the world, a book wrote by Fitz-Adam.

8th I went to Spindleston to breakfast - from there to Bambro' church to Betty Wilson's wedding. Came back to Spindleston to dinner - there was a large party - eight and twenty dined. The Miss Dinnings, John Younghusband and Mr Richardson came to Outchester to supper. We were all very merry when my Father and James made their debut - they were at Link Hall sale.

11th My cousin and Nichol are gone to Scotland. Was quite alone today, My Father and James are at Mr Wastall's neap. I dined at 3 o'clock on radishes. Mr Anthony Barber called in the evening - very drunk.

15th Wrote to the Iron monger and Cabinet maker. Mrs Weatherly and her family came from Dunbar today, Susan returned along with them. I was at Belford Fair but did not stop ten minutes

16th Mrs Weatherly, the children, Marion and I went to dinner at Newham Newhouses. Miss Young, John and I went to Link Hall to put the house in

---

[1] Tidy up

order. Miss Y went home, but I had to stop all night.

17th   Link Hall. Mr Young, my brother James and cousin David Weatherly came here after dinner. Miss Young was along with them. The company all went away at nine o'clock and I was again left in the house with only my cousin William and little John.

18th   Link Hall. My cousin has a sprained arm, so I had to be his amanuensis. I have been very busy today cooking the dinner for my Father and cousins - Mrs Weatherly came with the rest of her family about 5 o'clock, which gave me some relief.

19th   Nichol came for me to go home after tea.

25th   John Younghusband came here after dinner, and my cousin William of Link Hall. Miss Watson came up for us to go to a wedding that was at Spindleston Mill - we all went down and drank tea with the bride, and met with a great deal of civility.

31st   Made a sleeping gown, had a baking and bottled a cask of rum. This day has been uncommonly windy so much so that when I was out getting a walk, the wind blew me over. I was obliged to get hold of a plough stilt[1].

June

2nd   Mr Dinning, his brother and Mr Yellowly dined here, we had chicken and gooseberries to dinner for the first time this season. Miss Dinnings came down after tea to get some money from my Father to buy us hats in Newcastle - had a deal to do before he would part with the ready.

5th   I have been very busy today, flounced two petticoats, hemmed three yards of muslin, darned my thin sprigged muslin gown, made tea and last of all mended James small clothes.

9th   Took a walk to Bradford - had on my new hat for the first time, unfortunately got a shower on the road. Been busy packing my trunk for to be ready to go off on Monday.

Eleanor spent the rest of the month staying with relatives in Berwickshire - in particular visiting Blackburn, Boushiell, Townhead and Cambus, Cockburnspath and Cove. She arrived back in Berwick by the *Union* coach on

---

[1] Handle

2nd July. She had two days at Lamberton races, went to an Assembly and visited the theatre twice to see *She Stoops to Conquer* and *The Tragedy of Douglas*. Nichol came in to take her home to Outchester on the 7th.

13th *I was at the bathing[1] this morning before breakfast - a very fine day. We had young potatoes and green peas to dinner for the first time. The currant berries are ripe - bad crop of strawberries.*

26th *Met Mr Watson as I was going to the bathing[1] this morning. Was up at Newlands this afternoon and was regaled with strawberries and cherries. James went into Berwick, he is to be in for a week with the rest of the troop on permanent duty.*

Berwick Barracks
Courtesy of Jim Walker

30th *Stayed overnight at Link Hall, from there I went to Alnwick Fair. Got a gown from Mr Young, a dart from John Fawcus and a silk handkerchief from my cousin. Called upon Miss Wilson, drank tea with Miss Younghusband.*

August

2nd *Had a letter from my brother James, desiring Susan and I to come in to the Assembly tonight. We went in a chaise with Miss M. Younghusband. We went to the ball at 10 o'clock – danced the first two dances with Mr Fenwick Compton, then with Lieut. Tanner and Mr Tom Smith. Slept at the Kings Arms - went to bed at 6 o'clock.*

King's Arms Hotel, Berwick
Courtesy of Jim Walker

[1] At Budle Bay

3rd   Got up at nine o'clock, had breakfast with Mrs Todd, where I met a large party of gentlemen - got another breakfast at an inn with another party. Came to Belford in the coach - Miss Duncan the Actress was in the coach.

12th   We were all at Belford church today as there was no preaching at Warenford. My cousin Burrell dined with us, we went to Newlands for tea - my uncle James of Hoprigg and cousin of Linn Head were at Outchester when we got home.

16th   My uncle James and cousin of Linn Head went away just after breakfast. I was up this morning at 6 o'clock to bake muffins. Was at the bathing - weather showery.

22nd   Went up to Newlands from there to Belford Fair - drank tea at Mrs Broomfield - there was a large party there. The Scotch shearers came home today.

26th   I was at Belford church, sat in the Elwick pew - coming home I was for riding behind Mr Walton - I got on to the horse, but it would not carry double, so I was obliged to dismount again.

31st   James came in before dinner and said he had met Mrs Redpeth and Jane Humble - they had promised to come to Outchester to drink tea. So in the afternoon I posted off to meet them - I walked almost to Bamburgh but could see nothing of the ladies - I returned home very much disappointed for James humming me[1].

September

10th   I finished a little cap I had been working for Mrs Hood of Old Cambus Town Head - it has been my principle (sic) employment this last fortnight.

15th   I have hemmed half a dozen neck cloths today - the weather is warmer just now than what is has been this summer.

24th   Susan and I went to Newlands to dinner - went in the gig with Barbara to Belford races and returned to Newlands to tea. Mr Trotter was there, also Mr Bugg, Mr Cook, Mr Joe Mole, James and Nick, my cousin William Weatherly etc. Disagreeable wet day

---

[1] Hoax

28th   Mr Gibson of Lesbury dined here. We had the Kirn[1] tonight - had a
        pleasant dance.

29th   James and I were at Mr Scott's at Easington to tea - we called twice on Mr
        Yellowly but he was from home - very pleasant day. I have not had a good
        pen this month.

October

7th   Susan and I took the Sacrament for the first time today and afterwards
        we dined with Mr Ross[2].

12th   Susan and I called at Waren house to see John Watson who is very ill - we
        met Mrs Cap't Watson and Miss Grey there.

21st   Nickle and I went to Mr Thompson's meeting[3] - William Weatherly came
        to Outchester to dinner - Nick and I went with him to Newhouses to tea -
        the weather continues very pleasant.

29th   My Father went to Scotland this morning. We all went up to Newlands -
        from there to Wandylaw where we had a pleasant dance.

November

1st   Went up to Newlands to be ready to set off for Alnwick.

2nd   Barbara and I set off for Alnwick immediately after breakfast - went to Mr
        Wilsons - Miss Carples and Miss Wilson came back to Newlands with us. I
        called at Link Hall, we were back at Newlands before dinner. Our family
        were all up here - Mr Trotter, Laird Anderson etc - we had a dance -
        danced six couples and stopped to supper.

6th   My cousin Tom Weatherly of Hoprigg and Mr William Blackadder came to
        dinner - we had a large company to drink tea with us - sixteen in all.

8th   My cousin Tom, James and I were out hunting with the greyhounds - went
        to Link Hall to dinner.

11th   My cousin Thomas went away after breakfast. I won 2 shillings at Lieu
        this week - John Younghusband came here to his supper - had a busy day
        baking.

---

[1] Dance to celebrate the Harvest home
[2] Minister at Warenford Meeting House
[3] Minister at the 'Scotch' Church in Belford

21ˢᵗ *The colours were presented to the Glendale Troop today by Lady Haggerston.*

Chillingham Castle

Susan and I went up to Newlands after dinner and we began immediately to dress for the ball at Chillingham Castle. The chaise came for the Miss Dinnings and us at 6 o'clock, we called at Chillingham Barns for Mrs Younghusband, as we went in her party. We went into the room at nine o'clock, I was introduced to Lady Haggerston. Danced the first two dances with John Younghusband. There were between two and three hundred at the dance - kept it up until 6 o'clock in the morning - arrived at Newlands to breakfast at 8 o'clock.

25ᵗʰ *James and I were at Belford church - Harry Dinning treat us with milk punch. After dinner James, Susan Nickle and self went over to Chester Hill to see Miss Watson. Had a letter from Robert Younghusband, Dublin.*

29ᵗʰ *My cousin Joseph Burrell and his sister Nelly came to take leave of us before returning home to London. This is Miss Younghusband's wedding day.*

December
4ᵗʰ *Went up to Newlands after dinner, to go to the first subscription ball. Miss Andersons, Miss Dinnings, Susan and I all went in one chaise - led into the room by Mr George Selby. I danced the first two dances with John Younghusband, then with George Selby, Joe Mole, William Watson, Patrick Mole and Captain Humble. Returned as we came - very hard frost*

11ᵗʰ *I spent all this forenoon with Miss Watson at Chester Hill - Susan and I dined at Candle light.*

16ᵗʰ *James and I went to Alnwick, dined with Mr Wilson and then came to Link Hall to tea - a very stormy day, intense frost and hail.*

23ʳᵈ *Susan and I went to Chester Hill to see Miss Watson who has got herself very much burnt. Susan went home to dinner, but I stopped until eleven o'clock at night.*

25th *Mr Walton called - James and I went to Newlands to tea - called at Chester Hill and Belford. The weather is rather stormy.*

30th *Mrs Hall is here making my Leno gown I got from London. Susan, James and I were at Glororum to tea - met Mr Cockane - he was my partner at cards. James won 10 shillings from betting at whist. Weather neither frosty nor fresh.*

Begun this journal for to improve my writing - now been scribbling at it for a year, and still left room for improvement - will see what another year may do. I think this is the happiest year I have seen yet.

Interval

Unfortunately there was no transcript for the following year. It seemed possible that the original diary was mouldering away in an attic somewhere in the locality. Exhaustive enquiries proved fruitless. All that remained was to complete the research into the later years of the family, and assuming that was the end of the story, 'close the file'. Many months later, a lady who had read one of the 'Diary' articles made contact. As a keen spinner and weaver, she was curious about some of the old terms used, and consequently put a query into a national journal for 'spinners and weavers'. She only had one response. It came from a lady in Cumbria, who couldn't help with the spinning terms, but asked where the extracts had come from, as they matched word for word with a diary in her possession.

What an unbelievable stroke of luck!

The diary owner was Elspeth Orrom, née Oliver, whose family had lived for many years at Lochside House near Yetholm, The diary had been in that family's possession for over a hundred years - and in fact it was Elspeth's mother who had typed out the copy which had found its way into the hands of Anthony Barber in Northumberland. When Elspeth and I met up, it was a thrilling

Eleanor's diary
Courtesy of Elspeth Orrom

experience to actually hold and read the original diary, and quite a revelation for Elspeth to discover its provenance, for she knew nothing of this diarist, Eleanor Weatherly.

The 'missing' year for 1805 was continued in the same volume - but had not been transcribed by Elspeth's mother.

January 1805

3rd   Barbara and I went to Mr Thompson's of Scremerston for dinner. From there we went to Mungo Walls[1] in time for tea. A pleasant journey, but the road was so slippery we were obliged to get out of the gig - saw a beautiful house at Ninewell Mill.

4th   Mungo Walls. Barbara and I were sewing before we were out of bed, altering a gown for Bab to have on at the ball tonight. Bab and I were dressed alike, had on white gowns with scarlet velvet sleeves - lace veils on our heads with a crescent and wreath of brown velvet leaves. We went into the ballroom at 8 o'clock and danced reels with every gentleman in the room. I led off the New Claret, which was quite new here and very much liked. Had two smart beaux at supper - never liked a dance so much as ever I was at. No dancing after supper which was served up at 4 o'clock, we got home at 6 o'clock.

5th   Mungo Walls. Got up to breakfast at eleven o'clock, having had a sound sleep and dreamed of nothing but the handsome Dr Trotter. Bab, Sandy, George and I took a walk to Swinhoe - we each got a pair of gloves from George who bet that we could not walk so far after the dance. We had company all day and after tea Peter Tait came and insisted on stopping all night. What a charming day this was - had dancing, singing and everything that could be thought of to give us pleasure. Betsy Thomson and I went into Peter Tait's room after he was asleep - wound up his watch and put a new string to it.

6th   Mungo Walls. The beaux were not inclined to go to Church, of course the ladies did not wish to go either. It was proposed to go to the Crookses and see Mr George Thompson's house - the Doctor drove Betsy and Bab in the gig.- I rode Mr Thompson's mare escorted by Mr David Murray and Mr Peter Tait. Saw a great many gentlemen's seats, Nisbet, and Lord Swinton's at Hall Back, Lord Hume's at the Hirsell and Manderson. We rode up to the Hirsell Law, but the gig could not get up as the Water Leet was not fordable - only for horses - I rode it up to the saddle laps. Got whiskey punch at Crookses and came to Bogend for dinner. We returned to Mungo Wall's after supper - did not go to bed before we had a

---

[1] House near to Duns in Berwickshire

comfortable chat by the fireside. I was rather fatigued having rode above twenty miles before dinner - took leave of Peter Tait which rather affected me.

7th   *Was quite melancholy this morning as I did not wish to leave this enchanting country. The Doctor, Bab and I left Mungo Wall's at the same time. Mr Thompson of Scremerston had to take charge of us through Berwick, as the servant had taken the wrong road and missed us. I made several calls, paid an account for Miss Dinning, was at all the milliners shops in Berwick, called on a servant that once lived with us - got a scold from Barbara for stopping so long. Dined at Scremerston, we got to Newlands for tea, where we met Mr Bugg and his son Compton, who danced a hornpipe four times over.*

18th   *Nichol went off to go to Edinburgh this morning, Dr Turnbull from Dunbar came here just before we drank tea to spend a few days. I won 1/6d at cards.*

22nd   *We all went up to Mrs Bromfield to tea - we dressed there to go to the 2nd subscription ball - I danced the first dance with Doctor Turnbull - after the first 4 dances we changed partners every dance - danced 14 couples. Did not get home until 8 o'clock. Mr Bowlt[1] appeared at the ball with wedding favours having married Miss Haggerston the day preceeding to Sir Thomas Stanley. We had supper which improved the gentlemen's dancing - this was the first dance I was ever tired of dancing at.*

ZMD-167-1-98   ZMD-167-1-99
Reproduced with permission of Northumberland Collections Service

24th   *Doctor Turnbull left us today, I have had a busy day putting by my cloathes and mending them. Wrote to Nichol.*

---

[1] Mr Bowlt was then the Vicar of Bamburgh

February

1ˢᵗ   Miss Dinning, Miss Watson and William Watson dined and spent the day here. William hid Mary's fur tippet - never remember of laughing so much as I did this afternoon - tickling Mary Dinning's knees. Had a present from Miss D of a preserved orange.

5ᵗʰ   James and I went to Belford church - Mary Ann Selby and I walked three times up and down the West Street - met Captain Forbes. Wrote a very long letter to Nicholas and sent him 11/6d.

12ᵗʰ   Made the Marmalade today. John Younghusband came to tea and brought from Edinbro' a letter from Nichol. Won a shilling from my father at Whist.

18ᵗʰ   Mrs Hall and her apprentice were here today making a morning gown and pelisses - they stopt all night.

24ᵗʰ   At Doddington. Came here to tea yesterday, I won a shilling playing at Lieu and seven shillings at Whist. This morning a gentleman bet me a dozen pairs of gloves I would be married to John Younghusband. A guinea I will look plainer than I do now six years hence, and another half dozen pairs of gloves that, if I am not married in six years time, I will never be married. Left after breakfast and hunted all the way home, only got one hare.

27ᵗʰ   Susan went off to Edinbro' this afternoon.

March

5ᵗʰ   Went to Newlands to tea from there we went to Belford to see 'The Conjuror' and the players - never saw as many beaux at Belford, there were five officers in the theatre.

10ᵗʰ   Had a letter from Susan and Nichol. James and I were at Waren House to dinner, after tea we played at Commerce - Miss Watson, Mole and Weatherly were in Co - we won the pool which was 4/6d - we stopt to supper. I never remember seeing such a fine day at this season of the year, it was so warm and mild.

23ʳᵈ   I rode to the Warenford Meeting alone. After dinner I took a walk to see Miss Dinning - I met her on the Turnpike, she and Mrs Henderson came to *tea. I wrote until Monday morning, finishing a letter to Bab Dinning and Susan which was twenty four pages long - also wrote to Nichol in answer to one I had from him today.*

BY DESIRE OF

The STEWARDS of the RACE.

THEATRE, BELFORD.

On Monday Evening Sept. the 24th, 1810.

will be performed the Popular Drama of the

CASTLE SPECTRE

Osmond	MR. BRADY
Reginald	MR STANMORE
Motly	MASTER BRADY
Father Philip	MR. BRADY
Angela	MISS BRADY
Alice and the Spectre	MRS. BRADY

DANCING

BY MISSES BRADY.

To which will be added the Farce of

The Lying Valet.

Sharp	MR. BRADY
Justice Guttle	MASTER BRADY
Gayless	MISS BRADY
Kitty Pry	MRS. BRADY
Melissa	MISS M. BRADY

To begin when the Race is over.

PIT 1s. GALLERY 6d.

Tickets to be had at the Blue-Bell-Inn, and of Mr. Brady.

On TUESDAY Evening—the HEIR AT LAW, and LOVERS' QUARRELS.

Davison, Printer, Alnwick.

Belford Theatre notice from 1810 probably similar to the performance arrangements as visited by Eleanor on 5th March

28th James and my father were from home, Miss Dinning and I spent this day very comfortably by ourselves - she left me after tea.

April

2nd I went to Newlands to tea and got myself completely wet coming home, it was a very rainy evening. Cut off a dozen shirts for Nichol.

6th Had a letter from Susan sent with her green gown and a pair of bibles. Went to Newlands to tea and stopt all night.

7th Newlands - got downstairs to breakfast at 8 o'clock. John Younghusband came to escort Miss Dinning and I up to Learmouth. We called at Wooler and got to Mrs Compton's at 2 o'clock.

8th Learmouth. After breakfast Mr & Mrs Compton with Miss Dinning in the gig, and John Younghusband and I on horseback went to take an airing. We went to Coldstream and Cornhill, and got home to dinner about 3 O'clock. We had just drunk tea when in came Mr Givens the fiddler - we danced until we were all tired. I sported a green lustre which was very much worse of the excessive heat.

10th Learmouth. John Younghusband went away yesterday, my brother James came after breakfast to take us home. I made a bet with Mrs Compton that before this time twelvemonth she will have an addition to her family. Mary was very cross on our way home. We have got our tickets for the next Belford ball, I wish we may have plenty of beaux, but am rather doubtful.

13th We are all very dull today having heard of the death of my Aunt Catherine, my father is in low spirits. Went to Belford to buy mourning, I hope I will get to the ball next week.

17th Went to Newlands to dress for the ball. We danced 10 couples and were in great spirits - had an offer. Was dressed in a short blue gown with lace let in round the bottom - blue beads with brown net on my head, cord and tassle at my waist. Every lady was in the room before any of the gents made their debut - 19 ladies and 26 gentlemen - we gave up dancing at 5 o'clock.

18th Newlands. After dinner my brother and a number of beaux came in, we *danced until supper. Mary Dinning and I amused ourselves with knotting all the gents hats so they could not go home, and we sewed up the arms of Joe Mole's greatcoat. Am not fatigued with all the dancing but dull, that all the balls are over.*

26th *Had a letter from Susan and one from Miss Dinning for me to go to Ross with her - my father would not allow me to go. I have been very dull today as I see by the papers that Robert Younghusband is sailed for the East Indies.*

May

1st *After dinner I took a walk to Newlands - about 6 o'clock the party arrived from Edinbro'. Nichol is a great buck - speaks fine, has a stock up to his nose. Susan and Barbara dressed in velvet pelisses[1] looked quite stylish - the noise we made was ridiculous.*

5th *The whole family were at the Meeting - this being the Sacrament day.*

10th *Nichol and I went to Link Hall to dinner - from there to Alnwick, did a deal of business and then went on to Bassington to tea. This is the first time I have been to see Mrs Nichol Burrell - got several showers of rain.*

11th *Bassington. We came away after breakfast, called at Link Hall and got home to dinner. Miss Watson called upon us to go to Newlands - when we were half way on the road a shower of hail came on which wet us to the skin – the weather is colder and more stormy than it was a month ago.*

17th *Mr Walton and William Watson were here to tea and supper. Had a rubber at Whist - William and I against my father and Mr Walton - I won sixpence. Had two bowls of punch to drink Nichol's joy - he leaves Outchester tomorrow*

18th *Nichol left us this morning - we were all very sorry to part with him. James has gone to see him on board.*

20th *John Younghusband came here to tea and stopt to supper. He told us that Mr Werges, with him and James had seen Nichol over the bar at Berwick on Saturday.*

---

[1] 'Edge to edge' coat, usually calf length

22nd *Miss Dinnings were here to tea, I went up to meet them. We went a good deal out of our way to put up some of Mr Weddle's fat sheep that were laying awkward.*

24th *My father is very anxious to hear about Nichol - he is often looking out to see if the wind is fair. Susan and I walked to Chester Hill, then to Spindleston and from there to take tea at Glororum we had a long chat about the Bent Hall dance. We then went to Bambro' Friars and the castle to see Miss Maughan.*

27th *Got a letter from Nichol, he got to London on Thursday. After dinner Susan and I went to Newlands and with Miss Dinnings to the Middleton sale. We got a dreadful fright with some cows that were in a field, as we had a dog with us which attracted their notice. They ran after us and had Mr Jobling not protected us we might have been hurt. Barbara tumbled over with fear. As the dog belonged to me it got as close to my side as possible, and I was surrounded by cows. However we surmounted all difficulties and reached Middleton to tea.*

28th *We were at a bride's tea drinking. This is Belford Fair and we were not there – this is the first Fair we have been absent from this ten years. Had a ticket from William Humble for the Bent Hall dance.*

June

8th *We went to Swinhoe, the Dinnings, Sandersons and us, drank tea at Bent Hall. Joe Mole and John Younghusband drank tea at Outchester. Went into the Assembly room at 9 o'clock - Joe Mole and I led off the New Claret - had a merry dance but rather confused. Harry Dinning, Joe Mole and John Younghusband came home with us to breakfast, reached home at 7 o'clock - we did not go to bed.*

12th *Was up this morning between 5 and 6 o'clock and had a very busy day - baked as much bread as would last us ten days.*

17th *Had two wool buyers to tea, William Watson brought me a pair of gloves. After tea Joe Mole and Margaret Watson called, Joe was as usual in high spirits, had a talk about the ball which is take place on Friday.*

19th *Mr Richardson of Spindleston is taken unto himself a wife today - had 3 chaises at the wedding - the happy party dined at Holy Island. George*

Cornforth came after tea and gave us a full and particular account of the wedding.

20th   *I have since Monday been working at my ball dress – it is now finished.*

21st   *Miss Younghusband and I rode into Alnwick, single horse without a beau – James rode before Susan. We drank tea with Sandersons at the Black Swan. Went to the dance and returned to the Black Swan to sup and slept there – were very much disturbed with the noise in the house.*

22nd   *Got a very uncomfortable breakfast at the Swan, all the inhabitants were drunk, took a walk with the Sandersons and Dinnings to see the castle – this is the first time I was ever in it.*

Entrance to Alnwick Castle c.1825

30th   *My cousin Nichol Burrell came to dinner – this is their wedding visit. Afterwards we had a walk to Spindleston Hills and in the evening took a walk in Bradford Dean. The evening was so pleasant none of us could stay in the house – the Watsons are parading about, they seem as loth as us to go into the house.*

July

7th   *James and I took a ride to Belford church. A party of soldiers were marching north, some of them stopped in Belford. The band played in the church – I never saw as many people in the church – a great many of the soldiers were obliged to stand as they could not get seats.*

10th   *Was up at 5 o'clock, we were at Newlands before they were out of their beds- got a second breakfast there, and set out for Lamberton races. Miss Dinnings, Susan and I in a chaise and Harry and James on horseback. We had very little sport on the Raceground, the day was so unfavourable. Returned to Berwick to the Assembly, I had on a green lustre dress with silver tissue sleeves.*

11th   *Berwick. Got down to breakfast at 9 o'clock, walked about the streets for an hour and then the walls, we went out to the Race Ground at twelve. Lost 3 pairs of gloves and came back to Newlands for supper. I have got a very bad cold - bet Grieve Smith that he will be married in the course of a week - doubt I shall lose.*

16th   *Went up to Newlands and we all walked up to West Hall – Capt'n Humble gave us a dance on Belford Craggs. We drank tea in a marquee which was erected on purpose – our music consisted of a fiddle, drum, fife[1] and triangle, danced 12 couples till near 10 o'clock and then came to West Hall, where 34 of us partook of an excellent supper. Joe Mole was very drunk - I went to Newlands - James and I quarrelled so I would not go home with him.*

West Hall, Belford

20th   *The painter is here - he has painted the large parlour and now begun the small one - the furniture is out of them both and we have not a place to sit. Susan and I pulled the peas for dinner and were obliged to hull them in the arbour, we did not get into the house until 1 o'clock. I have been in a sulky temper this last two days.*

23rd   *Was at Belford this morning - saw all the officers which belong to the Westmoreland Militia. The Dinnings came down - Bab has promised a music book when I am married and Mary has promised me two pin cushion slips. My father and James were from home, so we were very happy.*

30th   *My father, Susan and I went to Link Hall to Watson Weatherly's christening. After dinner the ladies walked to Shepperton Hall[2] to see the garden - I was dressed in a sprigged round dress trimmed with chenele oak leaves and flounced with broad lace. A showery day, but very warm - I had on three greatcoats with two double handkerchiefs to keep off the rain - I was near melted with the heat. Am in low spirits tonight as I don't think my father will allow us to go to the Glendale ball A great crop of strawberries this year, more than ever before.*

[1] A flute
[2] Now demolished

Extract from the diary showing the supper table at West Hall

Head of the Table at Supper

Blamange Egg		Cockles		Sliced Ham
Butter		Apple Jelly	Lobster	
Beetroot		Preserved Oranges		Whipped Cream
Celery			Preserved Pears	
Carrots		Hedgehog		Potatoes
Brawn		Roast Chicken		Cranberry Open Tart

Ornamented with Boxwood
Hedgehog is a sponge covered with whipped cream, and spiked with almonds

August

2nd   *I am in a bad temper as I am disappointed for not getting to the ball - Harry Dinning and Mr Liddle came here to ask my father, but he is quite inexorable to their entreaties.*

5th   *I have bet with Thomas Henry Liddle this morning that if he is a Major in six years from this day, I will forfeit a sword to him, value twenty guineas, if he is not, I am to have a gold watch from him, value twenty guineas. If he dies before that, he is to leave me his gold watch enclosed in a box shaped like a coffin, to put me in mind of his death. He took leave of us before dinner.*

15th   *My father went to Scotland - we heard today that Miss Fawcus of Newham is married to a joiner she ran off with on Sunday evening.*

21st   *Had a letter from Miss Dinning saying she was coming to tea - we spent a happy evening as we were not interrupted by any male creature. After we were all gone to bed my father and uncles James and Thomas came from Scotland.*

23rd   *I have wrote two sheets of paper in a letter to Nichol - got a frank[1] from Mr Sitwell - I was at a tea drinking at Peggy Rogersons - she has got the seventh daughter.*

Drawing by Denise Adam

25th   *My uncles left us this morning. Susan and I went to the bathing and then to Belford Fair - the Lady Hays were there - drank tea as usual at Mrs Bromfields.*

September

7th   *Had another letter from Nichol, franked by Lord J Thynne. John Younghusband breakfasted here, he went to Alnwick with James and returned to tea. Afterwards Joe Mole and William and Margaret Watson called, they obtained my father's permission for Susan and I to go to Berwick to see the 'Young Locious'.*

11th   *Set off at half after one o'clock in Mr Yellowly's gig to go to Berwick – we had not got as far as the Grange when one of the straps broke – we stopped at Mr Moles until it was mended. Called at Elwick for John*

---

[1] Before the introduction of the Penny Post, letters could be 'franked' by M.P.s or Peers

Younghusband - he out of politeness got into the gig. - down it went, the limers had broke with it being too heavy a load. We got a boy to go to Belford for a chaise but they were all out - they had not a seat[1] at Elwick, all the females having gone to Berwick, so we borrowed one from the miller's wife. James took Susan behind him, I rode single on Joe Mole's mare - never have I had such a jaunt - got to Berwick in an hour. We joined a large party to go to the play, Master Betty performed Young Norval in the Tragedy of Douglas.

12th   James and I went to Smiths and bought a carpet and called upon most of my acquaintances. Went to the play, was very near squeezed to death in the crowd going in and disagreeably situated, could neither hear or see the performance - Mr Mole gave me his seat and stood himself. The first act was over when an alarm of fire was given, and people called that the gallery was coming down. I was dreadfully frightened, two men had to hold me - some ladies went into hystericks, others fainted. The performance was stopped for a while before they could get the folk persuaded the alarm was false. Two of the actresses fainted - this is the first time I knew what fear was.

13th   Did not go much out today - my cloathes were so much dirty'd. Mr George Bell is made a Burgess today, they are to have a large party to sup, but my father has sent for me and I shall be obliged to leave Berwick.

17th   Susan and I walked to Elwick - had a pleasant afternoon - made the buttonholes of a shirt for William - John brought us home in the gig, called at the Grainge, got pears from Joe Mole.

19th   Our Scotch shearers are gone this morning, our harvest was finished last night. Miss Dinnings were here to tea - Bab is in low spirits as George Younghusband is going on the secret expedition.

21st   This being Belford Feast we all went up to Newlands - they all went to the races except me, I stop'd with Mrs Dinning and helped her get the tea ready. The company did not come home until it was dark, I waited upon them as the Girls were not returned from the races.

25th   My father bought the houses off Easington today.

---

[1] Ladies' side saddle

BELFORD
Festival Races.

TO BE RUN FOR

On MONDAY, 25th of September, 1815,

AN ELEGANT
SILVER TANKARD,

By any Horse, Mare, or Gelding, that never started for Fifty Pounds, or won above the value of Thirty Pounds, at any one time, (matches excepted); to carry 8 Stone—Three Miles Heats—Three Horses to start, or no Race.

The Same Day,

A HANDSOME SADDLE,

By any Horse, &c. that never won above the value of Ten Pounds.— Two Miles Heats—Catch Weight.

ALSO,
A FASHIONABLE BRIDLE,

By Ponies not exceeding Thirteen Hands high—One Mile Heats— Catch Weight,

The Horses to be entered between the Hours of 11 and 12 o'clock on the day of Running, at Mr Scrowther's, Black-Swan Inn.

Entrance for the Tankard 5s.—for the Saddle, 2s. 6d and for the Bridle 1s.—Entrance at the Post to pay Double.

To Start precisely at 2 o'clock.

MR TAYLOR,
MR BURN,
MR SCROWTHER, } STEWARDS.
MR S. ROGERS,
MR M'DONALD,

MATTHEW ROBERTSON, *Clerk of the Course.*

Should any dispute arise, to be settled by the Stewards.

The Winner of the Cup to pay 5s. towards further diversion.

Stewards for the ensuing Year will be appointed upon the Race-Ground.

N. B. The Theatre will be open during the Race Week.

ASSEMBLIES AS USUAL.

Davison, Printer, Alnwick.

Belford Festival Races 1815   ZMD-167-1-62
Reproduced with permission of Northumberland Collections Service

27th Miss Dinning came down this morning - Bab is making me a nankeen hat. My father and James returned from the Fair, Mr Robert Blackadder along with them. John Younghusband and William Watson came to tea - we played cards for the first time this winter - I lost sixpence.

October

9th I have been very ill all morning and was in bed when Susan came up and told me she saw a gentleman with my father who had a star upon his breast. I got up in a great hurry to see our illustrious visitor - he is one of the Governors for the Hospital - Sir John Colpays - he was very chatty - sat a good while.

11th I was busy this morning baking a cake when in came all the Governors - I ran upstairs to dress - but in a short time in my room my father ushered in Sir William Bellingham, who it seemed wished to see the house.

24th Susan and I were busy at work this morning when in pop'd Bab Dinning, she told me her sister and a beau were following her. I made my escape to adjust my dress, that done came down and had the happiness to find Dr Trotter in the parlour - we went half way home with them. Miss Dinnings came back to tea - Bab baked us the best Nead cake[1] that ever any of us had eaten. It was too good, for a general sickness took place after tea - we spent an unhappy evening.

27th This is the Sacrament day at Warenford, all our family were there. Mr Atkin of Eattle assisted our priest Mr Ross, had an excellent sermon - dined as usual with the priest. Came home to find John Younghusband at Outchester - we expected Mr William Barber of Boomer today but he has not come.

28th I was at Warenford again this morning to hear Mr Atkin preach and was very much edified by his sermon. Went to Link Hall to dinner and then accompanied my cousins to Shepperton Hall to tea. Spent a delightful afternoon, Mrs Kay was very kind - her brother and sister were there, we danced after tea. I am quite in love with little Albert Kay he is so polite. Miss Kay played on the piano and sang - she is an indifferent singer, but I daresay she will improve. We were laden home with flowers, I went to Link Hall for my horse - wore my blue gown for the first time.

---

[1] Usually a cake for a celebration

November

1ˢᵗ   John Younghusband called for James and I to come to Elwick to tea - I could not fix as James was out hunting and did not come home until 5 o'clock. Although it was late we set of for Elwick, and were much astonished to hear that it was their Kirn night. We went out into the Granary for about an hour - was highly gratified with seeing the Girls - they were dressed so ridiculously. Slept with Miss Carr.

2ⁿᵈ   Elwick. Was busy this morning running the heels of William Younghusband's stockings - then took a walk to meet Mrs Oswald Younghusband who came up to dinner with her son and daughter. I came home to tea. Got very little work done this week, as I have visited so much.

3ʳᵈ   James and I were at Warenford Meeting, came out at half preaching, to go to hear Lord Grayson preach at Rock. James has gone into Berwick with the Glendale troop on permanent duty, the rest go tomorrow, but he has gone before to get lodgings.

7ᵗʰ   When the Girl came to tell me to get up this morning she gave me a letter from Miss Watson asking me to go down to fix how we were to go to Berwick for the dance. We fixed to go in a chaise and when we called for Miss Watson at Waren House, Mr Bell and Mr Nesbit were there - the Budle business was just finally settled, so we got a glass of wine to drink good luck to it. Next we called at Elwick, I almost made Margaret and Susan stupid I talked so much, got into Berwick about 5 o'clock. Had an excellent dance, and got back to Mr Bell's at 5 o'clock.

8ᵗʰ   Got up at eight o'clock, had breakfast at Mr Todd's and saw from there the Troop pass. The Berwickshire came first, the Glendale next and the North Durham brought up the rear. Then went out to make morning calls and walk upon the Walls, called upon Mrs Rankin, she gave me a full account of my cousin George's wedding. Went upon the bridge to see a ship launched and was joined by all the beaux of our acquaintance. We were dancing after tea and in high spirits when we thought of going to the play.
The play was bespoke by Cap't Bennett which was 'Diamond but Diamond'. It was just over when we heard a great noise in the street and shortly afterwards a flag of victory[1] was brought into the theatre with the

---

[1] The battle of Trafalgar fought on 21ˢᵗ October

joyful news that nineteen sail of the line were taken, but a damp was soon thrown over the general joy, when we heard that the brave Admiral Nelson had fallen in the action. Nothing was heard for some minutes for the shouts of the people, Sir Carnaby Haggerston began to harangue the nobility, but the wine had been too potent at dinner for anyone to be edified by his bright speeches.

Cap't Bennett got the newspaper in and read it 'pro bonna publico' - when he came to the place which announced the death of Lord Nelson, he spoke with such feeling it brought a starting tear into every eye present. Rule Britannia was sung by the players and joined in chorus by everybody that had a voice either to roar or sing.

Colonel Brown came down with us to Mr Bell's to supper - we sat up as the gents would not allow us to go away, for all the news was canvassed over and over again - the memory of Lord Nelson drank after supper. This is the busiest day I have had for some time.

9th   *We were through half the shops in Berwick trying to get a feather for Joe Mole. Got a letter from my father saying he could not send horses for us. A Mr Smith of Stockton offered to take a chaise for us - Susan had made a conquest of him at the ball - being a stranger, we cold not with propriety accept his polite offer. We went to a china shop to chuse a set of china, but so many beaux put me quite stupid, with the Dinnings help I chose a set with landscapes drawn upon them, next went to get a dozen knives and forks and pair of patent snuffers - was as stupid there. Susan went home with the Dinnings - John Younghusband, Margaret Watson and I paraded the streets for two or three hours. I had to bear with patience some severe rubs for saying that I was going home with John Younghusband in the Gig.*

14th *Mr Thompson of Scremerston called with Harry Dinning, and in a few minutes in pop'd Mr Smith, and if I am not mistaken may take up his abode here for a few days. I was engaged to go to Newlands, and although we had a beau it did not prevent me. Sandy Thompson was there - Mary smiled once upon him, which fluttered the poor fellow so much, he could not compose himself again. Bab and I took a ride to Belford to read the papers.*

16th *Mr Dinning called and kindly invited Mr Smith to his house. Mr Smith promised to follow him there, which he did, but was not long in returning, he had lost the road. Susan and I took compassion on the youth and* *walked up to Newlands with him. I very nearly blushed when I went in as it was the third time I have been there this week. We played at cards and had a merry dance - stop'd to supper. I went upstairs with Barbara whilst the Girl was laying the cloth for supper - what a shock did I get when Bab informed me that Mr Smith had offered to Susan and they were engaged for life - to a man she has only been acquainted with for a week.*

19th *I took a walk to Belford this morning to get each of us a dark blue greatcoat. After dinner James and I went to Newlands to call on the Dinnings to go to Elwick. Susan and Mr Smith came the other road. Played at Speculation, I won eighteen pence, William Younghusband never spoke to any of us, he was in the sulks the whole evening. We were 13 in company at Elwick - they told us something would happen, which was verified as Susan fell off the horse. Mr Smith was so foolish as to get off the horse before her, that it kicked her off at the stable door.*

24th *We were engaged to drink tea at Bambro' Castle with Miss Maughan and to meet the Dinnings there. Mr Bowlt, Mr Charles and Mr Lewis Perigle, Mr Robinson of Tugal were at Maughans. We played cards after tea, I neither won nor lost, but Susan lost four shillings as Mr Maughan kept teasing her about Mr Smith. The gentlemen were very civil to Bab - when we came away, Mr Bowlt threw Mr Lewis Perigle into the cart.*

26th *I have been nineteen times in a passion today - we expected a party to dinner at 2 o'clock, then James said three, Joe Mole came at 2 but none of the others came until four, we got dinner by candlelight - was at high words with William Younghusband.*

28th *James and my father were at a race today on Ross sands, it was a match between Colonel Hunter and Alder of Horncliff - they came home in great spirits.*

29th *Mr Horsington and Joe Mole were here to breakfast they went to hunt at Ellingham with Bailes hounds - they returned in a bad humour as Mr Beaug of Hoppen had spoilt all the sport by planting the ground before they arrived. After tea, James and Mr & Mrs Scott arrived, we were so busy at cards, I could not rise to receive them, so Susan got them their tea. Susan saves me a great deal of trouble now, as she gets the supper ready and goes far more about the house than she used to do.*

December

4th   A parcel arrived from Mr Smith containing a gold allegrech bandeau, cornelian brooch and earrings, a gold chain and locket, accompanied by a polite card - with the same to Susan.

5th   We went to Belford church, as this is the thanksgiving for the late victory. Called at Newlands before and after. Got cold meat for dinner as my father had dined before we got home. Mr Yellowly and Miss Watson came to tea, and as Susan and Margaret left me, I was under the disagreeable necessity of playing at cards with the old folk.

7th   Wrote to Nichol and sent him a box full of songs and catechisms.

11th   I walked up to Belford to the weavers, Bab Dinning was also there - we went to Mrs Broomfields and in jumped George Younghusband - nothing could exceed our astonishment, as we never heard of him being in the country.

12th   Susan is in a terrible dilemma as my father has to see Mr Smith's letter. Miss Dinnings came to tea, and their brother and George Younghusband soon followed. Bab is perfectly stupid - she ordered the Girl to place a candle on a table at the door to let them see to play at cards. I was Harry's partner and lost two shillings. I came to the other table and soon won my money back, George and I against Bab and my father. He was not so much in love as his partner and was heard to say Miss Barbara you are taking all my tricks. Poor girl, her confusion never let her see a card that was played. I think George is still very fond of her.

13th   This day is so stormy it is hardly possible to stir out of the house.

22nd   Whilst sitting at dinner a post chaise drove to the door and in a few seconds Mr Smith was announced. Susan was agreeably surprised - it had the contrary effect on me. Mr S looks much better than when we first saw him at Berwick.

23rd   Miss Dinnings, their brother and George and John Younghusband dined here. George and Barbara carried on a great flirtation. John Younghusband and Mr Smith got themselves beastly drunk.

24th *Called at Newlands this morning and from there went to West Hall, George and John Younghusband joined us. - a great number of farmers were in town today - I counted twenty four - a rare sight*

25th *We were all at Belford church - sat in the Younghusbands pew. John, George and James all behaved very ill - laughed immoderately, This being Xmas day we got goose pie at Mr McDonalds - we were a large party, Younghusbands, Dinnings, Miss Wood, young Selby of Twizel House, Mr Smith etc.*

26th *We were at Newlands to dinner. I spent a charming day, though I was sadly neglected. Mr Smith looked everything to Susan, George paid marked attention to Barbara as usual - Joe Mole was very sweet upon Mary and I never got a civil thing said to me except from Cap't Humble or Mrs Dinning. Mr Smith treat us with a chaise to and from Newlands. It was 1 o'clock before we got home, James was mildly drunk, Mr Smith stupidly so.*

29th *Was awoke this morning by Susan who said that Mr Smith was on the point of death. We were all very much alarmed as he said himself that he had only a few moments to live. He made his Will and left Susan six hundred pounds, and me his gold watch, James to have his chaise and a pair new boots. The Dinnings each to have Mourning rings. James & I were obliged to hold him in bed - Susan went to bed as she had not paid a visit to her pillow since Saturday. Anthony Barber came to tea - James & my father were under the necessity of drinking tea with his Lordship, and I was left with Mr Smith in high fever. A sorry nurse I make, as patience is not in the catalogue of my virtues. The doctor made his debut after supper and I was relieved of my charge.*

30th *Mr Smith still continues poorly although he got downstairs to see the doctor this morning. I'm afraid he is subject to these fitts, he tells me he was affected in the same manner some years ago, I paid him unremitting attention, for which he seemed very grateful.*

Expenses for the year 1805 (Eleanor's spelling)

Jan	£.	s	d.
A Comb		10	0
Gold fastener for beads		1	0
Lost a bet of a pr of gloves which cost		3	0
A ruby velvet bonnet	1	1	0
A box of lip salve			8
A shawl		12	0
A brooch		4	6
Spirit of Roses		5	0
Making a white morning gown		2	0
Feb			
Pr Pea green glove leather shoes		7	0
Bottle of Liquid Blue		1	0
Qtr yard of muslin		1	0
A dark morning gown		10	6
A brown calico petticoat		5	4
Making the morning gown		2	0
Making a cloth peleese		2	6
March			
Pr black morrocha shoes		6	0
To soaling a pair		3	0
Purple ribbon		2	2
Pink ribbon			6
Silk thread			6
Paste board			3
Silk thread			4
Silk thread		1	0
5 yds flannel at 2/2 per yard		10	10
Glass buttons		5	0
Silk cord		2	0
A spy glass		6	0
Postage at sundry times		5	0
Pair of gaiters		4	0
Cambrick muslin petticoat		14	3
Wine muslin for frills		4	0
Apr			
Cambrick for Habit shirts		12	0
For sundry expenses		5	0
A pair of bibles		13	0
Green ribbon		6	0
White ribbon			7

	£.	s	d.
Apr *continued*			
Black ribbon		6	0
Cottin cambrick muslin gown	1	16	0
Lining		1	11
Making		2	0
Tape and brown ribbons		1	0
Expences at Belford ball		4	0
Pair of short gloves		1	10
Pair of long gloves		3	8
May			
A cambrick muslin spencer		10	6
A straw bonnet	1	18	0
Ribbons		4	0
Making up & dying an old gown		4	0
A comb		3	6
Straw coloured ribband		3	0
Brown coloured ribband		1	3
A cheked muslin kerchief		2	0
Bloom muslin		3	0
Wine muslin		1	0
June			
Pair of glove leather shoes		6	0
Pair of morocco glove leather shoes		6	3
Altering a gown		1	7
For brown chineele		1	6
A Dimity bonnet		6	6
Pair of white gloves		1	6
Thimble		1	6
Lavender water			6
Pink ribbon			3
July			
A blue cotton gown	1	1	3
Green ribbon		1	4
Leno muslin		1	6
Aug			
Making & altering gowns		6	0
Lavender water		1	0
Pr of black morocco shoes		6	6
Pr of Habit gloves		2	0
2 pr of white cotton stockings		9	6
Sept			
A white leno half shawl		6	0

	£.	s	d.
Sept *continued*			
Black silk half neck kerchief		2	4
Qtr yd Cambric muslin		1	0
Pair of white silk stockings		12	6
A nankeen hat		4	6
Oct			
Flesh coloured ribbon		4	6
A nankeen peleese	1	3	6
Shoes		7	6
1 yd cambric		7	0
For making the peleese		4	0
For strings to it			8
A blue sarsenet gown	2	9	6
Lining and pad		3	6
Making		6	6
Cord and buttons		7	6
Cotton		4	6
Blue ribbon			8
Altering a gown		1	6
Nov			
White kid shoes		6	0
White kid gloves		3	9
Mending trinkets		3	0
Dying stockings		2	0
Hair band		5	0
Black ribbon		1	0
Dec			
Muslin for long sleeves		2	0
A great coat	2	12	0
A black velvet peleese	4	2	0
Altering gowns, mantua maker		3	0
Gloves cleaning 6 prs		3	0
Leno Habit shirt		4	6
Black shoes		7	6
Leno Habit shirt		4	6
Claret habit	4	15	0
Black boarder	1	5	0
2 pairs stockings at 6/6 each		13	0
Total	42	11	2

Some extra expenses I have omitted to mention –
I think £50 will cover the whole

Postscript

John Weatherly died in 1807, described in the Newcastle Courant as 'an honest and worthy man'. Not long before his death, he bought the 'Town Farm' and adjoining cottages in the nearby village of Easington, for seven and a half thousand pounds, and also left over eight thousand pounds in cash bequests to his younger children.

James inherited the Easington property, and spent the next four years trying to sell it on – eventually succeeding in 1811, although at a much reduced price. The lease of Outchester expired in 1811 - shortly afterwards he married Catherine Wilson of Alnwick and then settled with their five children at the farm at Budle Hill[1].

Papers from an Alnwick solicitor, concerning Easington and the Weatherly family were auctioned in 2010. It seems that James and his brother Nicholas used their inheritance to speculate in property. They bought the lease of a Brewery in Canongate and the Beehive public house in Alnwick, and the tenancy of another farm there - Stonyhills. However, these speculations appear

Extract from the partnership agreement between James and Nicholas Weatherly
Courtesy of Philippa Craig

to have been made before the transaction for Easington was completed, leaving his finances in constant disarray. At one point he was on the brink of bankruptcy, had not his friends come to the rescue.

---

[1] Budle Hill was the old Signal House, see Greenwood's map 1828

Debts due from the late John Weatherly 10 June 1807.

		£	s	d
Arch.ᵈ Mack	Belford	700	–	–
Executors of the late Phil.ᵖ Watson		1000	–	–
Ann Richardson	Whittingham	100	–	–
Jos.ᵖ Crea Surgeon	D.º	300	–	–
David Weatherly	Redheugh	506	16	4
Tho.ˢ Henderson	Belford	100	–	–
Tho.ˢ Hall	Grange Mill	100	–	–
Greenwich Hospital ½ yrs Rent		296	–	–
D.º	Tythe	80	–	–
John Dinning	Newlands	350	–	–
Property Tax and Leepes		70	–	–
Mr. Weddell	Mousen	20	–	–
Sundry persons / small Sums /		100	–	–
	Discharged and cancelled	£3722	16	4
John Scott	Belford / not paid /	700	–	–

Charged by Will

		Debts	4422	16	4
Eleanor Weatherly	2400	Assets	3320	7	–
Susan Weatherly	2400		£1102	9	4
Rich.ᵈ Weatherly	3500 8300				
Remains for Ja.ˢ Weatherly	3200				
The supposed Value of Estate	£11500				

Courtesy of Philippa Craig

Some of these debts would be in respect of the farm business. Puzzling, however, are the amounts owing to the Watson executors, his brother David and friend John Dinning. Clearly he had funds available but, for whatever reason, had chosen not to discharge these particular debts.

By 1825, whilst still living at Budle, he decided on a career change and advertised his services as an Auctioneer. By 1837 the Budle farm was put up for let, although noted as being 'in the occupation of Messrs Weatherly'. Whether James was still there is uncertain. However this certainly appeared in the local press:

29ᵗʰ April 1837. Suicide - on Sunday morning last, the body of Mr Weatherly of Budle was found suspended from a tree on a neighbouring plantation. The unfortunate gentleman had gone from home on Friday morning, and not having returned by night, a search was made for him at the adjoining farms: but no trace of him could be discovered at that time.

For a long time this was thought to be Eleanor's brother, until the discovery of a notice in the Newcastle Courant, announcing the death of James Weatherly, late of Outchester, in Edinburgh in 1853. The census for both 1841 and 1851 lists James, a Coal Agent, Catherine and their children living in Edinburgh.

By 1837, the occupants of Budle Hill were James and Young Weatherly, two second cousins who had moved to Link Hall with their parents in 1805.

Nicholas was serving his apprenticeship to be a Land Surveyor when his father died. He was to inherit three and a half thousand pounds when the Outchester lease expired in 1811 - meanwhile during his apprenticeship he was to be kept in a *full and affluent manner* and paid fifty pounds a year for *cloathes and other necessaries*. Although in partnership with his brother, somehow his reputation survived and he became quite a well known figure locally. When William Clark bought Belford Hall in 1810, Nicholas surveyed the town of Belford for him, and during the Dobson rebuild of Belford church in 1828 he was appointed secretary and treasurer .At the age of 35 he married an Isabella Cockburn from Dunbar - they had just one son.

However he disappears abruptly from the Belford scene after 1837; the family suicide marked the end of his career locally. His house, Belford Villa, was put up for sale and he moved to Newcastle. Shortly afterwards, his wife died and it seems he was in financial difficulties. Eventually his son joined him in Newcastle, taking a job in the Armstrong factory at the west end of the town.. Nicholas died in 1854.

Despite their father's careful approach to money and his determination to leave his family well provided for - within a few years his sons had squandered their inheritance.

Susan, it seems, in her father's eyes, was not to be entirely trusted with money, having already had from him 'four hundred pounds or thereabouts'. She was to inherit a thousand pounds on marriage and a further thousand in trust after her death for her 'lawful children'. In spite of her surprising engagement, she did not marry Mr Smith after all. Not long after the death of her father she married George Turnbull, a surgeon from Dunbar in 1808 at Bamburgh. Doctor Turnbull is mentioned in the diary as an occasional visitor to Outchester, although at the time not classed as a 'beau' and there was no hint of a romance with either sister. The wedding attracted a large gathering of Weatherlys and Dinnings, including George's cousin Matthew.

Susan of course moved to Dunbar where she and George had a family of eight - two of their sons also became doctors and carried on the medical tradition in Dunbar. Susan survived her husband by thirty years and died in her eightieth year from the 'debility of old age'.

Eleanor inherited nearly two and a half thousand pounds when she reached twenty five or married, which might have made her a sought after bride, but not so. Perhaps the behaviour and financial difficulties of her brothers may have damaged her marriage prospects. The anticipated marriage to John Younghusband did not materialise. After Outchester was given up and James married, it seems likely that she and Nicholas set up home together in Belford.

The *Berwick Advertiser* reported in 1821:
> *On March 20th at Dunbar, Matthew Turnbull, surgeon to Miss Eleanor Weatherly, eldest daughter of Mr John Weatherly Esq. of Easington. A large party of their friends were at the Kings Arms, Berwick to welcome their arrival, where the day was spent in the most convivial manner. The happy pair in the evening set off for Coldstream.*

The marriage was registered in Coldstream, not Dunbar, stating that Eleanor was 'of the parish of Belford'. Matthew was a native of East Lothian, born in 1792, and cousin of George Turnbull. They had obviously first met at Susan's wedding in 1808, although at the time, a worldly young woman such as Eleanor was probably not romantically inclined towards a seventeen year old medical student. At the time of their marriage, Eleanor was thirty six and Matthew twenty nine. They settled in Coldstream where Matthew had his practice, and some five years later Eleanor gave birth to their son Matthew James.

Little is known of Eleanor's life from this point, but she did keep a book - a 'Scriptiana' - in which, after her marriage in 1821, she recorded the names of people who visited her in Coldstream. She made notes of recipes and household hints, and also encouraged some of her acquaintances to record poetry and prose of their choice.

It seems likely that Eleanor saw a lot of some of her nephews. The 1841 census lists Peter, the son of Nicholas at school in Coldstream, and two of Susan's boys were also studying in the town.

Eleanor died in February 1841 aged 56 *esteemed, regretted and respected by a large circle of friends.* Her son was just fifteen and already studying medicine in Edinburgh. Some eighteen months later his father married a doctors' daughter from Dunbar, and in retirement moved to Bellhaven. Matthew James worked alongside his father in Coldstream - and took over the practice when his father retired. He became a magistrate and J.P. for Berwickshire, and appropriately for some one living on the banks of the Tweed, a keen fisherman.

Matthew James married three times, but nevertheless died a childless widower in 1894 leaving no direct descendants of Eleanor Weatherly

According to his obituary in the *Scotsman*, he appeared to be a 'larger than life' figure.

He was a man of striking presence and strongly marked individuality, a genial manner which was expressed in ready wit. He dispensed the most liberal hospitality at his board, and he was a most punctual man, his habits of punctuality amounting almost to eccentricity. By his death, perhaps the best-known figure in this part of the country has been removed.

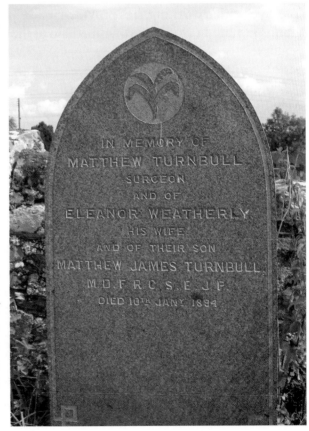

In the graveyard at Lennel, near Coldstream there is a headstone in memory of Eleanor, Matthew and their son Matthew James. The three wives, Janet, Sophia and Jane are remembered on an obelisk nearby.

Matthew James bequeathed his books to Robert Oliver, the brother of his second wife previously Sophia Oliver of Lochside House. The diary has been in the possession of the Oliver family since 1894, and whilst they certainly knew of the marriage between their ancestor and Doctor Turnbull, the family had no idea that the diarist Eleanor Weatherly was his mother.

The present diary owner, Elspeth Orrom, who inherited the diary from her mother, is the great, great niece of Sophia Oliver and related by marriage to Eleanor.

At the beginning of her diary Eleanor Weatherly wrote 'should curiosity induce anyone to look at this book I hope they will forgive repetitions'. She could never have imagined that some 200 years later, her diary would attract so much

Matthew James Turnbull
Courtesy of Elspeth Orrom

attention and reach such a wide audience. What began as a simple exercise to improve her handwriting, has provided a fascinating social commentary and glimpse of life in North Northumberland at the very beginning of the 19th century.

Acknowledgements:
The Diary extracts, edited by the author, are by courtesy of Elspeth Orrom.
I would like to thank Philippa Craig for the use of the Weatherly family papers.

Additional sources:
Berwick upon Tweed Record Office
East Lothian Local History Centre
Internet websites - ancestry.co.uk
    and Scotland's People
Newcastle Library
Northumberland Collections
    Service, Woodhorn
Scottish Borders Archive and Local
    History Centre

The Restored Diary

4

BELFORD HALL
TWO FAMILIES, TWO ARCHITECTS
by John Harris

Belford Hall is the most obvious architectural landmark visible from the A1 between Newcastle and Berwick. Surprisingly little information about the building is easily available in print. In *Aspects of Belford* Gillian Lee provided a detailed history of the Dixons and of the (Atkinson-) Clarks who were the two families associated with the Hall through most of its history. Only the essentials will be repeated here to provide a context for the building of the Hall to the designs of James Paine and John Dobson.

Belford Hall - from the South

The first phase of Belford Hall.
To establish himself as a member of county society, Abraham Dixon IV built a new house, part of the present Belford Hall, on a prominent site to the east of the village. The building was completed, to the design of James Paine, in 1756.

Paine was one of the most prominent English architects of the eighteenth century. He is thought to have worked in his early career under Lord Burlington, one of the chief proponents of the neo-classical Palladian style in England. He was approaching the height of his career in 1756. In the 1750s and 1760s he designed in the North, amongst other buildings, Cusworth Hall, Doncaster Mansion House, Gosforth Hall and Gibside Chapel. He worked on Alnwick Castle, Chatsworth and Sandbeck Park, and among landscape features, a bridge in the grounds of Wallington Hall. Such was Paine's success as an architect that Thomas Hardwicke commented:

A simple **chronology** for Belford and the Hall:

1726	Belford Estate purchased by Abraham Dixon III from James Montague for £12,000. The Manor house was then on the site of the present West Hall.
1746	Estate inherited by Abraham Dixon IV. He began development of Belford by building new farms, a cotton mill, and a tannery. He introduced agricultural changes including quarrying and burning limestone in new limekilns to improve the land by liming. He improved the roads in the area and developed the Blue Bell in its role as a Post House.
c.1750	James Paine commissioned to design a new Hall.
1756	Dixon's Hall substantially complete.
1782	Death of Dixon IV. Estate inherited by great nephew Arthur, later Lord, Onslow, aged five years. Dixon's widow continued to live in Belford until at least 1808. The estate was administered by Thomas Adams, lawyer, of Alnwick who was one of Dixon's Executors.
1808	After Onslow attained his majority, the estate was sold at auction and bought by Scottish entrepreneurs.
1811	Complete estate resold and purchased by William Clark of Longbenton for £127,000.
1818	John Dobson commissioned to extend and improve the Hall. Dobson undertook other work in Belford, including 'restoring' and extending St. Mary's Church.
1921	Death of George Atkinson-Clark. (The 'Atkinson' was a result of the estate passing to the daughter of William Clark, Jane Margaret, who was married to the Rev. William Atkinson. A condition of the inheritance was the adoption of the name 'Clark'.) The heir Henry George Atkinson-Clark, or his wife, is said not to have wished to live at Belford Hall.
1923	Estate sold by the Executors to Thomas Place junior for £85,000. At a further auction the estate was sold as separate lots, some of which, including the Hall which reached £12,000, were withdrawn unsold.
1924	After another attempt at auction, the Hall and 262.5 acres were bought by two local butchers. Various abortive schemes were proposed to find a use for the Hall. Start of deterioration.
1938	The same property was bought by McLarens of Belford for £9,500.
1939	Requisitioned by War Office. Hall not well treated.
1956	The property was returned to McLarens. Further abortive attempts were made to find a use for Hall. Deterioration continued.
1969	Hall listed Grade 2.
c.1980	Hall and garden (3.64 acres) sold to Stanley McKale for £5,250 to turn into hotel whilst surrounding land remained with McLarens. Project abandoned.
1983	Belford bypass completed. Hall had deteriorated to a point where demolition was imminent. Hall and garden purchased by Northern Heritage Trust for £11,000 with view to restoration.
1984-1986	Full restoration undertaken. Conversion into apartments. Listing raised to Grade 1. Hall and gardens leased to Belford Hall Management Company for 999 years. Apartments then leased individually to residents for 999 years.
1990s	Some of the parkland sold to create golf course, some bought by Belford Hall residents.
2002	Gardens and neighbouring land, most of the original parkland, placed on Register of Parks and Gardens Grade 2.

Sir Robert Taylor and Mr James Paine nearly divided the practice of the profession between them, for they had few competitors until Mr Robert Adam entered the lists...

Paine designed the central villa of Belford Hall in the Palladian style, as it is still seen from the south, but with extensive wings which were never built. A plan of the Hall and a drawing of the south elevation, as envisaged by Paine, are in Paine's own work of 1767: *Plans, Elevations and Sections of Noblemen and Gentlemen's Houses.*

Palladianism.

Andrea Palladio was a sixteenth century Italian who developed classical Roman architecture, as seen in the remains of temples and villas, into a style based on symmetry, proportion and harmony to design farms, villas, town houses and churches. The English architect Inigo Jones (1573 - 1652) visited Italy and his observations of Palladio's work influenced his own work, for example in the Queen's House, Greenwich.

Under the later Stuart monarchs, English architecture tended toward the freer, more ornate Baroque style. Vanburgh's Seaton Delaval Hall is one of the most notable examples. After 1714 and the Hanoverian accession, the Whig party gained ascendancy and a 'national' architectural style, free of supposed Catholic influence was sought. Colen Campbell and his patron, Lord Burlington, were influential in developing Jones's work into an English Palladianism used to design many town and country houses and even churches (e.g. Gibside Chapel).

Characteristics of Palladian country houses are external and, where possible, internal symmetry with simple mathematical ratios used to establish the proportions of the rooms and of even minor elements of design. The elevations typically have a low rusticated basement i.e. one with heavily incised and chamfered masonry, a high *piano nobile*, the main floor containing the most important apartments, and a low, half height, attic storey. Columns and pilasters are designed in one or more of the classical orders – Doric, Ionic or Corinthian.

The Hall was originally approached from the west and the first sight of it was of the restrained side elevation. This was followed by the revealing of the main façade at an angle that showed to advantage the advance and recession of its main architectural elements.

The villa has a frontage of five bays, with a rusticated basement, a *piano nobile* and a half-height garret storey. The central portico has four Ionic half-columns, flanked by slightly recessed Ionic pilasters. The outer windows are set back and then the frontage is brought forward again by twin Ionic pilasters at each side to frame the façade. The main door was originally in this south front, probably approached by a double stair from the terrace.

John Adam, an Edinburgh architect and a brother of the more famous Robert Adam, visited Belford in 1759 and was rather scathing of the design, especially

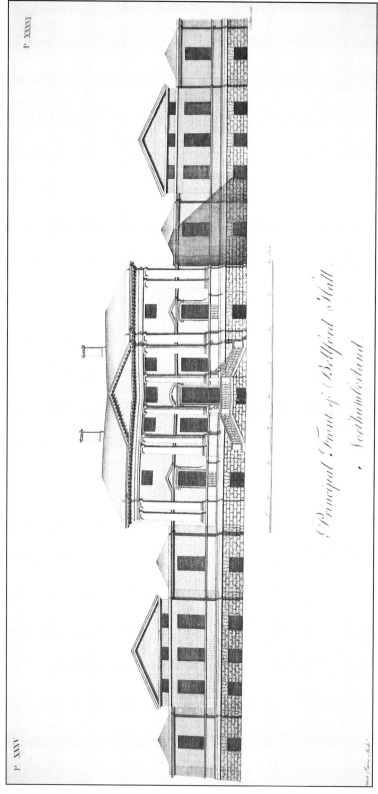

Belford Hall - South Elevation - James Paine - *Plans, Sections etc.*
Courtesy of Newcastle University Library

the façade which he described as in bad taste, possibly a case of professional jealousy. Leach, biographer of Paine, in contrast describes the façade as *a wonderfully complete and successful essay in movement.*

The rear, north, elevation was probably similar to the *front* elevation of Georgian townhouses in cities such as Edinburgh. Because of the slope of the ground, the rear entrance to the villa, into the *piano nobile*, is at ground level. The slightly eroded Ionic pillars in the present Portico Room are believed to be in their original position framing the, then external, rear door. A sunken area ran along the back of the house with two doorways for the servants into the basement of the villa. The area was presumably spanned by a slab bridge to allow access to the rear door. In the north wall of the area are doorways into two cellars, one of which has a coal chute from above. (Intriguingly, it also has the lower mullions of a blocked-up window, despite being below ground.) This is similar to houses in the New Town of Edinburgh where cellars are under the streets' pedestrian pavements. The lack of any plaster on the area walls and the

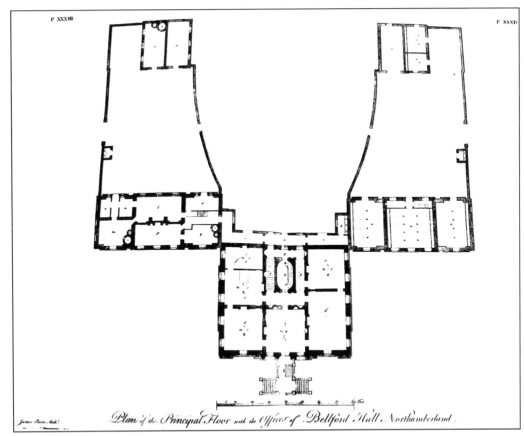

Belford Hall - Plan - James Paine - *Plans, Sections etc.*
Courtesy of Newcastle University Library

presence of two blocked-up windows in the wall on the villa side suggest that, at some time, some or all of this area, which now forms a covered passage, was open to allow in light.

Of considerable interest is a tunnel starting opposite the main servants' door in the passage and extending some forty yards northward. It was constructed in a 'cut-and-cover' method and roofed with a vault partly of brick and partly of stone. The floor consists of a central pavement of flagstones with cobbles to each side. Although it now ends in two large subterranean coal bunkers, with hatches and chutes from the surface, it is conjectured that originally the tunnel may have been built as a way for servants to enter the Hall out of the sight of the 'family' and their guests. Later when the Hall was extended and, it is believed, a new Servants' entrance was made under the South Entrance steps, the redundant tunnel could have been adapted readily for

Belford Hall - Tunnel

coal, with the addition of the much bigger, and newly essential cellars. Newhailes, an almost contemporary house in Musselburgh, near Edinburgh, has such a tunnel to admit the servants unseen, but many other Georgian houses have elaborate passageways, and even underground railways, merely to supply coal to the house. There are parts of hinges at the Hall end of the tunnel suggesting it was once gated. Despite the remarks in the English Heritage Listing description of Belford Hall, and in Pevsner's *Buildings of Northumberland*, the tunnel does **not** go to the Icehouse which still exists in the field to the north of the Hall and is visible as a grassy mound with some exposed masonry. In the corresponding position to the tunnel but at the other end of the passage is what appears to have been an opening, but blocked by very old brickwork.

As previously mentioned, Paine's originally planned wings were never executed. There is evidence however that two small wings were added to the rear of the house. The west wing consisted of a projection from the rear of the villa at the level of the basement, within which was the kitchen. Above that was a single storey with a pitched roof. The east wing appears only to have spanned the rear area, with a single storey and roof. These wings appear on the plan of

1820. A small mystery attaches to a circular window in the north wall of the east wing. It is too high to have afforded a view to anyone inside, but is of a size suitable for a clock face, with a square recess behind adequate for a mechanism. Many country houses had clocks mounted to be visible to outdoor workers.

Paine originally designed the main interior staircase as a concentric outer public stair and an inner servants' stair. This was changed to a three-sided staircase with separate servants' stair, probably during construction, *following the advice of a gentleman eminent in the law*. The original stair was built at basement level however and appears to have been made into a secure store or strongroom. There are hinge sockets in one side of its doorway and rebates cut into the walls for shelves. The roof is a brick vault. At a later date the space became a Wine Cellar. Paine was clearly unimpressed with the alterations to his plan, commenting sarcastically in 1767 that *the backstairs are almost one foot ten inches long…* The necessity of a separate servants' stair to the east meant that the main stair was to the west of the central axis of the building. It followed that the impressive Venetian Window on the half-landing is off-centre when viewed from the outside. This Venetian window was restored in the 1980s using measurements taken from the one remaining voussoir, a curved stone forming part of the arch.

The main staterooms, with much of their plasterwork, were to Paine's design. The **Saloon** is entered through a door facing the foot of the stairs. This room was the original Entrance Hall from the exterior steps on the South Front and formerly communicated with the other State Rooms on either side. The Drawing Room, Bedchamber and dressing room were to the west; the Dining Room and Breakfast Room were to the east. (By the time of the 1808 sale, the Breakfast Room had become the Library.) The Breakfast Room, Dining Room, Bedchamber and Entrance Hall could be entered separately from the Staircase Hall, but all the rooms could be passed through in succession. The Entrance Hall measured approximately 23ft x 25ft x 15ft and the Drawing Room, Breakfast Room and Bedchamber were similar. This was close to a desirable Palladian ratio of 1.5:1.5:1, whilst the Dining Room at approximately 33ft in length was close to 2:1.5:1. The windows of the rooms on the *piano nobile* are in the ratio 2:1 height to breadth.

Symmetry was an important element of Palladian architecture and in the principal rooms where a doorway was not in the centre of a wall it was invariably balanced by another at an equal distance from the centre, sometimes only giving access to a cupboard or even being 'blind'.

The fireplace in the Saloon is original, and a match for one in the Ballroom of

the Blue Bell Hotel in Belford, although much
repaired after an accident during the Hall's
restoration. The plasterwork is largely a 1980s
restoration of the original, which was criticised
by John Adam in 1759 as too heavy, as it had a
complete entablature i.e. architrave, frieze and
cornice. The restored areas can be
distinguished by the shallower nostrils of the
bucrania, the ox skulls, resulting from taking
moulds of the originals. Sufficient of the
original plasterwork existed in all the
Staterooms for moulds to be made. At the time
of the restoration, the Library, Bedchamber

Saloon, originally Entrance Hall,
fireplace

and dressing room were converted into bedrooms for two of the new
apartments. False ceilings were created and some of the original plasterwork
remains in the voids above them. The Drawing Room and Dining Room
ceilings were also restored and these rooms form the main rooms of the same
apartments. Plasterwork restoration was by James Phillips of Leeds.

Saloon, originally Entrance Hall, Cornice

The original doors, of
panelled deal (although
described as mahogany in the
1923 sale!), were sold abroad
during the Hall's dilapidation.
Later, when they were entered
in a London auction, the price
was too high to purchase
them. A photograph in the
Saloon shows one of them.
The present doors and
architraves were made during the restoration by Tony Smith, son of Alan Smith
of Holly Construction. The original floors were of oak but had been 'asset
stripped'! In the interest of economy they were replaced by pine.

According to the 1808 Sale Catalogue, on the first floor were five 'best'
bedrooms and dressing rooms and also servants' bedrooms. The basement
contained all the domestic offices of Housekeeper's Room, Steward's Office,
Butler's Pantry, Servants' Powdering Room, Servants' Hall, Kitchen, Scullery,
Larder, Pantry, Brew-House, Wood-House and Coal-House, Dairy and
Laundry, Wine, Ale and Beer Cellars. Perhaps surprisingly for that date, there
was a water closet, although James Paine is known to have installed *one* at the
much larger Kedleston Hall in 1760!

The same catalogue describes outbuildings for three carriages, stabling for twelve horses, granary, harness and saddle rooms with servants' bedrooms, out-houses, hogsties, small barn and shed for cattle. There was a house convenient for the resident Steward and a kitchen garden enclosed with a wall, eleven feet high, on all but the south side and with grape house and melon house adjoining. The kitchen garden was the still-existing walled garden to the south-west of the Hall and the other buildings may have been at Home Farm. There is no mention in the sale catalogue of a water supply, but on the 1754 Plan of the Hall a 'Draw well' is shown due east of the Hall near to a position where water still emerges through the surface of the drive. A well also existed close to the east end of the 'area', in what is now Garden Flat.

Since the estate was being marketed with a colliery, in which the occupier, Richard Pringle, had erected a steam engine, there was sufficient fuel for the house. There were also quarries for building stone and limestone, lime kilns and tile kilns. Presumably the building stone was the sandstone of which the Hall is built, but the quarry location is not given. A sandstone quarry existed on the Rogues Road on Belford Moor which was reopened as a large enterprise when the railway arrived.

Like most architects of his day, Paine could turn his hand to landscape design. He planned the layout of the whole of the Hall grounds, probably starting planting before building work began on the Hall. A plan of 1754 shows his original intentions. He later included a Pleasure Ground to the east of the Hall, taking in a craggy outcrop of the Whin Sill, on which he sited an octagonal Gothick Folly with castellated parapet, arrow slits and a flagstaff. Inside there was a fireplace. Views were afforded of Budle Bay and Holy Island. A serpentine lake was excavated below the crag and a fernery planted. A wooden 'Chinese' tea-house was also built. The whole area was protected by a ha-ha - a stock barrier consisting of a ditch and a sunken wall.

As previously mentioned, the Hall was originally approached from the Turnpike to the west. On the 1754 Belford Survey Plan, this drive is merely pencilled in, presumably as a work yet to be started. It starts at the east of the south front of the planned Hall, bends towards the south and then back to the west, emerging halfway up what is now North Bank. On the 1817 Estate Plan, the end of the drive is shown by gates halfway up North Bank, and on the 1820 survey by John Dobson, the course of the drive is shown clearly from the position of these gates to the front of the Hall. No Lodge is shown on any of these plans. On the 1754 plan, a track is shown coming from the Market Place, along what is now Clark Place, turning to the north, passing in front of the hall site and then heading roughly ENE. The track is labelled 'Path to Grains'(?). Another branch heads east as 'Road to Easington'. The track is absent from the two later plans, but the Walled Garden has appeared and lies across the route of the track. The removal of the track had been planned as early as 1754, since 'New Road to Easington' appears on the 1754 plan along the course of the present Quarry Bank. Clearly a public road immediately in front of the new Hall would not have been wanted.

The Walled Garden was a feature of most country houses, providing shelter for the cultivation of vegetables and quite tender fruit. After the beginning of the eighteenth century, the walls were frequently heated by hot air from furnaces, the air being passed through ducts in the thickness of the wall. At Fallodon Hall such an arrangement is believed to date from 1720, and the Belford Hall garden walls are apparently similar, with two furnace houses still existing. Belford Hall had, of course, ample supplies of coal from the estate's own resources. At some stage, a hothouse with elaborate underfloor heating was built.

The second phase of Belford Hall.

By 1811 the estate was owned by the Clark, later Atkinson-Clark, family. They commissioned John Dobson, a Newcastle architect still early in what was to become an illustrious career, to survey the estate and to complete the Hall.

Dobson was dismissive of Paine's habit of opening main entrances into the best rooms of his houses since this exposed most of the State Rooms to fierce draughts. Dobson built a new main entrance on the north side, complete with a single storey portico with four Ionic columns *in antis*, i.e. between, and in line with, two rectangular pilasters ending the side walls. Because of the slope of the ground, this

North Portico - Dobson's work.

portico is on the same level as the *piano nobile*. At this time he probably replaced the South entrance stairs with the present single flight. The original Entrance Hall then became the Saloon or main reception room. The staterooms were reorganized. The Bedchamber ceased to be used as such, becoming the Dining Room and its dressing room appears to have become a serving room with a 'dumb-waiter' to the kitchen below. There are still the springs for a set of pulley-operated bells in the void above the present false ceiling. At some point

---

The Apartments of the *piano nobile* of the Villa
(1. Apartments as intended by Paine. 2. Apartments after changes by Dobson.)

<u>North</u>
1. Rear Door
2. Main Entrance

| 1. Dressing Room | | 1. Breakfast Room |
| 2. Serving Room | | 2. Library (by 1808) |

Staircase Hall

1. The Bedchamber
2. The Dining Room

| 1. The Drawing Room | 1. Entrance Hall | 1. The Dining Room |
| 2. The Billiard Room | 2. The Saloon | 2. The Drawing Room |

<u>South Steps</u>
1. Main Entrance
2. Garden Entrance

---

the Drawing Room became the Billiard Room and the original Dining Room replaced it as a new Drawing Room. The Library continued in its 1808 position. These locations for the principal rooms were those current at the sale in 1923.

Dobson designed the current wings and pavilions. They were constructed between 1818 and 1820. They are four bays long, the end bay at each side being raised to form a pavilion. Dobson's style is similar to Paine's, but with subtle changes. The basement is rusticated and the first floor windows of the pavilions copy Paine's, but the pilasters are broader and flatter. For a short time, until outbuildings were constructed, carriages were kept in the arched area below the East Pavilion. It is not clear why this was necessary if facilities for carriages to be kept elsewhere already existed in 1808. The sash windows of the Dobson parts of the Hall have, as expected, finer astragals (glazing bars) than the windows of the earlier Paine villa, reflecting a trend through the Georgian/ Regency period. The ground slopes upwards from west to east and this has an unusual consequence. To retain the horizontal line of windows through both wings the floors of the rooms in the basement of the

East Elevation - Dobson's work
E. Pavilion with carriage house below.

East Wing are level with the window sills. This results in only the lower half of residents being seen from outside as they move about inside!

The Dobson north entrance leads into a large **Portico Room**, top-lit by a rectangular lantern. On the west side is a fireplace with the crest of the Clark family, a griffon, on the mantel. The fireplace has been dated by National Trust experts visiting the Hall as late 17th or early 18th century and no longer has a functioning chimney. It may have been brought

Portico Room fireplace with Clark crest

by the Clarks from an earlier house. Presumably it would have had a functioning chimney, as the Portico Room would have been heated. The griffon motif appears also on at least two hopper-heads for rainwater downpipes on the Dobson extensions to the Hall.

A doorway, framed by the Ionic columns mentioned above and thought to be the original rear entrance of Paine's villa, leads into the **Staircase Hall**.

Doorway to Staircase Hall

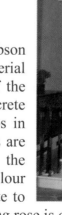

In his improvements for Clark, Dobson devised the present, more impressive, Imperial staircase to replace Paine's. The base of the previous stair is shown by the incised concrete which loosely mimics the sandstone slabs in the rest of the hall. Some of the balusters are original, some are copies made during the 1980s restoration. A difference in the colour of the brass of the brightwork is deliberate to allow their identification. The plaster ceiling rose is original.

Returning to the Portico Room, a door on the west side leads to a very worn stair needing care during descent. This gives access to a remaining part of a transverse corridor with 19th century tiled ceiling which gave access to most of the domestic areas. The kitchen was to the right (west). The **Wine Cellar** is visible with its original numbered brickwork bins. It was constructed from the storeroom in the base of the originally planned Servants' Stair, possibly in Dobson's time, since the bricks appear to be newer than those in the ceiling. Also in the basement were the Servants' Hall, kitchen in its original position, scullery, three larders and various store rooms and fuel cellars.

At the time of the 1923 sale, the upper floor of the Villa still had its original five bedrooms, but now also only two dressing rooms, two WCs and a bathroom. Domestic hygiene had advanced! By this time, too, the larders had tiled walls and shelves and, as was the custom, were probably dedicated to meat, fish, dairy etc.

The East Wing contained additional guest accommodation of six bedrooms and a bathroom and a study. In the West Wing, part of the basement was given over to a laundry, complete with a large 'copper' for boiling the wash. Also in this wing were the Butler's Pantry and bedroom, strong room and plate safe, a bathroom and two stairs leading to six servants' bedrooms. The custom of the time had the rooms of male and female servants located separately, which perhaps explains the two staircases. The basement of each wing appears to have had a boiler room.

The total accommodation of the Hall in 1923 was twenty bed and dressing rooms and three bathrooms. Perhaps it should be said at this point that it was the convention that upper class married couples did not normally share a bedroom. The husband would usually sleep in a single bed in the dressing room. Census returns show that the number of resident servants increased from seven in 1851 to thirteen in 1901, but this number would be supplemented on occasion by the servants of visitors.

In 1897, George Atkinson-Clark temporarily vacated Belford Hall to allow Princess Mary Adelaide of Teck, mother of the formidable future Queen Mary, consort of King George V, to use it to recuperate from an illness. The Princess brought her household of housekeeper and fifteen other servants! Her bedroom was in the top, front central room and her 'boudoir' was the Saloon which she refers to as the Music Room. She described it as a 'cosy' room which contained a self-acting piano. She was very impressed with the furnishings and pictures in the Hall.

A Land Valuation plan of 1824 shows the lower part of the Walled Garden as a 'Hop Ground', but by 1860, the Ordnance Survey 25-inch plan shows the garden as apparently part ornamental and part productive. By 1897, a fountain features in the ornamental area. There are stories that this fountain still exists in a garden in the Belford area and there are similar stories about large statues, possibly griffons, which certainly adorned the South Stair balustrade as late, at least, as 1910[1].

Dobson also built the South Lodge and a twin carriage drive on the line of the present drive from the south-west, the drive passing across the South Front and curling around the East Pavilion, as at present. The remains of a line of trees in the field to the west of the present drive mark the vanished second carriageway. At this time a drive was also constructed to the top of what is now Quarry Bank where a second, less elaborate, North Lodge was built. The site is now occupied by the modern 'Neralcm'. Squire's Pond was excavated at this time, and a dam with outflows capable of regulating the water level and dealing with overflows was built. A set of wide concrete steps now leads down into the water. If the steps were intended for bathing, the users were unaware, or unconcerned, that, according to a plan in the Hall's possession, the overflow of the Home Farm septic tank appears to drain into the pond, and probably always has! In 1923, so did the Hall's cesspool!

Large scale Ordnance Survey plans of the nineteenth century show that the paths through the Hall grounds continued across the other side of North Bank along Chapel Crags. The walled area surrounding the Hall is marked as a 'Deer Park' and a pheasantry is also shown. At that time both Paine's and Dobson's landscaping were treated as an integrated whole.

---

[1] Information about the present whereabouts of the fountain and the statues which might lead to their being photographed, would be gratefully received.

Mention should be made of Dobson's other work in Belford. He restored St. Mary's Church, then added the North Aisle, Porch and Tower, and built the Courthouse in the High Street. He built, or at least refaced, some terraces of houses in the village. The houses of Clark Place, for example, appear on the 1754 plan, surveyed for Abraham Dixon, but their present appearance clearly owes much to Dobson. The last house may have started life as a farm, and part of it used to be referred to by local inhabitants as the 'Office' - perhaps because it was the Agent's house. It is also sometimes referred to as 'The Dower House'. The widow of Abraham Dixon junior was still living in Belford in 1808 when the estate was put up for sale. A 'Dower House' could have housed her, although she is thought to have continued living at the Hall. At another time the

The Croft and stables
Courtesy of Mr & Mrs M. Nisbet

house accommodated the Presbyterian Minister, the Rev. Marcus Dods, and his small boarding school. Later it became a more up-market Vicarage than the original one, when the son of the Squire became the incumbent! 'The Croft', which has the appearance of a Dobson building, at one time housed the Land Agent, but was also known as 'The Dower House'. The widow of William Brown Clark may have been accommodated there, after his brother, John Dixon Clark, succeeded as Squire in 1840.

The third phase of Belford Hall.

The estate was sold at auction in 1923 and broken up. The Hall started to fall into disrepair. It was requisitioned by the War Office during the Second World War and a hutted camp was built in the grounds to the west of the drive. A large shed was built alongside the drive and, whatever its main use, was apparently used for dances also. Other sheds were built behind the Hall and even on one of the main lawns. Because the presence of the army put a great strain on the water supply of the village, the War Dept sank a borehole, at the council's expense, and additional water was pumped up to the reservoir at the top of Quarry Bank. The pump house still stands next to the gate of the Walled Garden. The camp continued to be used, sometimes by cadets, until the 1950s, with the Hall itself serving as an Officers' Mess. After being released by the War Office, the decay of the Hall continued despite abortive attempts to turn it into flats and a hotel, quite detailed plans for which are in the Berwick Record Office. By 1984 it had reached the state graphically shown in the photograph overleaf. All the lead was missing from the roofs, most floors were gone, walls were collapsing and dry rot was rife.

Belford Hall - Dilapidation

The building was acquired in 1983 by the recently formed Northern Heritage Trust under the leadership of Philip Deakin. Funds were raised from the Monument Historic Buildings Trust (linked to the Sainsbury family), English Heritage, Northumberland County Council, the Sir James Knott Trust and Berwick Council. The restoration was carried out by Reavell and Cahill, architects, and Holly Construction, the work being led for them by Ray Connell and Alan Smith respectively. The project was coordinated by Hugh Cantlie. The work included the clearing away of the last of the Army's huts and various odd lean-tos which had appeared over the years, and landscaping the gardens. At its conclusion, sixteen apartments had been formed with a small communal

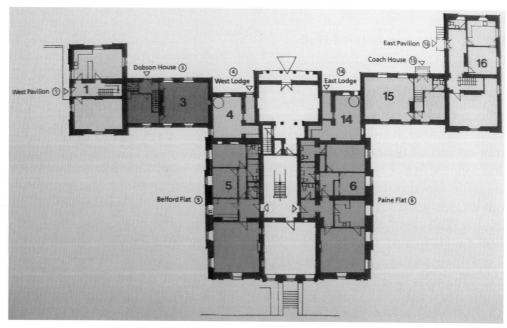

Belford Hall - First Floor Plan of New Apartments
Courtesy of Sale & Partners

area. The conversion was one of the earlier adaptations of a large dilapidated country house, partially inspired by the exhibition 'The Destruction of the Country House' at the Victoria and Albert Museum and the subsequent SAVE campaign. The quality of the Belford Hall project was recognized by its gaining two conservation awards.

Belford Hall Management Co. Ltd. and Belford Park Ltd own only a small part of the original Hall grounds. The vestiges of James Paine's Pleasure Grounds, the Ice House and the Walled Garden, in which is located a newly built Georgian style house, are in other ownerships. The gardens and park as seen today are largely the result of Dobson's work. The Hall's grounds are an important example of an 18th and 19th Century landscape and recognition of this has been made by their addition to the Register of Parks and Gardens, Grade 2.

Most of the area bounded by the A1, the north-south route through Belford, Quarry Bank and the southern link to the A1 is included.

Restoration of the Turret, which is now in a very dilapidated condition, dredging the serpentine lake and reopening some of the paths in the Paine Pleasure Grounds could provide an area of benefit to Belford's residents and to visitors, whilst continuing to be a haven for wildlife.

Paine's villa, the central part of Belford Hall, is now over 250 years old. After falling on very hard times, its restoration and continuing careful management should see the whole of the Hall through a similar span.

Turret from NE showing window, arrow slit & flag staff bracket
Courtesy of Cemex UK Ltd.

Belford Hall is now a Grade 1 Listed Building. It is one of the foremost examples of a Palladian mansion in England. The communal areas of the interior and the gardens are open to the public by prior arrangement. Visits may be made any day (Summer 11.00 a.m. – 4.00 p.m., Winter 11.00 a.m. – 3.00 p.m.), excluding Christmas, New Year and Easter, Contact details are available in various locations in Belford village. The Belford Hall Management Co. also usually participates in Heritage Open Days.

Acknowledgements:

Thanks are given for the help received from members of the B.D.L.H.S. especially Jane Bowen and David Morrison for providing copies of the 1808 Sale Catalogue and the Dobson Estate Survey of 1820. Thanks go also to Mrs Linda Bankier at the Berwick Record Office, Mr Hugh Cantlie, Mr & Mrs R Dodds, Mr & Mrs J. Nisbet, Mr & Mrs M. Nisbet, Mrs B. O'Connell, Mr A. Black at Cemex UK Ltd., Dr Melanie Wood at the Robinson Library of the University of Newcastle, and staff at the Northumberland Archives Study Centre at Woodhorn.

Sources:

Claridge, J., *Descriptive Particulars of the Belford Estate* Pall Mall, London 1808

Cruickshank, Dan, *The Country House Revealed* BBC London 2011

Dobson, H. G., *Dobson on Dobson* The Pentland Press. 2000

Faulkner, T. & Greg, A., *John Dobson, Newcastle Architect, 1787 -1865* Tyne and Wear Museum Service 1987

Leach, Peter, *James Paine* Zwemmer, London. 1988

Lee, Gillian, *Belford, the Hall, the Estate and the Owners* from *Aspects of Belford* Blackhall 2008

Paine, James, *Plans, Elevations and Sections of Noblemen and Gentlemen's Houses* London 1767

(Pevsner) Grundy *et al.* *The Buildings of England - Northumberland.* 2nd Edition Penguin Books 1992.

Wilks, Lyall, *John Dobson* Oriel Press (RKP) Stocksfield 1980

Wood, John D. & Co. *Belford Hall Estate - Auction Catalogue* February 1923

Woodforde, John *Georgian Houses for All* Routledge Keegan Paul London 1978

Worsley, Giles *Belford Hall, Northumberland* Country Life Magazine January 1988

Belford Revisited - The Rebirth of a Mansion. Northumbrian Autumn 1988

Belford Village Trail - Belford & District Local History Society 2006

Maps and plans (various) - Northumberland Communities website

Plans of Belford Hall (Hotel and residential proposal for Mr and Mrs McKale) – Eric G Hasler (Architect) Newcastle 1981 Berwick Record Office

5

PUBLIC AND PRIVATE EDUCATION IN BELFORD
by Jane Bowen

In the first volume of Aspects of Belford, *in* All ink is frozen, *Valerie Glass outlined the history of the Presbyterian School in Belford. It is the purpose of this chapter to survey what is known about the other educational establishments in Belford, between the late eighteenth century and 1940, when the original National School was closed and the children moved to new premises at the top of West Street, now Belford First School.*

Private Schools
It is clear from the records that, over the years, there were a number of different private establishments in Belford. Tantalisingly, however, only passing glimpses of them can be found, and many seem to have been of short duration.

There is mention of a school in St Mary's Church prior to August 1723. The first recorded schoolmaster in Belford however, was Franc Blinshall, described in the Church Register in 1736 as a church schoolmaster, but the nature of his role is unclear. In the 1760s, the Registers record the presence of a John Finny, Schoolmaster, who had children baptised in 1761, 1764 and 1766, and who died in November 1769, but nothing is recorded of his school. The first definite reference to a school in Belford, in October 1784, comes, almost as an aside, in a letter about the reletting of property from Henry Barber, the Belford Estate factor to Thomas Adams, the estate Lawyer.

> *Mr. Pool will bring you this: I understand his Business with you is to desire*
> *you to build an addition to his House & to repair the present House....*
> *My opinion is there is greater propriety in getting clear of him than in*
> *accommodating him .... The best parlour in the House is rendered out of*
> *repair by converting it into a school: he must be subject to a proper repair.*

Matthew Pool was the minister of the Presbyterian congregation in Nursery Lane from late 1776 to 1786, but where exactly he lived is unknown. It was common, however, for ministers, of whatever denomination, as among the few educated people within a community, to supplement their income by taking pupils either on a daily or boarding basis.

Two years later, in September 1786, property problems involving a school again have Henry Barber writing to Thomas Adams, and this time, as an extra,

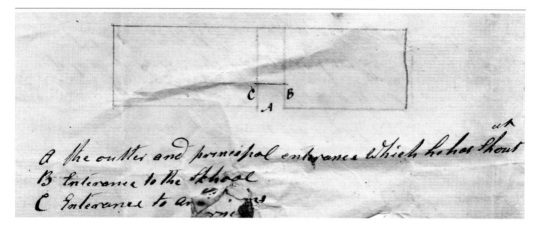

there is a sketch of the building involved.

John Anderson got home last Night and this morning has prevented the School Master and Children from access to the School by locking the outer door which are situated as below, and was always the only entrance to the different apartments.

From a later part of the letter it is clear that John Anderson was an on-going thorn in the factor's side, but there is no precise picture of the location of the school or who the schoolmaster was.

It is again from the Belford Estate papers, that a slightly fuller picture of the next school emerges. This time the reference is in a letter to Thomas Adams written by John Dinning, Henry Barber's successor as factor, and dated 14th June 1798. He refers to Mr. James's School in Belford. Clearly this was a boarding school, as amongst the parents sending their children there was a Mrs. Powditch of North Shields. The purpose of the letter, however, was to gain Adam's approval for the residence in Belford of a French émigré, M. Bernier, formerly Rector of Mounteburgh in Normandy. Bernier had presumably escaped to Britain from the Reign of Terror in France, and had now been employed *to teach the Young Gentlemen under Mr. James's care, the French language.* A little more information is given about Bernier, who was also to teach Mr. Watson's children at Spindlestone school.

Mr Bernier speaks tolerably good English, is of a pleasing address, and, I understand a Man of Science and literature. He lodges at Mrs. Ramsay's.

Sadly however, there is no further information about either the school or Mr. James.

In January 1817, Simon Coltherd advertised his school in Belford, offering a particularly full and wide ranging curriculum:

> · English,
> Arithmetic,
> Penmanship in all its branches,
> Book-keeping by single and double entry,
> Geography,
> Euclid's Elements of Geometry, superficial and solid,
> Trigonometry, plane and spherical,
> Navigation, with lunar observations,
> Surveying, Gauging, Mensuration, Gunnery,
> Fortification, Perspective, with the principles of Architecture,
> Algebra, Conic Sections, Mechanics, Pneumatics, Optics, &c.
> Spherics, Astronomy, with the use and construction of Globes,
> Maps, Planispheres, Dials, &c.

This was followed up at the end of 1818, by a further advertisement advising parents how to ensure their children got most benefit from their education. It seems that he continued to run his school in Belford until at least 1839, when he advertises a move to new premises in West Street. By 1841, however, Simon had moved to Newcastle where he continued as a schoolmaster. Interestingly, in 1850, the death of an Andrew Coltherd, schoolmaster, is recorded in Belford -

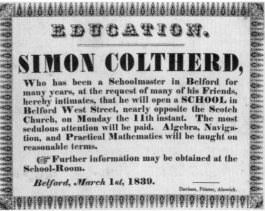

Ref: ZMD-167-18-51
Courtesy of Northumberland Collections Service

was this Simon's son, and if so, what brought him back to Belford?

In 1822, a Mrs. Barber, most probably Henry Barber's widow, advertised her school. As Henry's widow died the following year, however, this probably was a very short lived enterprise, and certainly there are no other references or advertisements for it.

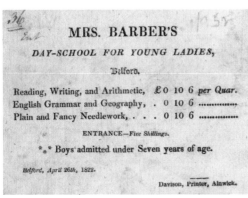

Ref: ZMD-167-1-952
Courtesy of Northumberland Collections Service

The Scots Presbyterian minister, the Reverend Marcus Dods, conducted a Boarding and Day Academy from his Manse in Belford c.1822-1838. We know the young John Bolam attended this school as a boarder in 1832. There is also a brief description of extra-curricular boarding school life in the Manse, (now 5 Clark Place), in a short memoir recorded by Dod's daughter, Marcia.

It was a great delight to get possession of the schoolroom on a Saturday afternoon, for there we could not spoil anything. Our father had always boys whom he taught along with our own, and there were always a few who lived in the house, so that the schoolroom was furnished with long desks and forms. Two long desks placed together made a splendid boat, so that seafaring was a very popular occupation on those indoor afternoons. We went innumerable voyages to every port we knew of, but I do not remember of ever arriving anywhere without suffering shipwreck and coming to port on strange boats and rafts, or by swimming, our baggage generally going through even more adventures than ourselves, and being fished out of the sea with much danger to life and limb.

Between 1822 and 1828 (possibly longer), George Curry also ran a Boarding School in Belford. The eight year old Thomas James from Kirknewton was presumably attending either Dods' or Curry's establishment, when, sadly, he died there in early December 1822.

William Hall ran a day school from no later than 1822 until at least 1828; George Young is listed as a schoolmaster in 1822 and Mr. Broomfield[1] ran a school in 1825. This last may well have been an apprentice school, training weavers to work in his mill, which was the other side of the lane from the Scotch Church (now Community Club) in West Street. Of longer duration was John Thompson's school, possibly at Detchant, which is recorded at various times between 1822 and 1840. None of these establishments, however, are recorded on the 1820 Belford Estate map, so that we can be fairly confident that all were new ventures in the 1820s.

In 1834, there is mention of Sarah Hindmarsh running a school in West Street, and John Lowrey holding one at the back of the *Horse and Groom*. This inn was where Well House Café now is, and it has been suggested that the schoolroom was in the upstairs back room, reached by a separate external staircase. Mr. P Scott's educational establishment is recorded in 1843, when he says that

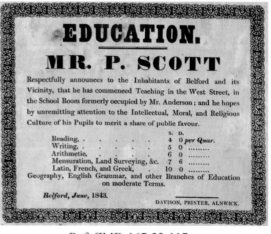

Ref: ZMD-167-22-117
Courtesy of Northumberland Collections Service

---

[1] The name is spelt variously as Broomfield and Bromfield in the records

he has taken over Mr. Anderson's schoolroom in West Street, but as there is a record of the death of a Peter Scott in 1844, this was possibly a very short lived school. In 1846, Peter Hilton of West Street, Belford, advertised for an experienced teacher:

competent to instruct in the general branches of a sound English Education, Geography, Mathematics, French and Latin. The number attending School till the vacation was upwards of 60, and the fees are liberal.

Berwick Advertiser 22nd August, 1846

Hilton is consistently recorded as a grocer and draper in West Street from the 1830s to the 1850s, so it seems unlikely that the advertisement relates to his personal school. He was, however, also a leading light in the Oddfellows, so possibly he was acting on behalf of a fellow Brother. Most probably, this was a continuation of the Anderson/Scott school, but under whose management is unknown.

The 1850s saw yet more private schools – both George C. Davison and W. Smith are listed in 1855 as having day schools. David Walker seems to have opened his Private Boarding and Day Academy in 1853. The *Berwick Advertiser* for November 19th of this year records a successful 'juvenile ball' organised by Mr. Dixon, the teacher of dancing, and held in the hall of Mr. Walker's school.

… a number of the parents and other friends of the pupils attended. It was the unanimous opinion of all present, that the pupils performed their various dances with such gracefulness and ease as is seldom displayed under so short a period of tuition…….Although the pupils were during four hours displaying their many evolutions, the same happy smiling faces and light step prevailed from the commencement to the close.

Unfortunately, the school itself must have been less successful since, in June 1855, Thomas Stamford of Belford sued Walker, who had now left the town, for 15/6 owing on goods purchased and delivered.

A private school of much longer duration was the Day and Boarding School for Girls run by the Misses Bromfield, at least between 1861 and 1897. Three sisters contributed to the enterprise over the years, Margaret, Dorothy, and Isabella. They were the daughters of James Bromfield, the weaver and grocer and it is possible that the school was run in the original linen weaving shed, as by the 1850s, James Bromfield seems to have been concentrating on his grocery business. In 1861, the two older sisters, Margaret and Dorothy, were running the school, with Isabella shown as an apprentice. In 1871, all three were teaching, but in 1875 Isabella married and moved to Ashington, leaving the two older sisters to continue the business on their own. From the 1871 and 1881 censuses, we know that most boarders were relatively local, Elizabeth and Annie Elliott from Preston, Mary Bolam from Chathill, Jessie Winton from Wooler, Beatrix Jones from Doddington and Eliza Waller and Elizabeth English from Chatton. Their fathers were reasonably well-to-do farmers, master tradesmen, or, in one case, a gamekeeper. Also attending was the Misses Bromfield's niece, Ellen Broomfield, daughter of their brother Robert, who, in 1881 was working in Liverpool, as manager for a Forwarding Agents or Carriers. At the end of July 1882, the *Advertiser* records that the Boarders and Day Pupils presented the school with a handsome octavo Bible, bound in Moroccan leather and with additional gilt. Given the time of year, it may have been intended as a leaving present from senior pupils. The school appears to have specialised in music education. Consistently Margaret Bromfield is recorded as a Teacher of Music. Also, in 1880 and 1881, there are reports of the successes of its pupils:

> *Misses Annie Ryan, Belford (with honours), Beatrix Jones Nesbitt, (with honours), Annie Elliott, Tynely, and Ellen M. Broomfield, Liverpool, attending Misses Broomfield's day and boarding school, have been successful in passing the Examination recently held here in Musical Knowledge in connection with Trinity College, London.*

Berwick Advertiser 26th August 1881

The Belford National School
Origins

Until the nineteenth century, education was largely restricted to the wealthy, whose parents paid for them to attend schools, often, as in Belford, run as a sideline by clergymen. Sometimes very basic teaching of the alphabet and numbers was given by elderly ladies in what were known as Dame Schools, and in this way poorer children may have obtained the rudiments of the 3 Rs. In 1780, a successful publisher, Robert Raikes, concerned about the welfare of poor boys in Gloucester, developed the idea of a Sunday School, in which education was provided to poor children on a Sunday, usually in the Church buildings. This initiative was immensely successful, and by the 1830s a quarter of the population attended such schools. Meanwhile, in 1811, the *National Society for Promoting the Education of the Poor in the Principles of the Established Church in England and Wales* was founded, with the aims of promoting church schools and Christian Education. The intention was to provide a day school in every parish, run by trained teachers.

Church of England Education in Belford

The first recorded drive to provide education for the children of the poor in Belford seems to have been the initiative of the Reverend John James, who became Vicar of Belford in 1803. In Belford, in May 1810, James preached a sermon on *The Usefulness of Sunday Schools*, and subsequently paid to have it published as a pamphlet. More importantly, he practised what he preached and, during the Clergy Visitation of that year, his curate reported that over 120 children attended such a school. The Sunday School continued in later years, though after the initial enthusiasm, numbers seem to have dropped. In 1835, when the Church first considered opening a day school in Belford, James's then curate, Edmund Wilkes, wrote that the only existing provision was a Sunday School for 30 boys and 20 girls which was held in the aisle and chancel of the church.

The origins of the plan for a day school are not clear, but in April 1835, Edmund Wilkes applied to the National Society for aid in establishing a National School in Belford. It was intended that the school would provide places for 66 boys and 50 girls. These children would each pay a penny a week for education, with the proviso that where the parents' circumstances warranted it, the charge might be increased to 2d. or 3d *when the child is writing & cyphering*. The school was to occupy the former Armenian Methodist Chapel of the 1820s, at the south end of the village, on the west side of the Belford Burn. The building is

Union *Belford*

1835

North
Application for Union.

To be signed by the parochial Clergyman, and other Managers of the Schools. In the absence of the Incumbent of the Parish it is requested, that the officiating Minister will certify the Incumbent's consent to the application for Union.

It is the wish of those who have the management of the Schools at *Belford in the County of* Northumberland

in the Diocese of Durham *that the same should be United*

to the NATIONAL SOCIETY.

In these Schools the National System of teaching will be adopted as far as is practicable; the Children will be instructed in the Liturgy and Catechism of the Established Church, and constantly attend Divine Service at their Parish Church, or other Place of Worship under the Establishment, as far as the same is possible, on the Lord's Day; unless such reasons be assigned for their non-attendance, as shall be satisfactory to the Persons having the direction of the Schools. No religious tracts will be used in the Schools, but such as are contained in the Catalogue of the SOCIETY FOR PROMOTING CHRISTIAN KNOWLEDGE. *Annual or other communications on the state and progress will be made as may be required by the regulations of the* SOCIETY.

The 9th *day of* April 1835. John James Incumbent

Edmund Wilks Curate

Application to join the National Society (NS/7/1/984) Copyright of The National Society described as being made of stone and blue slate. The cost of purchasing this from the Belford Estate was £150. The room, whose dimensions were given as 32 feet long, 22 feet wide and 15 feet high, was to be fitted out for a further £50. The annual salary for the schoolmaster was estimated at £50 a year. At the time of the application, donations of £100 had been received towards these costs. Mr. Wilkes planned to make a second approach to the landowners who had not so far donated. There was also a scheme to preach a special sermon in the summer, presumably on the importance of education, and to use the collection from that service for the school fund. Even then was a shortage of £80 to purchase and equip the building, far less to pay for the teacher. Apart from an acknowledgement, Wilkes received no immediate response to his application. In October he wrote again, asking if Parliament had voted money to aid the National Society, and if so whether some was available to assist the purchase of a suitable building in Belford. There is a note of despair in his letter:

> *I know of no place where an institution of the kind is more wanted than here - & for nearly two years I have been labouring to establish it... Unless it* (the National Society) *can afford us some support I fear it will be impossible ever to carry the plan into effect.*

In November 1835 he wrote a third time, indicating that the Managers would be willing to accept a lesser sum to *enable them to proceed with the undertaking,* and that *we are most wishful that the school be established this Winter if possible.* At the Society's end this letter was annotated: *Grant to qualify? – No.* At the beginning of February 1836, the *Newcastle Journal* published an article inviting the promoters of schools to apply to the National Society for money to help with the building. This prompted Wilkes to write again, now asking whether he should resubmit his application. On this occasion the Society's annotation shows that a grant of £58 was offered and accepted. There was still insufficient money to buy the chapel outright, and instead, in November 1836, the squire, William Clark, conveyed the former dissenting chapel to the School trustees on a 99 year lease. By the beginning of 1837, Belford had its National School.

The early years of the National School

Sadly very few early records of the school between the 1830s and the 1860s survive, but it is possible to piece together a little of its history from the pages of the *Berwick Advertiser*, and from the brief inspection entries recorded at the National Archives.

A year after its opening, the National School pupils enjoyed the celebrations accompanying Queen Victoria's coronation at the end of June 1838. Belford certainly celebrated in style - flags flew on the church tower and in the Market

Place and houses were decorated with banners. The squire provided strong ale in the Market Place for his tenants to toast the coronation. This was done at one o'clock *with tremendous shouts of enthusiasm, accompanied by several vollies.* The squire's wife decided, probably wisely, that such revelry was not for schoolchildren. They *were regaled with tea and cake by Mrs. Clark on the green before Belford Hall, and were attended by this lady and Mr. Clark, the Misses Gillum, Mr. Lockie, teacher of the National School and others.* The day ended with the burning of tar barrels to the cheering *of a joyful and happy people.* This account of the coronation celebrations is the first record of the Master appointed to the school - Mr. Lockie. By 1840, he had been succeeded by Robert Lightfoot, who was still there in 1841.

Despite the grant from the National Society, finance was still a serious problem for the school, and in 1838 there was a major drive to improve the situation. This took the form of a Grand Bazaar, held on the 24th of September, the day of the Belford Races. The main organising spirit seems to have been William Brown Clark, the new squire, and his wife and friends were called upon to provide items for sale and raffle and to run stalls. Entry to the Bazaar was 6d. Among those helping were the Squire's wife, Mrs Dinning of Newlands, Mrs Selby of Twizel, Mrs. Mitford, Mrs. Forster, Mrs. Gillum and her daughters from Middleton Hall, and Miss Smith from Buckton. The contents of only two of the stalls are recorded - Mrs. Clark's stall contained drawings and fancy work together with snuff boxes, ring stands and other items turned by her husband. Mrs Dinning of Newlands provided fruit and lemonade. The Countess of Tankerville had donated a *handsome piece of needlework,* subsequently purchased by the Duchess of Northumberland, who did not attend herself, but had sent £10 to be spent on items at the Bazaar. Overall, some £200 pounds was raised from the stalls with another £5. 17s. 0d. from entry money, suggesting an attendance of over 200, assuming the 'great and the good', who were on duty did not actually pay to go in. Overall it was a remarkable achievement, equivalent today to just over £9,000, and must have gone a very long way to put the school on a sound financial footing. In 1842, the school gained another supporter when the Bishop of Durham agreed to subscribe two guineas annually to the school.

The first recorded inspection was in 1843. It reads:
School not at work in consequence of there being a fete at Belford. Discipline Tolerable, Progress V.G., Religious & Moral condition – small.

Though, if the children were not at school, how did the Inspector know? Perhaps because there was little available school work to inspect, the inspector took a detailed interest in the finances of the school. Income was made up of subscriptions and donations (£40); Endowments (£8); and Fees (£27. 10s. 0d.), amounting in total to £78. 10s. 0d.   The Expenses amounted to £77. 3s. 3d. accounted for by stipends: £60; Repairs: £12. 19s. 1d; Furniture: 16s. 4d; Books £3. 1s. 0d.; and other items 6s. 0d. Interestingly, he notes that there were no costs for either heating or lighting, though no reason is offered for this omission.

The probability is that the Inspector had arrived on the 5th of June 1843, when the school was on holiday due to the wedding of the new Squire, the Reverend John Dixon Clark, brother of William Brown Clark. By now there were 163 children on the roll, and they were treated to *a dinner of roast beef and plum pudding with wine* (*Berwick Advertiser* 10th June 1843). There followed a range of noisy entertainment, peals of bells, firing of small arms and cannon and fireworks; though what probably provided the young people with most entertainment was a group of youths vying with each other to climb a 24 feet greasy pole to reach a leg of mutton at the top. The prize was eventually won by seventeen year old John Arnot, an apprentice cooper from Miller Square.

A clearer picture of the school is obtained from the inspection by the Reverend Frederick Watkins HMI in August 1845:

Reading: Moderate; Writing: Good; Arithmetic: Fair; Progress: Fair; Tone: Good. A fair school, decreasing in numbers; master steady and sensible.....strap not often. Economically it was now making a small loss– *Income £68.14.8; Expenditure £69.9.11; overdrawn 15/3d.*

The following year there was a change of Master, for we know that Mr. Mitchell moved from Branxton to Belford to take charge of the school in November. By the early 1850s, the school hit a bad patch, though whether this was under Mr. Mitchell or a successor is unknown. In 1851 the Inspector was the Reverend D. J. Stewart, and his report reads: *This school is apparently not a successful one. There is a great want of method.* Nevertheless pupil numbers were rising, with 33 extra pupils gained during the year. There were now 123 on the roll. Stewart's criticism must have had some effect, as in 1852 the entry reads: *The attainment of the children is very moderate. New Master to be appointed.* Even so numbers had now risen to 153, but they began a rapid decline shortly afterwards. Stewart's inspection of 1855 records only 56 pupils.

Mr. Moor 1856 - ? 1864

In 1856, the Managers obtained a new and more effective teacher, Mr. Moor. For the period of his mastership most information derives from the *Berwick Advertiser's* detailed accounts of the annual school sports, held in the grounds of Belford Hall. These include some additional information about the general state of the school. After two years in post, the *Berwick Advertiser* praised Mr. Moor *for his devoted attention to his duties and his kindness to his pupils....To his steady perseverance in his office we can only attribute his success in raising the school during the time he has been amongst us...from about fifty to nearly three times that number.* (24th July,1858). The Education Report for the same year shows that the school received a parliamentary grant of £2. 6s. 0d. for apparatus and books.

In January 1860, there was a further significant development. With the support and encouragement of the Countess of Tankerville, who gave £15 per annum towards the teacher's salary, a separate Infant School was opened under the overall management of Mr. Moor. Its first teacher was Miss Acton and, by July 1860, there were already 70 infants enrolled. The Education report for that year shows that Mr. Moor's teaching was also supplemented by the presence of a pupil teacher, - an able senior pupil, with aspirations towards further education who received higher grade lessons from the master, generally in the mornings between 8 and 9 o'clock, in exchange for which he or she taught a class of pupils under the Master's supervision. After five years of such apprenticeship, pupil teachers could either be employed as uncertificated teachers, or apply for a scholarship to attend training college for a year, setting them on the path to obtaining their teaching qualification or 'parchment'.

In 1862, the *Advertiser's* report states that the infant teacher is now Miss Caswell. Also, despite the competition offered by the opening of the Presbyterian School in 1858, the National School numbers were again rising, with 146 attending the sports. There was little change in this number in 1863, but in reporting the celebrations for the marriage of John Dixon Clark's daughter in 1864, the numbers attending the National Schools (infants and mixed) were given as nearly 200.

Charles Redhead Brown 1866 – 1872

It is not clear when Mr. Moor left the National School, but possibly about 1864, as when information is again available, in 1866, attendance had fallen to approximately 100, including about 30 infants, while the Presbyterian school had grown at the National School's expense. In 1866, however, the Managers were fortunate to appoint Charles Redhead Brown at a salary of £11. 0s. 0d. a quarter. Nothing is known of his previous history, but it is from this time that the School Log Books and other records date, suggesting a well organised and experienced teacher, although he was only 22 when he took up the post. By the time of H.M.I. Mr. Wilkinson's inspection in July of that year, there were signs of improvement. Of the infants he wrote: *A clean, orderly & excellently conducted Infant School*; and of the Mixed School: *This school is conducted with considerable energy, industry & ability, & is in a very satisfactory condition.* Pleased with this success the Managers increased the Master's salary to £13. 10s. 0d. a quarter.

As with many Masters in charge of rural schools, Brown's first challenge was to secure his pupils' attendance. In his first year in post, among the activities which kept the children from school were mushroom and raspberry picking (August); looking after the house while their mothers worked as bondagers during the harvest (August and October); gleaning (September); potato picking (October); crow scaring (January); herding cows from the young crops (March); potato planting (April), in May, the massive disruption caused by families moving to new farms, following the Hirings; and finally, in July, the Lamb Fair. Clearly for many families existing close to the breadline, education was all very well, but helping with the farm work was the priority. In an attempt to minimise the disruption caused by the farming year, the main five week holiday ran from late August to late September. There was considerable flexibility given to the Managers to fix these dates as seemed best, but closing sooner to accommodate an early harvest, meant that school resumed before the week of Belford Feast - and that was a disaster.

> *Belford Feast takes place here on 26 September & the two days ensuing. It is a generally recognised matter that no school can be held during the feast week. I have tried it once and failed.* (National School Log Book)

Even when it was possible to delay the school closure till later in August, so that the Feast week was included in the holiday, there was no guarantee that the weather would be accommodating – *The backwardness of the Harvest also causes many to stay away* (10th October, 1866).

Brown noted another less common work-related cause of absence in June 1869:

> *Eight of my scholars have been absent now for several weeks, gathering on a species of bivalve known here by the name of 'cockles'. In most instances the usual excuse is given for the necessity of this step, viz.:- the parents are poor & a little – a very little money – is to be made; & therefore go the children must. The gathering, however, is very trying work as I know from the experience of adults who put their hands occasionally to this same work. What then must it be to boys & girls – some of them far from strong – when they are day after day, irrespective of weather, engaged in this work.*

To his credit, Brown involved George Walker, the Vicar, in the problem and was successful in getting at least three of the children back in school.

In an attempt to improve attendance, Brown, together with the Squire and the Vicar, introduced prizes for attendance and good work in 1867. In July, 21 prizes were awarded, but even those who did not qualify gained some benefit – the Vicar distributed *a plentiful supply of sweets* and a half day's holiday was given.

Illness, too, could significantly disrupt teaching. In January 1867, a measles epidemic caused problems; more serious was the outbreak of scarlet fever in September 1868, which continued to affect the village until February 1869 with 13 fatalities in the village, although only one girl from the school died. Such outbreaks resulted not only in the absence of the invalids, but also of healthy children kept at home for fear that they would become infected. The same was true of the outbreak of smallpox in January 1872.

At a time when almost all children had to walk to school, wherever they lived, age and poor weather created problems. Families were reluctant to have young children walk long distances, often on poor tracks, an issue highlighted in the log book entry for April 27th, 1868, but one which continued to cause difficulties for the school well into the 1870s.

Two boys were admitted to the 'infant' school today. They are both nine years of age – the one can say part of his letters – the other has never been to school before, and does not know a single letter. Their homes are about 4 miles from this place.

Then as now, heavy snow made access difficult, but rain also resulted in bad attendances - tracks could deteriorate into streams of mud, but more significantly, children who had walked several miles in the rain arrived sodden at the school which had no effective way of drying them.

The severe weather of this winter has punished many of the children & several younger scholars have not yet put in an appearance (National School Log Book 20th January, 1871)

The school pupils also enjoyed a number of treats, often designed to encourage them back to school after the holidays. In October 1868, John Towlerton Leather entertained the pupils at Middleton Hall. It must have been quite a sight - the children processed through the village, headed by banners. Once there they received presents from their host, took part in sports and *enjoyed an excellent tea, to which they did ample justice.* In later years tea and sports took place at Belford Hall. Also, when school reopened after the Christmas holiday, on January 6th, 1872, a tea and magic lantern show was provided for those who attended - a strategy which worked as it produced an attendance of 123 pupils.

The Headmaster, assisted by the infant mistress, Mrs. Treble, the sewing mistress, Miss Mabon and a pupil teacher, James Treble (Mrs Treble's son), worked particularly hard and imaginatively to raise the standards in the school. Although the Inspection reports were generally good, consistently areas for criticism were reading which *lacked fluency and expression,* and readiness to respond orally. January 1870 saw Brown focussing on reading and dictation. He remained dissatisfied with the results of the latter, and so, in 1871, began to involve both the Vicar and the Curate in taking dictation lessons, to accustom the children to listening to different voices. In May of 1871, Brown was concentrating on word building and ensuring the children understand what they read. In June 1871, he introduced spelling homework. Arithmetic was used to encourage independent thinking, both through questioning and the setting of problems rather than simple sums. The Vicar also provided good support – he introduced a prize for reading in 1869, which he examined himself, and, in September 1871, is described as being most energetic in hunting up absent scholars. It all paid dividends. The Inspection Report of February 16, 1872 states that *all the Standards* (classes) *were higher than they need have been.* It was his final achievement in Belford. At the beginning of March he left for pastures new.

The Infant School and Mrs. Treble

The Countess of Tankerville's infant school, although monitored by the Headmaster of the National School, had originally opened in separate premises. In 1866, however, the decision was taken that it should be housed together with the main school. Subscriptions were sought and a letter to the National Society records that some £200 were raised for alterations and building work. This was not without its difficulties. Adaptions intended for the summer holiday of 1867, were incomplete when the school was due to reopen on September 30th, and the delighted pupils found themselves with an extra week's holiday. It was not until January 1868, however, that the new infant room was formally opened. The Inspector reported in February:

> *The Infant section, under a most efficient Teacher, is now in the same building as the Mixed School & forms part of the Master's charge. It is taught in a very good new Room, & I found things in very good order.*

Mrs. Treble, the teacher, had taken charge of the Infants in the autumn of 1864, when she was still unqualified, but at the end of 1873, she received her certificate, and the Managers decided to treat the Department as a separate school, a situation which continued until 1889. She clearly appreciated the importance of visual aids, recording with enthusiasm the arrival of new pictures for the schoolroom in October 1874, a multiplication table on rollers in March 1876, and of using letters formed of strips of coloured pasteboard to help her pupils learn their alphabet (May 1875). She also seems to have brought a very necessary sense of humour to her work, recording in February 1875 that she had started teaching a new group of pupils to sew *or rather to hold their needles*! Nor did she become set in her ways. Even in her last year in the school, 1881, she took on the teaching of a new subject, Callisthenics, exercises performed to music, designed to promote graceful movement. Her methods were certainly effective. The 1875 inspection of February 24th recorded:

> *This Infant School has always done well. The Reading and Arithmetic were very good, and the Writing excellently good. The Singing and the Marching were very fairly done, the discipline good and the Needle work very good.*

So good a teacher was she that the Inspectors encouraged other local teachers to visit the school and learn from her.

> *December 18, 1875: Miss Louise Henry attended for the 14th to the 17th – by kind permission of the Vicar - to receive Instruction in the Management of Infants previous to taking over the North Sunderland Infant School.*
>
> *June 3 1876: Had a visit from Mrs. Sanglier, Infant Mistress Bambro to see the routine of the School Work as her school has been put under Government lately.*

In 1881, when her husband, Sergeant Major Henry Treble, in charge of the Belford Northumberland Fusiliers Volunteer Force, was appointed Master of the Belford Workhouse, she resigned to become the Workhouse Matron.

Thomas Simonson 1872 – 1874

Mr. Simonson's arrival coincided with a number of other changes - James Treble had successfully completed his pupil teachership and applied for a scholarship to go to college. His replacement was James Johnson. The Vicar, George Walker, retired and was replaced by Thomas Atkinson, younger son of the Atkinson-Clarks at the Hall. The new Master's first year at the school was marked by some additions to the curriculum - Sergeant Major Treble was brought in twice a week to give the boys 'drill' which Simonson recorded *the boys appear to like very much.* He also introduced poetry learning as homework for the upper classes. May and June saw him also concentrating on singing and music. Over the two following years, history was introduced.

A variety of events also impacted on the school. The visit of a circus to the town in June 1872 resulted in significant pupil absence in the afternoon; a formal half day's holiday was given in July when there was an inspection of the Volunteers in Belford, and in October, the Prince and Princess of Wales passed through the village en route to Chillingham Castle again resulting in many absences. Less enjoyable happenings were the epidemic of whooping cough which began at the end of June, and resulted in the early closure of the school for the summer on the 11th of August; and the October storm which caused the flooding of the school and the children being sent home. Even the annual summer treat at Belford Hall was not without its problems, as a break in the weather meant the children had to leave early.

Simonson took his responsibilities for his pupil teacher seriously, and the log book records the setting of a number of subject examinations which Johnson passed satisfactorily. As a supervisor of classes however, he was possibly less effective. The Inspection report of February 1873 records:

> *The children passed a very fair examination on the whole. This report should have been considerably better had not the whole of the fourth standard failed both in spelling and handwriting. The rest of the children passed very well, and the Infants are thoroughly well taught. The discipline is also good throughout the school.*

Over the next year, however, the Master concentrated on ensuring his pupil teacher knew how to make lesson notes, and supervised his teaching from them on a range of topics including salt, sugar, silk and the whale. Johnson himself was clearly conscientious and, in July 1873, obtained a First Class pass in the externally set Divinity examination.

In October 1873, Miss Mabon, the sewing teacher left to get married, the children presenting her with *a very handsome teapot.* Her successor was Mrs. Pearson, who generally contributed well, but whose teaching of buttonholing and darning came in for some criticism in subsequent inspections.

The new Vicar, Thomas Atkinson, also gave good support, both hearing dictation like his predecessor, and taking on the teaching of Religious Instruction to the school. As a son of the Hall, he also arranged the summer treat, but in 1873, as on the previous year, the event was rained off. This year, however, it was rearranged for early October, just after the long holiday. This time the weather held and the children enjoyed tea and cake and a variety of games organised by the Vicar.

In February 1873, Simonson requested that attendance fees for the school be increased from 2½d. to 3d. a week, and this was agreed, but the managers made it a condition that the children had to be given their copy books free, and that the master had also to supply the coal to heat the school - a sixth of the money raised from the school pence were to be used in this way. In December of 1874, Simonson resigned his post, presumably to move to another school, and the school presented him with an inkstand as a token of remembrance.

Samuel Barrass 1875 -1880

From the point of view of the pupils, 1875 got off to a very good start. The oldest son of the Squire, George Dixon Atkinson-Clark, had just been married, and before he and his bride departed on honeymoon to St. Vincent, they laid on a treat for the schoolchildren. Tea was served in the school, and then the pupils went to the ballroom of the Blue Bell, where they were treated to a Magic Lantern Show.

The arrival of the new Master, Samuel Barrass, in January 1875 brought a significant change in the fortunes of the school. Although the records are not entirely clear, he seems to have been markedly weaker than his two predecessors. As early as January 22nd he records;

> *On Thursday there was a meet of the foxhounds near Belford, and according to custom I allowed the boys to dismiss at 11 a.m. and reassemble at 2 p.m.*

Previous Masters had complained about truancy on Meet days, but certainly there was no custom of allowing pupils to attend. He next records problems getting the children to march between the school and the Church for the Lent service. When the Hunt returned to the town in March, he again allowed the boys leave, but, on this occasion, 14 did not return. The week ending April 30th saw him setting class examinations, but not finding time to mark them. In June matters took a more serious turn.

> *On Monday Morning when James Blackhall went into my desk for some pens, he was detected putting his hand into the pence bag, and to have taken sixpence. I punished him before the school and reported him to the Master of the Workhouse as he lives there……Before this, I had often missed money. Also several times children had had their dinner taken out of their bag when hanging in the porch; but on Thursday a boy in the Infant School was found to have taken some that day.*

There were more truancies in relation to the Hunt in October. There were also problems with homework.

> *October 29: On Wednesday and Friday mornings those that could not say their home lessons had to stay in at Play-time and learn them, and on Friday there were so many that there was no time for the third lesson after I heard them.*

By custom, in this part of North Northumberland, the last Friday in November was Barring-out Day - a day in which the pupils sought to gain control of the school and lock the teachers out. The two previous Masters had wisely used their discretion to have a holiday on that day, thus avoiding problems. Not so Samuel Barrass.

> *Nov. 26: Friday the last in November was according to custom, Barring-out Day, but we discontinued the custom, although two boys got in, but were got*

out by the breaking of a pane of glass.

The overall extent of the problems became obvious when the school had its annual inspection on February 11th, 1876. The report which followed was damning.

> *The children passed an examination which was decidedly below par. Although it was Eleven o'clock when I arrived, nothing was ready; and half an hour was fully occupied getting the children into their places & supplying them with slates, and then they were badly placed for Dictation. There was also too much talking. The Reading was poor in the first Standard, fairly good in the second Standard, and just fair in the other Standards. The Spelling was Poor indeed in the first and third Standards, and just fair in the other Standards. The Arithmetic of the first Standard was fair, of the second Standard fairly good, but below par in the other Standards, the third Standard doing very badly indeed. All the work should be more neatly done. Order should be preserved in a quiet though firm manner, and then the Standard work would be better done.*

In the year which followed, Barrass seems to have made a determined effort to improve matters, and also presented pupils for examination in History, Geography and Animal Physiology when the Inspector next visited. Again, however, results were very mixed, and the parting shot of the inspection report was to the effect that the Master should confine himself to the teaching of the compulsory subjects.

The year also had its highlights for the pupils. Just after the 1876 inspection, Thomas Atkinson, the Vicar, laid on tea and a Magic Lantern Show; in April, for the first time, the children received a school photo; an unexpected holiday came at the end of the month when the burn was so swollen that the school had to be closed early to allow the children to get home with dry feet; and in May, a half day holiday was given when the circus came to town. More memorable still was the visit of the Duke of Connaught to the village on 28th July, travelling north to Berwick with his regiment, the 7th Hussars. A triumphal arch had been erected, and the children waited there to cheer the Duke on his arrival. One of the infants presented the Duke with a bouquet, before they all returned to the school for a spiced bun, before being dismissed for the rest of the day. This visit was no brief march past – the regiment rested overnight at Belford, the Duke first visiting the Earl of Tankerville at Chillingham Castle, before returning to dine (and presumably sleep) at Belford Hall. The following morning, the villagers turned out in force to cheer the party on their way.

A number of staffing changes affected the school. One pupil, William Dixon, had been appointed a Monitor towards the end of 1875. Then in October 1876, a second pupil teacher joined the staff, when William Clark Rutherford's parents moved into the area and he was transferred to the National School - with so much help, one of the young men was assigned to assist Mrs. Treble. At the end of 1876, James Johnson completed his pupil teachership, but it was agreed that he should stay on as an unqualified assistant master. He continued to make a good contribution, introducing Evening Classes in the autumn. Although not a teacher as such, Thomas Atkinson, the Vicar, who had consistently given Barrass good support and contributed to the teaching, also left in April to a new parish. Rutherford's time in the school was short lived – his parents moved again in May 1877, and he went with them. A new pupil, Ralph Bewlay was given a trial as a pupil teacher. The young men, however, were not entirely successful. In June, Barrass wrote:

> *The Reading in the Third and Fourth Classes is not so good as I might expect, through the laxity of the younger teachers, so I will have to look closer to it. I have complained several times to them about the noise in their Classes when in the class-rooms.*

By September, Bewlay had decided he could earn more helping with the Harvest, and his place was taken by another of Mrs. Treble's sons, George. In November news came that Johnson was one of the top few in the Queen's Scholarship examination, and so left to train at Durham in the new year, complete with portmanteau and hatbox purchased with the £3 the children had collected for him. His replacement as Assistant Teacher was William Green from Newcastle.

At the same time, external events were putting pressure on the school. Pupil numbers had fallen drastically at the West Street Presbyterian School, apparently due to a number of bad Masters, according to the *Advertiser*. When the Government Grant was withdrawn towards the end of 1877, the school closed. This brought an influx of pupils to the National School. In July 1877, eight were admitted taking the school roll to 212, and numbers continued to rise for the rest of the year. This put intense pressure on the school buildings, and creating significant teaching problems, since repeating work for the 'new' pupils, who had been taught differently, prevented the teaching of new lessons. It was finally decided to reopen the Presbyterian school in January 1878, and there was further disruption as 20 to 30 children left en masse.

The next Government Inspection occurred on the 12th of February, just after all this upheaval. Although Geography was good, History fairly good and Reading very fair, there were problems in the other subjects, most notably in Arithmetic, where some copying was uncovered. This, together with the fact that *the order and discipline was very lax indeed*, resulted in part of the Government Grant being withdrawn. Other serious criticisms referred to untidy writing and the dirty state of the toilets. Finally, the overcrowding of the school received attention. Its maximum capacity was said to be 135, and the warning was issued that should that average number be exceeded in the following year, then the entire grant would be withdrawn.

At this point, the school log book ceases, and there is a gap of over ten years before the next one begins. The bare outlines of the next events can be obtained from the National School Account Book and the pages of the *Advertiser*. There are no records for 1879, but in 1880 there was a further bad inspection report, which brought matters to a head.

> *In consequence of the unsatisfactory report of H.M. Inspector on the condition of the School as also in view of the fact that a Fine had been imposed for defective instruction, it was unanimously resolved that the Resignation of Samuel Barrass, Principal Teacher...should now be accepted.*
> National School Account Book 16th March, 1880

Barrass left the school at the end of May, and was presented with an electro-plated inkstand as a parting gift.

Enlargement of the School 1880

Meanwhile, the managers had to deal with the problems of the overcrowded school. Over the years, inspection reports had commented on the need for a porch, the poor state of the toilets, and roofing problems. The difficulties with the Presbyterian School had also brought home to them the desirability of a larger building, capable of accommodating all the children in the parish, should such a crisis arise again. In April 1880, the Managers decided *that an addition be made to the buildings and the original premises be put in repair.* The plan was to build an additional classroom on the side of the school opposite the Infant Class. The Managers discussed the best way forward with the new Squire, George Dixon Atkinson-Clark. He made two suggestions - either he could pay for the building of the extension,

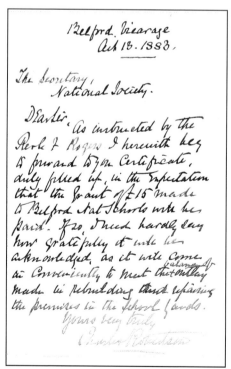

NS/7/1/984
Copyright of The National Society

estimated to be £250, and then increase the annual rent to cover 4% of his outlay; or he would redraw the lease, and the Managers would pay for the building themselves. It was decided to accept the first proposal, and the building was erected at an actual cost of £300. In addition there were the expenses of furnishing the room which amounted to another £52. The difficulty of raising this money prompted the new Vicar, Charles Robertson, to seek financial help from the National Society. On this occasion, after some delay, they gave a grant of £15.

James Munro 1880 -? 1885

James Macintosh Munro from Aberdeen was appointed to succeed Barrass. He brought with him twelve years teaching experience in large town schools and a First Class Government Teaching Certificate. The School Committee advertised the appointment with the expectation that *the greater efficiency of the Belford National School will in due time be assured.*

An additional Assistant Mistress (unnamed) was appointed in August 1881. The practice of having two pupil teachers and a monitor seems to have continued, but in 1884 one of the pupil teachers, Charles Howard, and the paid monitor, Elizabeth Pringle were dismissed, after poor reports. Financially things must have been a little difficult for the managers in 1885, as it was decided to once more amalgamate the Infant School with the

BELFORD NATIONAL SCHOOLS,

1 8 8 0.

HARVEST HOLIDAYS.—Six Weeks, from August 13th. The School will re-assemble on Monday, Sept. 27th.

SCHOOL FEES.—

INFANTS,		2d per week.
STANDARDS I., II., III.,		3d ,, ,,
,, IV., V., VI.,		4d ,, ,,
OVER STANDARDS and SPECIFIC SUBJECTS,..		5d ,, ,,

When three children of one family attend the Upper School, the youngest is charged half the above rates. Not more than three children from the same family will be charged for. Example :—If four children attend, the youngest will be admitted free, and so on for any number above three; but, in such cases, the full rates will be charged for the three eldest children.

SCHOOL BOOKS.—These must be provided for at the parents' expense; but not more than one Standard Reading Book for each child will be required in the course of the School year. If additional Reading Books are required before the end of the year, such books will be provided at the expense of the School Committee.

Mr. George Gibson has kindly consented to undertake the sale of all books required in the School at a discount to the parents at the rate of 2d. on every shilling of the advertised price. Copy and Exercise books will be charged in full.

SCHOOL STAFF.—While Mrs. Treble's capabilities as Infant Mistress are already well known and appreciated, the Members of the School Committee congratulate themselves on the appointment to the Standard Department of the School of Mr. Munro, whose personal attainments as a Scholar, experience as a Teacher of 12 years' standing in large town Schools, and exceptional efficiency, as attested on his Government Certificate of the First Class, justify the expectation that the greater efficiency of the Belford National School will in due time be assured. The Managers meanwhile venture to express the earnest hope that the parents will take pains to secure the early and regular attendance of their children; as, without this, Teachers and Pupils labour under great disadvantage and discouragement.

On behalf of the School Committee,

C. ROBERTSON,

Correspondent.

BELFORD, 13th August, 1880.

main school, although this does not seem to have been fully implemented until 1889. Also in 1885, the Managers altered the way in which the Master's salary was paid. Instead of receiving a guaranteed £120 per annum, he was to be paid £60 per annum and two thirds of the Government Grant for the whole school, presumably an incentive to see that he attracted more pupils. It was possibly this arrangement which decided Munro to seek a post elsewhere.

In terms of the running of the school, without the log book, there is very limited information available. The Master seems to have introduced a formal annual prize-giving. The first such event is recorded in the *Advertiser* for 25th March 1881. The book prizes appear to have been personally provided by Munro, and were presented by the Vicar. They were given to the top six pupils in the two senior classes: Class 1 - Wilhelmina Bird; William Lillico; E. A. Pringle; J. H. Mabon; Margaret J. Mabon and Robert Bennett. Class 2 - William White; Alfred Gibson; William G Hogg; William McCoard; Sarah Jane Clayton and Sarah Howard. He revived the Evening Classes begun by Johnson and introduced science as one of the subjects. He also launched a school cricket club, with Robert Bennett, the best player, as Captain, and Alfred Gibson as sub captain. Mrs Robertson, the Vicar's wife, provided cookery lessons for the girls.

National School c.1900

Personally, Munro's time in Belford brought unhappiness - on June 2nd, 1882 the new Infant Mistress, Magdalena Stevenson noted that the Master's wife had died that week.

From the pupils' point of view, the only events of note recorded were Christmas and summer treats, which continued much as previously, save that in January 1881, rather than a Magic Lantern Show, the children enjoyed a professional juggler from the Newcastle firm of *Mawson and Swan*.

James Mole 1886-1900.
Records show that James Mole was appointed to the Mastership of the school on October 11th, 1886. Earlier that year, on February 8th, a new Infant Mistress, Frances Louisa Alderson had also taken up post. The infant school log for 1886-1889 records the school closed by snow for three days in March 1886; the village flower show in the school on August 25th 1886, and a successful attempt to bar out the teachers on November 12th. There is little else of note.

When the main school log resumes in April 1889, in addition to Mole, there was an assistant teacher, previously pupil teacher, Wilhelmina Bird, the Infant Mistress Miss Alderson, and an unnamed sewing teacher. J. Hope was the pupil teacher. There were 72 pupils on the register. In September of that year, however, Miss Alderson left and it was decided Miss Bird should take over the infant classes. The Inspection report of February 3rd 1890, suggests that generally the school was doing well - *the children have passed a very fair examination in the elementary subjects* - although there were problems with the Infant Class – a bad examination and very poor lessons was recorded, but this was markedly better the following year.

Both Mole and the school experienced significant changes in 1891. In April, the basis of calculating the Master's salary was again changed – he was now to receive a guaranteed sum of £85 per annum, paid quarterly, in addition he would receive any additional sum above the fixed grant which the success of the pupils earned at the annual inspection, and his house would be rent free. On August 14th, he recorded his dissatisfaction with a visit of the Attendance Officer, who clearly had been before, but had not previously featured in the Log Book
> *The monthly visit of the A.O. seems to have become a mere matter of form; as nothing is ever heard of the cases, not is the attendance of the reported children anything improved.*

Later in the month, the Managers made the decision to accept the Fee Grant, which increased Government control over the school, but for the first time made education free for the pupils. This, Mole noted in October, resulted in a marked improvement in the regularity of attendance. Lastly, also in October, Mole was married, and received as presents from the children *a handsome lamp & set of jugs & paper knife*.

In 1892, Mole underwent an operation and was absent from March until August, during which time there was a temporary, unnamed master. In October the sewing mistress left to get married and was presented with a clock by the girls.

Her replacement was regarded by the Master as a considerable improvement – *the tone of the girls has materially increased. Strict discipline is now observed*; there was however a degree of bias as the lady in question was his wife! Nevertheless the Inspection report of 1893 confirmed his view - *the school has generally improved.*

During 1893 and 1894 he made a determined drive to improve attendance. In March 1893, he hung up a chart showing the fluctuations in attendance over the year, with a view to identifying causes. He encountered problems, however, when he tried to pin down individual children - in several instances the parents merely removed the offending child to the West Street School. Interestingly, the Master of the West Street School recorded the same problem in reverse! Mole also made an effort to improve his personal situation, writing to the Managers:

> *Seeing that the School house provided by you is unsuitable and not at all*
> *conducive to our comfort, both as regards space and necessary*
> *conveniences, I desire to remove from it, and hope you will use your influence*
> *in procuring for us a better and more comfortable home.*

This was agreed, provided the Moles paid the estimated difference in rent, and it seems to be from then that the Schoolmaster's house moved from the Cottage across the Burn from the school, to North Bank.

From the pupils' point of view, school life was fairly uneventful. At the Christmas treat, laid on by the Atkinson-Clarks at the Hall, a Punch and Judy Show now provided the entertainment. In 1893 they had a day's holiday to celebrate the marriage of the Duke of York to Princess Mary of Teck, and, in 1894, the taking of a school photograph is again recorded.

In 1895 there were again a number of staff changes. J. Hope went off to Durham Training College with a travelling bag provided by the teachers and pupils, and was replaced by Mary Jane Angus as pupil teacher. A new member of staff was added, Annie Ord, who also was to take over the sewing from Mrs. Mole. As a result of the good inspection report, Mole was now to be paid £120 per year,   subject to annual revision. Also, the arrangements for providing schoolbooks were changed. The books were to be bought from school funds, but the Master was made responsible for selling them to the children. On the positive side, the managers agreed to provide more equipment for the kindergarten pupils. The year ended less well, as the Master fell seriously ill in November and was absent from school until February of 1896, his place being taken by a Mr. A. J. Hall previously at St. James' School, Morpeth. Although Mole returned to the school in February, the Easter holidays were extended by a week to give him further recuperation time.

A combination of Mr. Mole's drive to improve attendance, and further difficulties at the West Street School, resulted in a rise of pupil numbers – in 1896 the number on roll was recorded as 124. The previous year's staffing changes, however were not all positive. In October, Mole recorded the need to reorganise the staff as the discipline in the Middle Room, where Miss Ord and Mary Jane Angus taught, was very unsatisfactory.

In 1897 a second pupil teacher, Ellen Forsyth, was added to the staff complement in an effort to provide further support for Mole, whose health, the Inspector recorded in February 1897, was still far from good. Arrangements for pupil teachers were now becoming more formalised - no longer were they solely dependent on the teaching of their own Master, but attended classes organised in the area and in June, one of them began going to classes at Berwick Art School two evenings a week. The school also received a Grant of £20 for increased teaching power and apparatus. Possibly it was spent on the new infant desks which arrived in January 1898.

A number of events impacted on school life during this year. The first was the Diamond Jubilee of Queen Victoria, which was celebrated in the village with a whole day holiday, and with a special tea provided by Mrs. Atkinson-Clark for the children at the School. Two days later, her husband presented all the children with a commemorative mug. During September and early October, the Duchess of Teck moved in to Belford Hall, and added interest to village life generally by visiting the inhabitants and opening a number of events. It came therefore as a major shock to the whole community when, three weeks after leaving, news came of her sudden death. Then, in November, the Vicar celebrated his silver wedding with an event in the school building at which he was presented with a silver tea service from the congregation, and the children were given an extra afternoon holiday so that the building could be decorated.

During 1898, the Vicar began to teach the senior boys Latin, and on the suggestion of H.M.I. Mr. Scott, mental arithmetic was slotted in just after registration, when the children were fresh. A further grant of £25 was received which seems to have been used to replace the old blackboards with new 'swing boards' which arrived early in 1899. The new year, however, did not get off to a good start, as a measles epidemic prevented the school opening until February 3rd. Over the summer holiday, the whole school was redecorated, and a clock installed in the middle room. Perhaps, however, Mole was losing interest in his post – the 1900 inspection report begins ominously - *this school seems to be deteriorating in the teaching of some of the subjects of instruction.* Nor was the situation in the Infant class any better - *the teaching is wanting in method and interest and the children are somewhat listless*.

Whatever the reason, in April 1900, Mole left the school. On behalf of the pupils and teachers, two of the senior boys, Alfred Weallans and Thomas Clark presented him with gold cufflinks and a case of briar pipes with silver mounts.

Richard Davison 1900 – 1928

Richard Davison, the longest serving of the National School's headteachers, came to the school from St. Andrew's Mission Hall School in Alnwick, and rapidly gained himself the nickname of 'Tarry' on account of his small black moustache and beard, which it was said made him look as if a tar brush had been smeared across his face. He began by having another drive on attendance. He brought new approaches to this perpetual problem - all staff were instructed not to register pupils who arrived late, and as a keen photographer, he also took a series of class photos, giving one to each of the 100 children with best attendance. Then latecomers were marked in red on the register and letters sent to parents at the end of the week. Certainly these initiatives had some success. In November, he was able to record that the average attendance was now 116 compared with 80 when he arrived, although there were now fewer pupils on the register. By the autumn of 1903, he was regularly achieving over 95% attendance. In 1902,

Probably one of Mr. Davison's class photographs

he began sending home school reports at the end of the year, and from 1903 these were accompanied by an attendance report.

The school inspection of January 1904 recorded Davison's achievements:
The children are in very good order; they are kept well employed and interested in their work and satisfactory attempts are made to develop their intelligence....Infant Class: the order is good and the teaching is careful and painstaking....

In his time in post, Davison sought to broaden pupils' learning experiences. On his arrival he introduced the teaching of singing using the tonic sol-fa method. In 1901, he brought a working potter into the school, so that the children could see for themselves how pots were thrown, an experience which was repeated several times over the years. In 1903, after he discovered that his pupils knew virtually nothing about the wild flowers around the school, he introduced nature walks, and began to teach the children about the plants they saw. In 1904, one of his teachers, Miss Mabon, visited Gateshead to learn more about using phonics to teach reading, and to investigate options for practical work. In March 1913 he introduced light woodwork for the boys and 'industrial work' for the girls, but these were suspended the following year due to staffing problems.

Davison also showed a commendable concern for pupils' problems. When he arrived at the school, he was particularly exercised over James Falla, apparently a child with significant learning difficulties, who refused to come to school. He noted that, when James Falla had attended, he had begun to develop some understanding of number and of social skills such as discipline and tidiness, and involved the attendance officer in trying to get him to return to the school. From 1907, he made arrangements for pupils from the country areas to enjoy soup at lunchtimes over the winter months at a charge of one halfpenny. Although this did not cover the cost, he made the scheme work by getting donations of vegetables and meat.

Davison's years in post were bedevilled by staff changes. Between 1900 and 1914 he had to contend with eleven changes of teacher, together with several extended absences. Even when there was some continuity, as in the case of Miss Rachel McLeish, the sister-in-law of the Vicar, who taught at the school between 1905 and 1913, significant bouts of ill health limited her contribution to the school. Insufficient staff was noted as a problem in the inspections of January and May 1908, and blamed for the poor standards achieved by the infant pupils. By the inspection of 1913, it was clear that staffing problems were impacting on the overall effectiveness of the school and of the headmaster, who himself had been unwell. The inspection of that year refers for the first time to *the lack of progress shown in the work of this school*. Although not immediately obvious, the appointment in March 1914, of Miss Torrance to replace Miss McLeish, marked the beginning of greater stability. She was to remain at the school until her retirement in October 1937, providing stalwart support for Davison and his successors.

Another problem was the teaching time lost through pupil illness. Most years, the outbreak of an epidemic resulted in the closure of the school for several weeks. In 1901, scarlet fever closed the school; 1904, mumps; 1906 measles;

1907   and 1910 whooping cough; 1908 February attendance was greatly reduced because of an influenza epidemic, although there was no official closure; and, in 1913, a combination of measles and diphtheria closed the school for 3 weeks.

By the start of the twentieth century, the buildings too were showing their age, a difficulty not helped by the apparent reluctance of the managers to address the identified problems. Lack of effective heating in winter (in February 1907 the temperature in the school was only two degrees above freezing), and adequate ventilation in summer were persistent problems, as were blockages in the boys urinals. In 1904, the Inspection report stated that the cloakroom was inadequate; a new stove was required; the ceiling needed repair and there was no gate between the boys' and girls' playgrounds. A storm in May 1906 resulted in the school being flooded to a depth of eighteen inches, destroying books, maps and pictures. It took a cleaning team of six women and constant fires for a week to make the buildings habitable again. There were problems with cracked downpipes in 1907 and the Inspectors called for better lighting in 1908 and better heating in 1910. By 1912 a very dry spring resulted in problems of dust in the playground and loose stones in the playground walls. In addition one of the classroom floors was dangerous and window panes needed replacing. Despite some internal painting carried out in 1911, it was not until 1913 that some attempt was made to address the other issues. When the school returned after the summer holiday that year, a new fireplace had been provided, and grates, the window panes and the playground wall repaired. An attempt was also being made to deal with the urinal problems, but, by mid October, they had blocked again.

Events of National and local importance also had an impact on the life of the schoolchildren. The first of these was the end of the Boer War. Before Davison's arrival, the pupils had already enjoyed a half day holiday for the relief of Ladysmith, followed, on May 21st 1900, by a further afternoon off to prepare for the torchlight procession to celebrate the relief of Mafeking. Exactly a year later, the school closed again for the return of the Belford Volunteers from the War, and ten days after that, the village children all enjoyed tea and sports in a further celebration of the soldiers' return. The peace celebrations for the end of the war resulted in another day's holiday in June 1902.

Queen Victoria died on January 21st, 1901. There was no school closure for this, but Davison interrupted lessons to give the children an overview of the life of the Queen. In June 1902, there was a two day holiday for the Coronation of Edward VII. The most noted excitement of the following year, however, came in the November. While the children were lining up at the end of playtime, one of the sheep belonging to Gordon, the Butcher, escaped and ran into the school, breaking the legs of one of the new desks in its panic! In 1904, the marriage of the Squire's son, George Atkinson-Clark, resulted in the children being given sweets and a half day holiday, as did the arrival of Buffalo Bill's *Wild West Show* in Berwick. King Edward VII's visit to Alnwick in 1906 resulted in a half day holiday, while his death in 1910 merited a full day's closure. The next year, the coronation of George V was celebrated with the children being presented with a Coronation mug and a Union Jack, being taught maypole dancing, having a day off school and taking part in sports held on the cricket field. Meanwhile, in September 1910, Mr J. N. Jarvie of New Jersey, U.S.A., made arrangements to have each child presented with one shilling in memory of his mother, who came from Belford. He also gave Davison money for a Christmas treat for the pupils. This took the form of tea, oranges, and a book for everyone, with the girls also being given a workbag and doll and the boys sets of pastels. Mr. Jarvie was to remain a benefactor of the school until his death in 1929.

In 1907, the managers of both the National and the Presbyterian (West Street) schools agreed to take common holidays, thus ending a long running source of complaint in the village. About the same time travelling children were required to attend school. From 1910 the school log records the admission of these children while the Hiring Fair was in town, but they rarely came for more than three days before moving on, and in March 1914, Davison noted that their previous admission had been responsible for an outbreak of measles in the school.

The War Years 1914-1918
When the school resumed in September 1914, after the outbreak of war, the first problem to be faced was the shortage of water, the result of a long summer drought. Dobbs Well, from which the school obtained its drinking water, was completely dry. The heat also resulted in the Burn smelling badly, and the stench penetrated the Cloakroom and Infant Room. Davison himself was one of sixty men from the area sworn in to act as special constables in case of any problems. The rest of 1914 was fairly uneventful, although it ended with the Squire's daughter giving the children a Boxing Day tea, complete with crackers and oranges.

There were more staff changes in 1915. Bad snow blocked all the roads into Belford in March, and Davison was ill for a month with influenza. By May, a shortage of paper meant that pupils had to return to working on slates. The reality of war was brought closer to the children, when, in July, a party of wounded soldiers marched through the town, and the Managers requested that the children line the street to welcome them. As part of the government drive to promote savings, Davison launched a Penny Bank in the school in September, and by the end of the year had 99 depositors. At Christmas, he gave those children who had an account and were present, 82 in all, an additional shilling to deposit *from money placed in my hand for certain purposes*. Rather than expecting a party, this year the children themselves gave a concert for their parents, and were rewarded with an orange from the Vicar.

At the beginning of 1916 one of the lady teachers married, and, due to the war, was enabled to retain her post but left shortly afterwards. On June 27th - Belford General Holiday - Davison organised an excursion to Ross Sands for the older pupils, some 60 of whom went. The summer holiday began early due to another measles epidemic. Then, in October, Davison took stock of the pupils of the school who had been killed - to date six former pupils had died - William Cameron, James Clark, William Turnbull, Ernest Currins, John Jeffrey and John White. By now, the extra work of running the school bank was beginning to tell, and, in November, the headteacher advised his depositors to transfer their savings to the Post Office Bank or into Savings Certificates. Still concerned to widen his pupils' experiences, in November he persuaded Mrs. Summerfield of Buckton to come into the school to talk to the pupils about her visits to Australia, Tasmania and Ceylon. At the end of the year, food shortages forced the school to give up totally the provision of lunchtime soup, it having already been cut back to one day a week. Davison remained very concerned about the rural children having nothing to warm them, and, with the help of donations from Miss Blenkinsop of Ross and Mrs. Summerfield, he offered instead a mug of cocoa or Oxo daily for a halfpenny a day, later reduced to twopence a week. This year, at Christmas, the children performed three short plays for their parents, and at the beginning of January, Miss Clark again provided a tea party for them.

In 1917, the senior boys, unable to do woodwork due to shortage of materials, instead took on gardening at Mr. Appleby's in West Street. There they planted 21 lbs of potatoes as well as doing more general gardening and pruning. With the aid of Miss Torrance, another visit to Ross Sands was organised on Whit Monday. For some of the children, it was their first visit to the seaside. Then in June, following a lesson about Holy Island, Davison organised a visit there one Saturday. In the event, only two boys, Cecil Dunn and J. Turnbull went, and the day was spent examining Lindisfarne Castle. Despite such efforts to provide for his pupils, when the Inspection took place in July, the subsequent report was damning, with Davison being blamed for much of the problem.

The condition of this school is very disappointing, owing to the absence of teachers Standards III & IV are in a distressingly backward state. The infants are badly grounded. The teacher of I & II (Miss Torrance) *works hard and her children are making progress…… The Headmaster must be prepared to exercise a more vigorous and effective control of the whole school. It is for him to realise how far short the work falls of what it is fair to expect in thoroughness and enthusiasm.*

Such severe criticism must have come as a blow to Davison, who certainly had been trying to do his best under difficult circumstances. Personally, too, he was coping with the knowledge that two of his sons were in the war, and the strain of this was affecting the health of his wife. Nevertheless he took stock, introduced a new timetable in the autumn from which the practical subjects of clay modelling, cookery and woodwork were excluded. He formally closed the school bank (which incidentally had raised over £800 for War Loans). Lastly, and with most regret, he abandoned the custom of having a table in the Infant Room formally set with cutlery and cups and saucers for the country children's lunch - something he had introduced to accustom the children to the rituals of more formal eating. The setting of the table, however, had caused some disruption to the teaching of the youngest children; given the criticism, he felt that this could not continue. The year did not get easier. The autumn brought more staff changes, and two months without a teacher. Then he was told that he had overspent his requisition money. Yet more economies had to be introduced. White chalk was dyed to provide colours, slates continued to be used, but in order to have paper for writing and drawing, old minute and account books were reused and even brown wrapping paper. Old books were repaired, cloth begged from friends for sewing classes, the teachers made their own arithmetic cards, and test and song books were purchased with non county council money[1]. By the end of the year, the national food shortage was impacting on the village, and the need to economise became another topic to be taught. As a result, the children enrolled in the *Junior League of the Anchors* and took its pledge, which seems to have been to economise in every way. The senior pupils also decided to forego a Christmas treat. Instead they put on a play on the last day of term, and on Christmas Day put what money they could into the Fund for Blinded Soldiers. They also distributed envelopes to people not connected with the school – all of which raised the not inconsiderable sum of £9. 11s. 6d.

The last year of the war began badly. When the school resumed in January, the snow lay on the floor of Davison's classroom all day without melting. When the thaw came the playground degenerated into mud which rose over the boots of the younger children, and to add to the misery, a craze for buying locust beans induced vomiting sickness in the children! Shortage of labour saw more and more under age children employed illegally, something Davison tried to counter by personally visiting the various farmers involved. Then, there was a specific inspection of needlework in the school, which recommended the use of better patterns and that the parents supplied better material. Davison recognised the

---

[1] It seems likely that this was from monies gifted by Mr. Jarvie.

problem in this:

> *There is difficulty in getting the parents to do this and some give as a reason that the garments are not particularly useful while others say that they are unable to afford to buy materials for garments of which they may not be particularly in need.*

At the beginning of April, another teacher resigned, and once more the school had to cope with a shortage of staff.

With the spring, however, things began to look up. At the beginning of April, Miss Torrance organised a Cantata and Concert in the West Street Hall, raising £19 for various charities, while the senior pupils made a silver collection which resulted in £6. 5s. 0d. for the Northumberland Prisoners of War fund. In mid-June, Davison organised a picnic on Holy Island for the Senior pupils – some cycled, others took the train from Belford to Beal before they all walked over the sands, and spent the day visiting the Castle and the Priory. Later in the month, the children who had taken part in the Cantata had a day's excursion to Bamburgh, travelling there and back by cart.

The summer holiday was cut short by a week to enable the pupils to have an extra holiday in October to help with the potato harvest. As luck would have it, the October weather was bad, and the one week's task became a fortnight's for a number of the children.

They were scarcely back at school, when the news of the Armistice brought a further school closure from 11.45 on Monday 11th November, when the news of the signing of the treaty reached Belford, until the Wednesday morning. Two days later, it was closed again for the rest of the term, as a result of the influenza epidemic.

The Post War Years
The new term began in 1919, with Miss Atkinson-Clark again providing the children with a festive tea, followed, on this occasion by a lantern slide show. Thereafter the term proceeded normally until late March, when influenza again resulted in the closure of the school, this time for three weeks. During this period, Sergeant Major William Dunlop was presented with his Military Medal at the West Street Hall, and as he had been a former pupil of the school, Davison was asked to see that the children attended this event.

June was both a personally and professionally critical month for Davison. His wife's health had not been good, attributed in her obituary to her concerns over her sons in the war. On June 11th, the crisis came.

> *11 June: My wife is very ill.*

*12 June: My wife died last night and I shall have to leave school occasionally
today and tomorrow.*

While he was coping with his bereavement, he had also to deal with new
admissions, arising from problems at the Presbyterian School. Although the
additional pupils brought financial benefit to the school, there was a serious
problem – insufficient desks, and due to some of the desks being 12 feet long
with multiple seating, he could not rearrange things as he would have wished.
He had to make do with trestles and table tops. Then, twelve days after the death
of his wife, there was another Inspection. It must have been the last thing he
needed. All was well, however. The school had turned the corner.

*I am glad to be able to report a general improvement in the condition of this
school. The lower groups are now being systematically taught and a
gratifying feature is the number of children who reach the higher standards.
The Head Master has been at pains to correct the children's exercises and to
see that there is a methodical procedure in the lower groups. His own oral
lessons are interestingly given..... the tone of the school is good and the
Head Master takes a kindly interest in the children's welfare both in and out
of school.*

The year 1921 brought significant changes which impacted both on the school
and the village. Canon Robertson, who had consistently provided good support
for the school, died at the end of January, and, two months later, the Squire,
George Dixon Atkinson-Clark followed him to the grave. His death resulted in
the sale of the Village, including both Davison's house and the school itself –
not surprisingly Davison attended the second day to see what happened and
bought his cottage in West Street for £100.

Generally Davison's post war years in the school differed little from those
which had gone before. There continued to be unresolved building problems
including the surface of the playground, the urinals, the repair of downpipes,
cording on blinds; stove repairs, roof repairs; plaster falling off the walls in all
the classrooms; a dangerous stone in the doorway of the Infant Room; badly
worn step in the girls' cloakroom; broken panes of glass; and a fastening needed
for the school gate. If the building problems were bad, they were worsened by
the coal miners' strike which began at the end of the 1919. Even with fires,
winter conditions in the school were bad. Without them, they were close on
unbearable. On 12th February 1920 the Headteacher suspended lessons for the
senior pupils, and took them out wood gathering in the plantation, until they had
collected enough to keep all the fires in the school burning for the rest of the
day. Coal shortages remained a problem until well into April of that year, and
recurred at intervals thereafter.

Other previously unknown problems presented themselves after the war. Someone, presumably a returning soldier, disposed of unused ammunition by dumping it in the burn, from where it was retrieved by the more adventurous boys. There was an on-going need to remind children that some war mementoes were potentially dangerous. Then there were the cars. As all supplies of fresh water came from the well outside the playground, it was not possible to confine the children to the school grounds. Now, however, a considerable rise in motor traffic on the main road greatly increased the risk of accidents.

The organisation of classes and teachers was again an issue. There were another seven changes in staff between 1920 and 1925. A further strain was the final closure of the Presbyterian School in May 1924, resulting in the block admission of a further 24 pupils, taking the overall roll to 131, which in turn required yet another rearrangement of classes. Despite it all, attendance remained good and in both 1923 and 1925 the school was awarded a picture by the Council in recognition of this. One pupil, Lucy Falla, achieved a nine year record of unbroken attendance on June 8th 1926 and received a special presentation Certificate from the Council Education committee.

National, village and school events punctuated the day to day work of the pupils. The first change was probably ill received by the children - the introduction of a weekly half day holiday for farm servants resulted in the ending of the Belford Feast Days, and consequently of the children's holiday. The school continued to organise summer outings and to help the children mount plays and concerts. The senior boys used some of their drawing lessons to manufacture the necessary props. In 1924, Davison also personally paid for the pupils to visit Wombwell's Menagerie when it was in town.

The Comrades of the Great War organised a children's sports on the cricket field in 1920, and in 1922 the children attended the unveiling of the War Memorial in West Street. Then, in 1924, the school held its own first Armistice Day Celebrations during which all the children were given a Flanders poppy. The service began with the National Anthem. Then Davison talked to the pupils, and they sang *Land of Hope and Glory* before a two minute silence. There followed a second hymn *The Saints of God their conflict past*; then two pupils, Lucy Falla and Alice Shell, recited Kipling's *Recessional*. A boy, George Gordon, then played a violin solo before they all concluded by singing *Rule Britannia*.

The pupils gained extra holidays from two royal marriages, that of Princess Mary in 1922 and of the Duke of York in 1923. That year also brought a new experience - the school received a gramophone record with a recording of the

King and Queen's message for Empire Day, May 24th. The classrooms were decorated with Union Jacks, the children listened to the record and then sang the National Anthem. The fact that Standards III and IV then had to copy out the full message, which had been put up on the Blackboard, must have taken the edge off the experience!

Davison retired at the end of 1926. The final inspection of his school came in the September of that year.

Richard 'Tarry' Davison

The Headmaster retires shortly after many years of faithful service. He leaves the school in a fairly efficient state.

Victor H. Bryson 1927 – 1931

With the retiral of Mr. Davison, the detailed keeping of the log books came to an end, and so information about the latter years of the National School is more limited.

During Mr. Bryson's five years in post, staff instability continued. While Miss Torrance continued to serve the school, the third teaching post was held by five different women in that time.

When the school was inspected in March 1929, Bryson himself received praise: *The new Head Master is doing well. His own class is in good order and some of the work reaches quite a high level.* The same could not be said for some of his colleagues, although who was who is not made clear. *Class III is less satisfactory – both here and in the Infant Room the teachers appear satisfied with much too low a standard of speech and constantly accepted answers that to the Visiting Inspector were quite unintelligible!* Other issues which were raised by the inspection were lack of adequate reading material in all the classes, the willingness of Bryson to teach gardening if a suitable site could be found, and the absence of a woman on the Board of Managers. The Inspector also took a particular interest in the arrangements for the children who lived outside Belford, particularly praising the lunchtime arrangements which had been introduced, but expressing concern that the local library only opened at times the rural children could not attend and suggesting that it be opened over at least one lunchtime.

The following year, the Education Committee took steps to purchase the house on North Bank which Mr. Bryson was privately renting, with a view to providing suitable accommodation for the school's Headteachers. The purchase was completed in 1931, but as Mr. Bryson left the following year, it was his successors who benefited from this arrangement.

Clifford Staynes 1932 -1935

Clifford Staynes brought with him a strong determination that both the staff and the pupils would work in satisfactory conditions. In his first week in the school he complained to the managers about the rat nuisance and the broken floorboards in the building, and more remarkably, given the difficulties of his predecessors, the floorboards were replaced three days later! The beginning of the 1933 saw him logging the low temperatures in the classes, and, on January 23rd, sending the infants home when the temperature did not rise above 33 F. On April 4th, he recorded that, for the tenth time, he had reported the unsatisfactory state of the urinals to Rev. Hull, followed up by a further report on the 13th. On this occasion his persistence paid off as Messrs Tully cleaned out the urinals the following day. July saw him taking issue with the state of the Belford Burn and the stench which came from it. He involved Dr. David McDonald, the Medical Officer of Health, and posted an official complaint to the Sanitary Office, but only achieved limited success. The Surveyor became involved and confirmed *that owing to the exceptionally dry weather and the discharge of sewage into the stream, conditions recently had been very objectionable.* He added that *arrangements had been made for cleaning out the burn, though no marked improvement could be expected until there was some flood water.* In 1934, Staynes again did battle over the urinals and also complained to the managers about the footbridge over the burn.

Under Staynes' leadership, woodwork was once more introduced for the senior boys. The previous inspectorate criticism of Library arrangements was also addressed when, in 1933, the library van began to call one day a week at 1.15 p.m. The Headteacher also seems to have been an enthusiastic supporter of school sport, recording both cricket and football matches played against neighbouring schools. Nevertheless, when the County adviser called, she was very critical of the standards of physical education, as was the Inspector about the senior pupils' English.

Belford National School Netball Team c.1935
Courtesy of Nance Turnbull

A new feature of school life was the introduction of a House System, about which, sadly, few details are given. Staynes recorded that for the first two weeks the *Mastiffs* were top house, which rather prompts the question, what were the names of the other houses. Other apparent innovations from this time were senior pupils attending an armistice service in the Church, the holding of fire drills, the introduction in 1934 of staff undertaking lunchtime supervision, the delegation of corporal punishment - no more than two strokes on the hand - to the class teachers, except for the infants; and the serving of Horlicks milk at the morning interval.

There continued to be a turn over of teachers. But the changes in staff presented Staynes with a chance to fight for improved provision for the infants. In August 1933, he succeeded in having a certificated teacher, Miss Newbould, appointed to take charge of them. He was also ready to support other colleagues. Noting that Miss Forster, having trained to teach seniors, was struggling with the younger pupils of Class 1, he arranged to spend extra time with that class. At the end of February 1935, however, he himself left to a new post in Bradford.

Robert Graham 1935 -1940

There was a two month gap, during which a D. Elliott took over as acting Headteacher, before the new appointee, Robert Graham arrived at the end of April. He came just in time for the celebrations for George V's Silver Jubilee. Both this and a Royal Wedding at the end of the year earned the pupils additional holidays, as did the Funeral of the King, in January 1936.

At the end of 1935, the school had a major fund raising effort, holding both a jumble sale and a bazaar on December 14th. Exactly how much was raised is not recorded, but it was sufficient for the purchase of a fifteen guinea wireless set. For the first time, this now allowed the school to take advantage of the schools' programmes now being broadcast by the B.B.C.

In December 1936, the school was again inspected, and the comparatively full report of that year gives a very good overview of the education it provided for the children of the area.

Since his appointment in 1935 the Head Master has introduced several new features into the training, bringing it more in touch with modern ideas; and the small measure of specialisation which has been introduced gives him an opportunity of making contact with the other classes. The staff do not spare themselves and the children respond well.

An encouraging start is made in the entrants class, where the teacher is doing some particularly useful work in training the children to talk. This should be

continued in class 3. In both classes Reading is taught satisfactorily, and
ideas of Number are introduced sensibly by the use of suitable apparatus.
There are also some commendable features on the activity side.
The teacher of class 2 (Miss Torrance) *has been here many years and, as this*
will be the last Report before her retirement it is fitting to pay a tribute to
her thorough and conscientious work. Her Needlework scheme is well
planned and the girls do some creditable decorative work. Weaving has
recently been added to their crafts.
In class one, the children are reading a number of good books and they make
free use of the Rural Library. The written work of the majority is reasonably
satisfactory, but there is some carelessness in the St V group. Arithmetic is
taught effectively although examples might be brought more in touch with the
life of the village. In Geography the regional survey has proved a very useful
exercise and this attempt to make use of local material might well be extended
to history. The introduction of Bookbinding has made possible developments
in the teaching of art.
In several subjects wireless lessons are taken.
The children are well mannered and friendly.

It was a measure of how the village had changed in the fifteen years since the
Squire's death, that on this occasion, the pupils' Christmas Party was organised
by the Women's Institute. Transport had also improved - school outings in the
following years took the pupils to both Glasgow and Edinburgh, destinations
unthinkable in earlier times.

The Coronation of George VI was the main event of 1937 and pupils received a
Coronation beaker, a penny with the new King's head and a special sports day.
International affairs, however, were beginning to cast a long shadow over the
country. On June 15th, Graham attended a meeting in Alnwick about air raid
precautions. There was growing concern, too, about the health of the nation's
children. Inoculations against diphtheria were introduced in April, and, in
October, all the pupils were examined by the School Doctor to determine who
should be given a free third of a pint of milk each morning. The barrier must
have been set quite high, as only 13 pupils qualified. Nevertheless the morning
break had to be lengthened to let these children drink their milk.

As in earlier years, there was a high staff turnover, with five staff changes in as
many years. The most significant of these was the retirement of Miss Torrance
at the end of October 1937, having taught in the school for 23 years, during
which time she had provided invaluable support to four headteachers, and
through her encouragement of concerts and plays, given her pupils a whole
new range of experiences.

By 1939, the belief that Chamberlain had gained *Peace in our time* was fading fast. In April, Graham received official letters about evacuation arrangements, and in July met with the designated billeting officers to discuss the practicalities. It was as well he and the school were prepared. On September 1st, Chillingham Road School from Newcastle arrived in Belford and the old school had to accommodate two lots of pupils. How this played out is described elsewhere in this book.

A New School
The days of the school were numbered. After a hundred years, as could be seen from the constant complaints of the recent Headteachers, the physical structure was well past its sell-by date. Indeed in the words of the County Council
> *This building is old and seriously defective judged by any reasonable standards[1].*

Equally important it was not properly equipped to provide the facilities needed to teach the range of subjects required for young people growing up in the middle of the twentieth century. From the beginning of the 1930s, the Northumberland County Council Education Committee had been considering the best way of addressing this problem. One option was to purchase Belford Hall. In 1931 the Director of Education for Northumberland wrote to the Government Board of Education:
> *We are contemplating the provision of a Senior School at a place called Belford, for 250 -350 pupils and we have been offered, for the sum of about £3,500, a country mansion and 15 acres of land. We have surveyed it and find we could get*
>
> | | |
> |---|---|
> | *On the ground floor -* | *Three ordinary classrooms* |
> | | *Three special classrooms* |
> | | *Two work rooms* |
> | *On the first floor -* | *Two science rooms* |
> | | *Two ordinary classrooms* |
> | | *Library* |
>
> *We should have to build a separate hall and other conveniences.*
> *In many respects it would be an admirable place for the school, and even if it costs £4,000 or £5,000 to adapt, it would be considerably cheaper than a new school.*
> *But there is this difficulty, while the rooms on the ground floor are 15 ft. high, those on the first floor are only 9 ft. Although the Board have no building regulations we assume you still require a minimum of 10 or 11 ft. Is it of any use do you think, to further consider the acquisition of this building for school purposes?*

There was an initial positive reply saying that height was not an insurmountable

---

[1] National Archives ED97/360 Belford Area File

problem, although there might be lighting difficulties. This was followed up by a visit from the District Inspector Mr. Adams, who wrote to London that having visited Belford Hall with the Director, he felt that *the general amenities offered would be sufficient to justify us in stretching a good many points over the details of the plan*[1]. Despite such a promising response, at some point the County Council dropped the plan. Instead, in 1935, they put forward a plan to build a school for pupils aged 5 to 14, from Belford, Middleton and Lucker, together with senior pupils from Warenford, at an estimated cost of fifteen and a half thousand pounds. The site selected was on the edge of Belford, on the southern side of West Street. Although this was approved and work began before the outbreak of the war, it was not until 1940 that the buildings were completed. From the beginning of April, some use was made of the new school grounds for gardening and games, but by May 10th, the building works were complete, the children moved into their new school, and together with Middleton and Lucker, Belford's National School was closed.

Commemorative mugs given to school pupils

Coronation Beaker
Courtesy of Edie Bowmer

Silver Jubilee mug
Courtesy of Mary Tait

Particular thanks for their help to: Edie Bowmer; Roy & Marjory Dodds; Mary Tait; and Nance Turnbull.

---

[1] National Archives ED21/37504

Appendix: The known Staff of Belford National School

NAME	STATUS	ARRIVED	LEFT
Mr Lockie	Master in charge	c. 1837	c.1840
Robert Lightfoot	Master in charge	1840	1841 or later
Mr. Mitchell	Master in charge	1846	unknown
Mr. Moor	Master in charge	1856	unknown
Miss Acton	Infant Mistress	1860	by 1862
Miss Caswell	Infant Mistress	by 1862	By 1864
Charles R. Brown	Master in charge	1866	1872
Mrs. Treble	Infant Mistress	1864	1881
Miss Mabon	Sewing Teacher	by 1867	1873
James Treble	Pupil Teacher	1867?	1872
Thomas Simonson	Master in Charge	1872	1874
James Johnson	Pupil Teacher then Teacher	1872	1877
Mrs. Pearson	Sewing Teacher	1873	
Samuel Barras	Master in Charge	1875	1880
Wm. C Rutherford	Pupil Teacher	1875	1877
Ralph Bewlay	Pupil Teacher	1877	1877
George Treble	Pupil Teacher	1877	
*	*	*	*
James Munro	Master in charge	1880?	1885
Charles Howard	Pupil Teacher		1884
Magdalena Stevenson	Infant Mistress	1882	1886?
Frances L. Alderson	Infant Mistress	1886	1889
James Mole	Master in Charge	1886	1900
Wilhelmina Bird	Pupil Teacher then teacher	Pre 1889	1901
J. Hope	Pupil Teacher	by 1890	1895
Mrs Mole	Sewing Teacher	1892	1895

continued on next page . . .

* Absence of Log Books between 1878 and 1889 means some records are missing

NAME	STATUS	ARRIVED	LEFT
Mary Jane Angus	Pupil Teacher then teacher	1895	1902
Annie Ord	Teacher	1895	1903
Mr. J A Hall	Locum Master i/c	Nov 1895	Feb 1896
Ellen Forsyth	Pupil Teacher	1897	1900
Wm. Angus	Monitor/ Pupil Teacher	1899(?)	1905
Richard Davison	Head Teacher	1900	1928
Mary Mabon	Teacher	1902	1910
Mary Jane Billson	Monitor/Pupil Teacher	1899	1901
Isabella Clark	Pupil Teacher	1903	1903
Edith Rose Scott	Pupil Teacher	1904	1907
Mary Jane Angus	Teacher (formerly Pupil Teacher)	1904	1905
Rachel McLeish	Teacher	1905	1913
Isabella Clark	Teacher	1908	1912
Miss Hughes	Teacher	1910	1912
Agnes Paxton	Teacher	1912	1915
Martha Leighton	Teacher	1912	1917
Miss Torrance	Teacher	1914	1937
Miss Grey/ Mrs Stuart	Teacher	1915	1916
Mary Louise Wright	Teacher	1916	1918
Elizabeth Laing Young	Teacher	1917	1923
Jane Clark	Supply Teacher	1918	1920
Effie Purvis	Teacher	1920	1921
Edna Mitchell	Teacher	1921	1922
Winnie Hull	Pupil Teacher/Supply Teacher	1922	1926
Adeline Jones	Teacher	1922	1923
Albert Ford	Teacher	1922	1923
Annie Clark	Teacher	1922	1927
James Wood	Student Teacher	1923	1924
Jane Fell	Teacher	1923	1925
Isabella Elliott	Student Teacher	1924	1925
Georgina Rule	Teacher	1925	1926

continued on next page . . .

NAME	STATUS	ARRIVED	LEFT
Frances M. Gray	Teacher	1925	1933
Miss Elliott	Teacher	1933	?
Miss Foord	Teacher	1933	1933
Victor H. Bryson	Head Teacher	1927	1931
Miss Craggs	Teacher	1927	1928
Miss Redpath	Teacher	1928	1928
Miss White	Teacher	1928	1930
Miss Burns	Teacher	1930	1933
Clifford Staynes	Head Teacher	1932	1935
Miss Allan	Infant Teacher	1933	1933
Miss Newbould	Infant Teacher	1933	1940?
Miss Forster	Teacher	After 1932	1934
Miss D. F. Shipley	Teacher	1934	1935
D. Elliott	Locum Head teacher	1935	1935
Miss Stewart	Teacher	1935	1937
Robert Graham	Head Teacher	1935	1940
Miss Hall	Student Teacher	1936	1936
Mary Elliott	Supply Teacher	1937	1939
Mr. Rudd	Student Teacher	1937	1937
Miss Forrest	Student Teacher	1937	1937
Miss Tait	Supply Teacher	1937	1937
Hilda Forrest	Teacher	1938	1940
Miss Hall	Teacher	1940	1940
Mr. McKay	Student Teacher	1940	1940

Sources:

Dods, Marcus, Ed. *The Early Letters of Marcus Dods* published by Hodder & Stoughton 1910
Wright, Joan. *The Parish Church of St. Mary, Belford* from *Aspects of Belford* Blackhall 2008
Belford National School Log Books.
National Archives - Belford Area File ED91/360 & Belford NS File ED21/3759
Reports in the *Berwick Advertiser*
Adams Correspondence (private)
Jarvie/Davison Correspondence (private)
The Church of England Record Centre Collections. (National Society)
Northumberland Collections Service, Woodhorn - The Davison Collection
Northumberland County Council - Belford School and Education Files

6

BELFORD GETS A RAILWAY - JUST!
by Brian Rogers & Dennis Cromarty

This is on-going research into the railway around Belford. There are still many unanswered questions and avenues to explore. What follows is something of a flavour and brief history of the period from the first thoughts of a railway in 1836 to the year after the opening, when the railway had settled down, in 1848.

Belford before the railway
Life in Belford at the start of the 19th Century mainly revolved around the market place and the ribbon development along the Great North Road. Building, agriculture and related trades, small scale coal mining in the vicinity, services to the users of the London to Edinburgh road including provision of horses and refreshments at the Blue Bell Inn, and retail of domestic goods were the main occupations. With the mail coaches picking up and setting down passengers and mail daily, news from far and wide would travel quickly to the village, at the Post Office standard speed of 10 m.p.h.! The lumbering stage wagons were also a regular sight, carrying all manner of goods up and down the country.

Wood or coal was used for heating and cooking. There were coal mines on Belford Moor and at Chatton Colliery, plus other open cast type sites. This was not the only source for fuel.

> *The bay of Waren affords a safe harbour for vessels of about 80 tons. Wood and coals are still imported here and considerable quantities of corn and flour are shipped to London.* Berwick Advertiser 17th July 1847

Coastal shipping brought goods to the ancient port of Waren on Budle Bay and from there to the village. There were only two available routes into Belford from Waren and the east of the village. From Waren Mill the most direct and relatively flat route went by Outchester and along the road towards Mousen before joining the Great North Road and turning north into Belford. The down side of this was the toll gate just south of Belford and the associated costs! The cheapest route was from Waren, through Easington to Crag Mill, then up a very steep hill to meet the Great North Road at the top of North Bank, before descending the bank into the town.

Although most inhabitants walked or used horses to travel, the news the mail coach brought after Wednesday 28th September 1825, that a steam locomotive had hauled passengers between Stockton and Darlington on a railway engineered by George Stephenson, might not have been a great surprise to some. They may have been aware of the use of steam engines and locomotives at pits in the north east and Scotland; some may have seen them; but how many would have guessed that this news would change their world completely in just over twenty years.

Plans for a railway

It is important to look chronologically at the various plans for railways, between Newcastle and Edinburgh, to show the 'rag bag' approach to the development of a system that might just include Belford. Just over ten years after the opening of the Stockton & Darlington Railway, we first hear of Belford possibly getting a railway. This was not for transporting the coal reserves on Belford Moor to the port of Waren, but rather part of plans to link London with Edinburgh. Would Belford get a railway station? Not necessarily.

In July 1836, a railway from Newcastle to Dunbar named *The Grand Eastern Union Railway* was proposed to link up with a planned line from Edinburgh to Dunbar, extending the Edinburgh and Glasgow railway. A local committee to progress the proposal was formed at Berwick on Tuesday 19th July 1836. Of the 33 people on the committee, 20 were from Berwick and only two from further south - Thomas Scott from Beal and John Strangeways Donaldson, a farmer and Assistant Tithe Commissioner from Cheswick. The latter was so keen on the future of rail transport and what it could do for the area and its farmers that he published two substantial letters in favour of this route. Sadly for Belford, the proposed line from the south went just west of Spindlestone, then within a quarter mile of Budle Bay before heading towards Elwick. In other words, it would run on the seaward side of the whinstone outcrop at Easington, missing Belford by about two miles!

At this time, George Stephenson ('the father of railways') was employed by the Edinburgh and Dunbar Railway Company to look over and report back on the oppositions' ambitious route for a line from Newcastle to Edinburgh via Otterburn and a two mile long tunnel under Carter Fell. His verdict was one of utter surprise that such a mammoth and costly task should be undertaken on a route that would be closed by winter weather. He was all in favour of the east coast route, which was on lower ground and so better for levels and, above all for the promoters, cheaper.

On 21st August 1838, George Stephenson attended a meeting in Newcastle of 'Gentlemen' interested in forming a railway from Newcastle to Edinburgh. The Committee asked him to undertake an inspection of the country, prior to a full survey to determine the best line of railway between those places. As far as Belford is concerned, his report dated 13th September 1838 and recorded in

Herapath's *Railway Magazine* makes interesting reading. North from Newcastle, his proposal was to take a coastal line:

> *It proceeds in a pretty direct line to Bamburgh Castle, which it leaves to the east, it then crosses Waren Flats on the land side of the small harbour, and runs parallel and near to the coast all the way to Berwick. There are, however, two lines presenting themselves here, one about a mile west of the other, which I can better decide upon when the levels are taken.*

Clearly from this, it was Stephenson's intention to give Belford a miss, preferring to hug the coast, almost literally, at Budle Bay. He then goes on to qualify his chosen route:

> *After leaving Bamburgh, some cutting will be required to fill up Waren Flats; this can be obtained close at hand, and will be the means of straightening the line at that place. In looking at the map, it will appear as though the sea might form a difficulty at this place, but it does not, as the sand is at present warped up, and forms a bank across this small bay, which is scarcely covered at high water.*

He then offers a route nearer to Belford.

> *There is another line which presents itself nearer Belford, and which has a feasible appearance, but I think the country will be found too high. I would, however, recommend that levels should be taken before the direction of the line is finally decided upon in this district. If the more westerly line should be found feasible, as regards levels, it will possess the advantage of approaching the town of Belford nearer than the line at Bamburgh. From Waren Flats the line will be found nearly a dead level, and remarkably easy of construction to within three miles of Berwick……. By carrying the line near the sea-coast nearly throughout the whole distance, I avoid the great expense entailed upon most railways, that of the building a great number of occupation and public road-bridges. In looking at the subject in a local point of view, I may state that it has always been my practice to lay out main lines of railway through the lowest country, unless some important consideration, such as a large and populous town, induced me to diverge into a higher country.*
>
> *The towns of Morpeth, Belford, Alnwick, and Kelso, may be easily accommodated by branches up the different valleys in which they are situated.*

So, Stephenson really did not want the main line to approach Belford on account of the contours, preferring to serve Belford with a branch line, which would have marginalised the village.

George Stephenson visited Belford Hall in November 1838, two months after his report. He breakfasted at the Hall with William Brown Clark and no doubt sort permission to enter his land to make a full survey and brief him on the prospects of the railway. At this early stage there must have been agreement in principal to a route across Clark's land as Stephenson remarks to a friend in a letter, *I think we will have no trouble with him.* William Brown Clark died in 1840 and his younger brother the Reverend John Dixon Clark then took charge of the Estate.

The east coast route was to become part of *The Great North British Railway*, with Grainger and Miller the engineers for the line from Edinburgh to Berwick, and George and his son Robert, the engineers from Newcastle to Berwick.
Perhaps Robert persuaded his father to rethink his plans, for, as shown on the deposited plans for the GNBR dated 1839 the line is shown approaching Belford, albeit still about a mile from the village. (see map page 146)

Belford, however, was not to get a railway just yet. Lord Howick objected to the plans for the line south of Craster to run to the east of Howick Hall between his 'long walk' and the sea. He could not oppose the line because he was the only person affected, his only option was, at great expense, to propose another railway which he did, called *The Northumberland Railway*, employing Stephenson's arch rival, Isambard Kingdom Brunel, as engineer. Obviously, this route avoided Howick Hall but, as it approached Belford, kept east of the village on a similar line to Stephenson's. The proposal was for an experimental engineless 'Atmospheric Railway' where the underside of the carriage was attached to a piston running in a cylinder between the rails. The piston was driven forward by atmospheric pressure produced by stationary steam engines. The upshot was that a committee of enquiry threw out the proposal as it would only be a single line, and incompatible with the systems already at Newcastle and Edinburgh. Stephenson took fresh levels and agreed reluctantly to move his line to the west of Howick Hall, on a steeper gradient and on higher contours. The move inland and to higher ground, brought the route nearer Belford.

The Edinburgh to Berwick line had now become *The North British Railway* and the southern part from Berwick to Newcastle, *The Newcastle & Berwick Railway*. The building of the *Newcastle & Berwick Railway* was paid for by the issue of shares. During January 1845, 435 people signed the Subscription Contract, mainly gentry, merchants or financiers, predominantly from York, London and West Yorkshire. George Hudson of York, 'The Railway King,' was the single biggest investor with £200,000 of shares. Perhaps this missing link in the London to Edinburgh route did not appeal to the investors of Tyneside and Northumberland who may have already had money tied up in coastal shipping of coals to London. There were only 10 investors from Tyneside, including James Joicey, the colliery owner, who bought only 22 shares costing him £550. There were two subscribers around Morpeth and only one in Berwick-upon-Tweed, Henry George Charles Clark, a Physician from Bank Hill, who bought

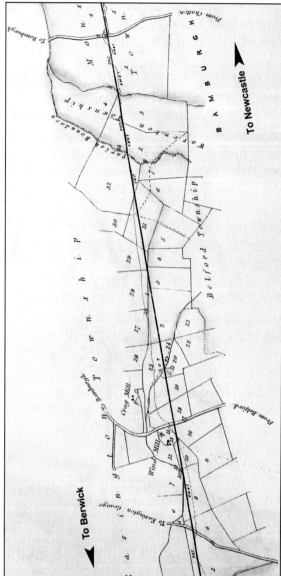

The Great North British Railway
plan through Belford 1839
Ref: QRUP47a
Reproduced with permission of
Northumberland Collections
Service

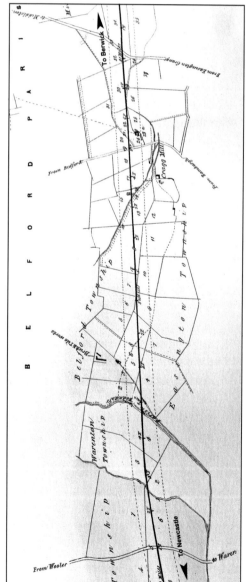

The Newcastle & Berwick
Railway route through Belford
Ref: QRUP58a
Reproduced with permission of
Northumberland Collections
Service

25 shares for £625. The absence of subscribers from the Belford area would suggest that local people either didn't have the money to invest, were not really interested or were very much against the railway, perhaps with good reason. Belford relied on trade from the Great North Road and, in other areas, the railway had forced the horse-drawn coaches off the road *leaving nothing but grass to grow along the highways.*

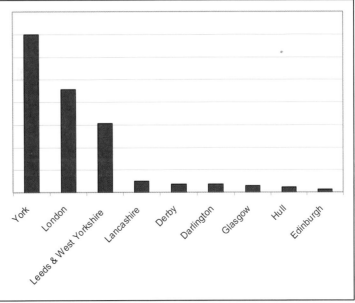

The majority of the shareholders in the Newcastle & Berwick Railway were from York

Lord Howick eventually agreed to Stephenson's new route around Howick Hall and so the *Newcastle & Berwick Railway Company* was finally incorporated in an Act of Parliament on 31st July 1845. Because of the delays with Lord Howick's opposition, the northern end of the line from Edinburgh to Berwick (*The North British Railway*), had received Royal Assent a year earlier and construction was already well under way. George Hudson was determined that the *Newcastle & Berwick Railway* would open on the same day as the *North British* line into Berwick from Edinburgh, as reported in Herapath's *Journal & Railway Magazine.*

> *A week after the royal assent was given, Mr. Hudson was reported to have said, that the North British line would be opened in May or June 1846, and the Newcastle and Berwick[1], he hoped, at or about the same time.*

The Belford section of the proposed *Newcastle & Berwick Railway*, (see map page 146) passed through the Parishes of Mousen, Warenton, Easington, Belford, back into Easington then on to Middleton and land owned by Stephen Fryer Gillum of Middleton Hall. Very little of the line was actually in Belford Parish as will be seen from the plans. The main landowner affected by the railway was the Reverend John Dixon Clark of Belford Hall. His estate, which

---

[1] Until the temporary railway bridge across the Tweed was opened in October 1848, the northern terminus of the *Newcastle & Berwick Railway* was actually Tweedmouth, although contemporary documents always referred to 'Berwick' a convention followed in this chapter.

he inherited from his elder brother William in 1840, was not only in Belford, but extended into Easington Parish which is where most of the land for Belford's railway was located. George Hudson, the Chairman of the *Newcastle & Berwick Railway* liked to meet and deal with the landowners personally when acquiring land for the railway. No doubt, because of the extent of land affected, he would have visited the Reverend Clark, and would have secured a good deal for the investors in return for avoiding the 'pleasure grounds' of Belford Hall, or for bringing the railway nearer Belford.

Railway contracts

Having found a route that included Belford, the next stage was for the *Newcastle & Berwick Railway Company* to accept bids for different contracts. So sure was Hudson that he would have his line of railway accepted, he even advertised for the supply of railway sleepers and iron rails six months before the railway received the Royal Assent, as these two advertisements in *The Railway Times* show.

NEWCASTLE AND BERWICK RAIL-WAY.—TO TIMBER MERCHANTS AND OTHERS.—The Provisional Committee of this Railway are ready to receive Tenders for the supply of 100,000 Railway Sleepers.

Tenders will be received for the above Sleepers of the following descriptions, viz:—

Of American White Rock Elm and Memel Timber, the dimensions being not less than 8 feet long, and triangular in section, being not less than 12 inches base, and 6 inches deep in the centre when cut.

Of sound Larch Timber, the dimensions being not less than 8 feet long, and semi-circular in section, and not less than 10 inches diameter at the small end, measured without the bark.

Of natural growth Scotch or Spey Timber, the dimensions being the same as for Larch.

Tenders will be received for any portion of the above, but not for less than 10,000 Sleepers in one lot.

The whole of the Sleepers will be required to be delivered in equal proportions, to commence immediately after the letting of the Contract, and to be completed within six months; the delivery to be made at the Ports of Newcastle, Blyth, Warkworth, Alnmouth, Beadnell, North Sunderland, Warren, or Berwick-upon Tweed.

Sealed Tenders, addressed to the Secretary, must be delivered at the Company's Office, in York, on or before the 4th day of March next.

GEORGE HUDSON, Chairman.
York, January 30, 1845.

NEWCASTLE AND BERWICK RAILWAY.—Tenders for Iron Rails and Chairs. The Provisional Committee are prepared to receive Tenders for the supply of 20,000 tons of Iron Rails, each Rail to be 15 feet in length, and weighing 65lbs. per yard. The quality of the iron in the Rail to be equal to No. 3. The tender to state in detail the process of manufacture which it is proposed to follow to produce the quality. No tender will be attended to without this statement, and the Company will stipulate with the party whose tender may be accepted, that the Company may at any time send an inspector to the works to satisfy themselves that the specified process of manufacture is fully adopted.

A tender, also, will be received for the supply of 7,000 tons of Iron Chairs.

The Chairs to be cast with a mixture, composed of equal proportions of Scotch, Staffordshire, and Welsh Pig Iron, from the cupola or air furnace. The Joint Chairs to weigh 28lbs., and the intermediate Chair 18lbs.

The delivery to be made at the Ports of Newcastle, Blyth, Warkworth, Alnmouth, Beadnell, North Sunderland, Warren, or Berwick-on-Tweed; to commence in April next, and the whole to be delivered in equal proportions before April, 1846.

Tenders to be delivered on or before the 4th day of March next, at the Company's Office, in York.

The section of the Rails to be in accordance with a drawing or template, which may be seen at 24, Great George-street, Westminster; or at the Company's Office, at York, where also models of the Rails and Chairs may be seen, and further explanation obtained.

GEO. HUDSON, Chairman.
York, January 30th, 1845.

Adverts for supply of railway sleepers and iron rails 1845

Adverts for tenders to actually build the railway were placed on 21st August 1845. The 53 miles of Railway from Netherton to Tweedmouth was let in five contracts. Contract No. 4 Belford covered the line from a point 30 chains (about 600 metres) south of Stamford (west of Craster), to Smeafield Burn, the boundary between North Durham and Northumberland, nearly 15 miles long. On 1st October 1845 the tenders were awarded. The No. 4 Belford Contract was awarded, with an unspecified completion date in 1846, to a Cumbrian stone mason and railway contractor, James McKay of Wigton, Cumberland, and his partner, John Blackstock for the sum of £87,555. They had just completed work on the *Maryport & Carlisle Railway* (also engineered by George Stephenson). The same contractors were to win the contracts to build Newcastle Central

Station and the Royal Border Bridge over the River Tweed at Berwick. Robert Stephenson (son of George) was the chief engineer for the line, although George was named as the engineer on the original plans, and Thomas Elliot Harrison was the day to day resident engineer for the line.

The Arrival of Strangers

In August 1845, surveyors, employed by the contractors, arrived to peg out the land acquired by the *Newcastle & Berwick Railway*. Local people became aware that life was changing. Land that had been farmed by successive generations had now passed into the hands of a railway company, apparently to be wrecked. Large productive fields were marked out into odd shapes to make way for the railway. When the land was marked-out, and the levels obtained, the labourers, or navigators arrived to make the plans happen. The term 'navigator' dates back to the eighteenth century. Originally these were the men who dug the canals, but in the railway age, the 'navvy' was anyone who worked on building railways. Navvies had a reputation for hard working and hard drinking. Their diet was one of meat, ale, spirits and anything else they could buy or even steal! They were generally feared by local populations, who were not used to such a large groups of itinerant workers on a single construction site. Where lodgings were available, the navvies lived in local towns and villages, but in remote areas, either they, or the contractors built wooden huts to house them. Many of the navvies were loyal to a good contractor and probably followed McKay & Blackstock from one contract, to the next. We do know that a great many of the navvies lodged in Belford, and some stayed on to marry local girls and settle down. There are references to incidents from which we can draw some inferences about their impact on the neighbourhood.

As early as 13th January 1846 there was trouble or suspected trouble in the Belford area. At the annual general meeting of the *Belford Association for Prosecuting Felons* (a group of mainly influential landowners) held at the *Blue Bell Inn*, Belford:

> *It was resolved that every means should be used for the apprehending and prosecuting all persons committing or suspected of committing felony* (serious crime)*, breaking down fences or trespassing on any of the grounds belonging to any of the members of this association, and that <u>ample rewards</u> should be given to persons giving such information so that any offender or offenders may be convicted.*

Such a resolution would not have been announced to a peaceful neighbourhood. It came as a veiled threat to the 'navvies'. Perhaps it was after reading about the ample rewards, that William Robson, the gamekeeper to Stephen Fryer Gillum at Middleton, doing his rounds in the dark on Friday 17th January, saw and identified four men and a dog on his employer's land. On this weak evidence, the four were brought before the Magistrates on Tuesday 20th. The *Berwick Advertiser* (24th) reported on the case and subsequent actions to deal with the misbehaviour of railway workers - were the two connected?

> *At the petty sessions at Belford on Tuesday last, - before P. J. Selby, Esq.,*
> *S. F. Gillum Esq., and the Rev. J. D. Clark[1].*
> *William FERGUSON, James BURNS, William BROWN and Robert HALL*
> *Were found poaching on land owned by S.F. GILLUM Esq. Gillum's*
> *gamekeeper William ROBSON swore to them being in a field near Middleton*
> *about ten to seven in the evening of Friday last with a black dog. ROBSON*
> *said he could positively identify them having seen them in the lights of the*
> *'Royal William' coach which passed at the time. They denied the charge and*
> *produced four witnesses named: THOMPSON, PEARCY, OLIVER and HALL.*
> *They said the defendants were at the house of Mrs HALL in Belford and not*
> *out from twenty to seven, till twenty past ten. The case 'fell to the ground'.*
> *The magistrates stated that someone must have given false evidence and that*
> *a case of Perjury had been committed by someone. It would be well for the*
> *Magistrates to find out who was giving false evidence.*
> *The magistrates resolved upon swearing in a number of special constables, in*
> *consequence of the misbehaviour of the men employed on the railway on*
> *Saturday last. The appointment will take place before Saturday next.*

The navvies had arrived in Belford!

McKay, it appears, made sure his workers ate well. In May, according to the *Berwick Advertiser*, he purchased *some of the best beeves (sic) in the neighbourhood for his men*. The contractors also had their own butcher, who lived in Belford and delivered the meat to the workers, as mentioned in a report in the *Berwick & Kelso Warder* of 6th June 1846:

> *We regret to hear that on Tuesday, the butcher connected with the railway in*
> *returning home from Newham to Belford accidentally fell from his seat on the*
> *cart and that being overrun by one of the wheels, he had several ribs broken*

Perhaps the red meat was having an effect on the navvies, as in the same paper we hear that Joseph ROUTLEDGE, employed on the railway, appeared at Belford Petty Sessions to answer a charge of assault brought by William Robson of Middleton (Gillum's gamekeeper from the January incident). After hearing several witnesses, the Magistrates (same three as before) could not

---

[1] These three Magistrates were related by marriage, Selby's sister Margaret married William Clark, the Rev J.D. Clark's father, after his first wife died, so Margaret was Rev J.D. Clark's step mother. His other sister Elizabeth married Stephen Fryer Gillum

decide who struck the first blow and so the case was dismissed with each of them paying half the costs. We are told that *a number of the navvies attended to hear the case.*
Perhaps the navvies took their revenge for the first incident?

Statistics give some idea of the impact of the navvies on Belford. The 1841 census gives the population of Belford as 1157. The *Berwick and Kelso Warder* of 13th June 1846 reported that the contractors were employing between 1200 and 1400 men, including masons at wages ranging from 18s. a week to 26s. for a skilled mason, at a time when farm labourers' weekly wages 9s. 3½d. (1850). The article goes on to comment on the overall effect of the navvies on the town:

> At Belford <u>where a great number of the workmen lodge</u>, they have on the whole behaved very well and a considerable number of them attend places of public worship. There has been none of that extreme turbulence among the workmen here so often reported of railway labourers in distant parts of the country ...... The abundance of employment for the working classes and the good wages obtained by them, the demand for lodgings and the increased expenditure of money in the shops must all tend to promote the prosperity of Belford. Although it cannot be foreseen what effect, beneficial or injurious will be produced in the town by the railway when it is finished, and its traffic fully established.

Building the railway
All three deposited plans, showed a similar route, staying east of Belford Tile Sheds and passing just to the west of Crag Mill as they crossed the Belford to Bamburgh road. The chosen Newcastle & Berwick Railway route was fairly level with few earthworks, except for two cuttings and a slight embankment to the south of the present station, and a more substantial cutting through the whinstone, just south of the Belford to Bamburgh road, at Crag Mill. Where possible, the engineers tried to avoid cutting through the hard whinstone rock, but this was unavoidable around the Belford/Middleton outcrop. Beyond the Belford to Bamburgh road (when travelling north), the land suddenly drops about 35 feet, then ascends briefly before dropping another 30 feet to the flat land around Fenham Flats. As a result, the engineer had to provide a large embankment across wet ground, on a gradient of 1 in 264.

Another problem was where the line met the road leading from Easington Grange to Middleton as shown in a cross section marked No. 41 on the cross section plans for the *Newcastle & Berwick Railway*. The proposal in the cross-section was to lower the road by four feet six inches and cross the road by a rail bridge. As noted already, Stephenson did not like to build bridges if he could avoid it. In looking at the cross section and the hard rock at this location, it

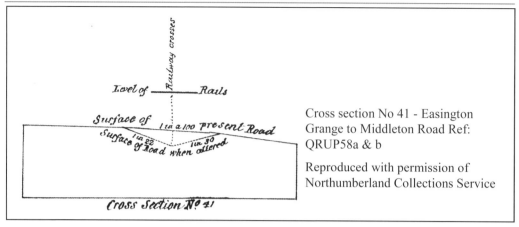

Cross section No 41 - Easington Grange to Middleton Road Ref: QRUP58a & b

Reproduced with permission of Northumberland Collections Service

is clear that without adequate new drainage, the road descending on both sides to a point directly under the railway would be a giant puddle after rain. It looks as if the Rev. John Dixon Clark and Prideaux John Selby came to the rescue - with the aid of the surveyors of the highways for Easington Grange and Middleton. On 9th March 1846 these two Magistrates applied to the Quarter Sessions to block off this road, never to be used again - all one thousand six hundred and six yards of it (over 9/10ths of a mile).

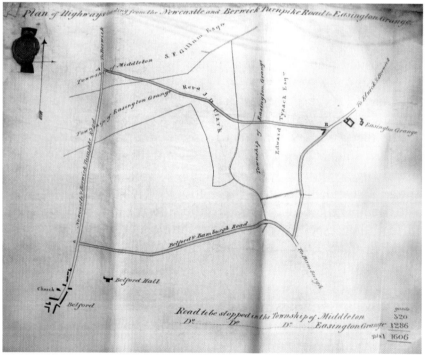

Plan of Highway 'stopped up' from Easington Grange to the great North Road at Middleton Ref: QRH148 Easter 1846. Reproduced with permission of Northumberland Collections Service

The reasons they gave were:

First. Because there are other and better roads leading from the said Newcastle and Berwick Turnpike Road to Easington Grange and more particularly that the Highway laid down on the said plan hereunto annexed and coloured green & between the points thereon marked with the letters 'C' and 'B' now answers all the purposes which the said Highway so proposed to be stopped up doth answer being a much better road and more commodious to the Public.

Second. Because the said Highway so proposed to be stopped up as aforesaid is not at anytime passable by a loaded cart with safety from the steepness of the hill leading to the said Newcastle and Berwick Turnpike Road and that part thereof is contracted to such a degree as not to admit two carts passing each other.

The outline of this road west of the current A1 can still be seen today descending the hill from the Middleton road. The railway was never mentioned, but this closure allowed the contractors to build a continuous embankment without a bridge.

Many things were needed to build the railway at Belford. In the early days, it was mainly equipment for removing spoil and stone, and taking what was cleared when cuttings were blasted, to where embankments to be built. For this, temporary lines of rail were laid on which horse drawn tipping wagons were to be used. Heavy goods - wagons, rails, sleepers and other equipment, had to be brought from Newcastle to the Belford area. Transport by the Great North Road would have been expensive both in tolls and in the numbers of horses needed to draw the loads. Fortunately, the original tenders (dated 30th January 1845) stipulated that the deliveries were to be made at various ports including, in the Belford area, Waren on Budle Bay, owned by the Greenwich Hospital, *to commence in April next and the whole to be delivered in equal proportions before April 1846.* Shipping the railway connected goods did not commence at Waren until 20th February 1846, when the sailing ship *Hope* arrived from Newcastle with *Railway Materials.* In the following week, three more ships arrived, *Coaster, Good Intent* and *Waren Packet,* all with railway materials. The Waren Packet was part owned by Philip Nairn the lessee of Waren Mill from Greenwich Hospital. There then followed a steady flow of shipping into Waren, as can be seen in the table on the next page. Although it is hard to imagine when looking at the area today, these boats could sail up to the mill on the high tides often two at a time, carrying in the region of 25 to 50 tonnes. The port was busy. The ships needed to be unloaded quickly, but there was a shortage of dock workers. Here, as elsewhere, navvies were used to speed up the works, not always successfully. The *Berwick & Kelso Warder* of 20th June 1846 reported:

Accident at Waren

ARRIVAL	NAME OF SHIP	SHIP OWNER	FROM	COMMODITY
20/2/1846	Hope	Alexander	Newcastle	Railway Materials
21/2/1846	Coaster	Forster	Newcastle	Railway Materials
23/2/1846	Good Intent	Bigelon	Newcastle	Railway Materials
23/2/1846	Waren Packet	Wake	Newcastle	Railway Materials
5/3/1846	Equity	Smith	Newcastle	Slates
6/3/1846	Coaster	Forster	Newcastle	Railway Materials
7/3/1846	Diane	Weatherston	Newcastle	General Cargo
23/3/1846	Maria	Reid	Shields	Railway Materials
24/3/1846	Clipper	Bennet	Newcastle	Railway Sleepers
24/3/1846	Waren Packet	Wake	Newcastle	Railway Sleepers
5/4/1846	William Thorp	Carter	North Sunderland	Railway Materials
11/4/1846	Coaster	Forster	Newcastle	Railway Materials
11/4/1846	Diana	Smith	Newcastle	Coal and Goods
12/4/1846	Mars	Dunton	Newcastle	Coal and Cinders
15/4/1846	William Thorp	Carter	Newcastle	Railway Sleepers
22/4/1846	Brothers	Swinhoe	Newcastle	Sleepers
3/5/1846	Brothers	Swinhoe	Newcastle	Railway Materials
3/5/1846	Hopper	Etherington	Newcastle	Railway Materials
9/5/1846	Ranger	Cook	Newcastle	Timber
10/5/1846	Mars	Dunton	Newcastle	Railway Materials
16/5/1846	William Thorp	Carter	Newcastle	Railway Materials
27/5/1846	Hannah	Moore	Shields	Railway Materials
27/5/1846	Hotspur	Brown	Shields	Railway Materials
31/5/1846	Hopper	Etherington	Newcastle	Railway Materials
1/6/1846	Village Maid	Walker	Shields	Railway Materials
1/6/1846	Isabella and Jane	Walker	Newcastle	Railway Materials
13/6/1846	Hannah	Moore	Newcastle	Railway Materials
14/6/1846	Hotspur	Brown	Newcastle	Railway Materials
16/6/1846	Diana	Weatherston	Newcastle	Railway Materials
16/6/1846	Isabella and Jane	Walker	Newcastle	Railway Materials
24/6/1846	Clipper	Bennet	Newcastle	Railway Materials
28/6/1846	Village Maid	Walker	Shields	Railway Materials
28/6/1846	Hannah	Moore	Newcastle	Railway Materials
6/7/1846	Diamond	Aiselie	Newcastle	Wood
16/7/1846	Village Maid	Walker	Shields	Railway Materials
21/7/1846	Clipper	Bennet	Newcastle	Railway Materials
13/8/1846	Clipper	Bennet	Newcastle	Railway Materials
15/8/1846	Agnes	Morrison	Dundee	Bricks
15/8/1846	Village Maid	Walker	Newcastle	Railway Goods
27/1/1847	Diana	Weatherston	Newcastle	Goods
15/2/1847	Clipper	Bennet	Newcastle	Railway Goods
15/2/1847	Oak	Elsdon	Newcastle	Railway Goods
9/5/1847	Coaster	Greenfield	Newcastle	Railway Iron
21/5/1847	Coaster	Greenfield	Newcastle	Railway Goods
28/5/1847	Coaster	Greenfield	Newcastle	Sleepers
5/6/1847	Hope	Alexander	Newcastle	Sleepers
12/6/1847	Gleaner	Johnson	Newcastle	Sleepers
3/7/1847	Good Intent	Paterson	Dundee	Sleepers

Railway goods arriving at Waren by ship 1846/1847

On Monday last on board the sloop Hotspur, while delivering a cargo of railway materials, a young man from Cumberland, a railway labourer was struck a very severe blow on the head by the winch handle which cut him in a very dangerous manner. He was taken to his lodgings in a cart, but we understand he is in a fair way of recovery.

Once landed, where did the materials go? From Waren, there were only two ways to bring the materials to the line by road, either to Crag Mill (2.1 miles) or to a point between Mousen and Outchester (1.5 miles). The materials would be stored at the chosen point until such time as they were needed. Of the two options Crag Mill lay towards the northern extremity of the contract area; Mousen was more central, nearer to Waren, and the land adjacent to the railway was relatively flat.

In early April 1846, the residents of Belford were treated to a rare spectacle. The *North British Railway* had ordered a number of passenger and freight engines from R. W. Hawthorn of Newcastle for the opening of their line. These were delivered by road from Newcastle to Berwick and passed through Belford. The *Berwick Advertiser* of 18th April reported that *the engine was drawn by fifteen horses.* One can only imagine the awe and wonder of the spectators on the High Street. At Morpeth, the engine had been hauled out of the town by one circus elephant - but only extra horses were used to negotiate North bank! The *North British Railway* line from Edinburgh to Berwick opened on the 18th June 1846, but sadly the *Newcastle & Berwick Railway* was way behind the tandem opening predicted by Hudson. There was, however, a steam locomotive working the area. McKay & Blackstock were now using their own locomotive named "Balentine" for moving the spoil wagons and the railway materials.

The building of the railway continued, as reported in the *Berwick Advertiser* of 2nd May 1846:

The Gullet-cut at Middleton is finished, the whole length of the cut being 24 chains (528 yards) and of the whinstone nearly 5 chains (110 yards).
Tomorrow (Saturday) the contractors expect to finish the gullet-cut at Crag Mill, immediately below Belford, the whole length of this cut nearly 60 chains (1320 yards) and of the whinstone 7 chains (154 yards). The extreme depth of the whinstone excavations here were expected to be only 4 feet, whereas it has turned out to be 12 feet.
Not withstanding this untoward occurrence the contractors have no doubt that their portion of the line will be open, so far as to permit engines to go between end to end of it in the month of August.

Large numbers of horses and carts were also needed to transport the materials to the nearest point on the railway. This is confirmed in an account in the *Berwick & Kelso Warder* of 20th June 1846.

It may be mentioned that Messrs McKay & Blackstock employ about 90 horses on their portion of the line and that they have used in blasting above 50 barrels of gunpowder. The excavations at Middleton, Crag Mill and Brunton will be found in a geological point of view very interesting.

There were a number of accidents to the navvies in constructing the line, but very few in the immediate vicinity of Belford. On Wednesday 30th June however, one occurred at Newham and was reported in both Berwick papers. The account also provides information about the number of navvies and the work involved. Alexander Gordon, aged about 28 years, from Greenlaw, Berwickshire, who had only been 12 days on the works at Newham, was killed.

He was guiding a wagon to the tip or bank end and was pitched from the loaded wagon on his face both wheels travelling over his body about his shoulders he was killed on the spot. His body was interred at Bamburgh where nearly three hundred of his fellow workmen were present.

That is a lot of people at the funeral, not forgetting that the works would be stopped for the day.

At the half yearly meeting of the Newcastle & Berwick Railway the Chairman George Hudson reported that:

The works are now progressing satisfactorily but difficulties have arisen in some parts of them which could not have been anticipated, and which will prevent the completion of the entire length of line until the early part of next year .... The Directors however, hope to be able to open that portion which extends from Newcastle to Morpeth and probably twenty or thirty miles at the northern terminus in the course of a short time. In February next the line would be open throughout.

This was August 1846 and beyond the original date when Hudson wanted the Newcastle & Berwick line opened. There was a need to rush the works to keep to the new deadline, in doing so risks were being taken and the accident rate continued to rise along the line, but not so much in the Belford area.

A workman was injured slightly whilst blasting at Middleton, he was sheltering behind a bank for safety, a stone hit him on his shoulder and back of neck, he was able to walk home.   *Berwick & Kelso Warder* 1st August 1846

It seems that at this stage, Hudson was playing for time. There was a shortage of masons for building the bridges south of the Belford contract, at the same time he was convincing shareholders with new deadlines for openings, but there were other troubles involving the workers. The Mayor of Berwick, at a meeting on

11th August, raised the question of the conduct of navvies working on the *Newcastle & Berwick Railway*. He complained of disgraceful scenes of drunkenness and riot on public streets and compared them unfavourably with the *North British Railway* navvies at Berwick:

> *a man or party of men might be seen drunk for an entire day, but not*
> *continuously drunk for a whole week at a time.*

Hudson addressed this problem at the half yearly meeting, saying they had given a sum of money towards the religious instruction of the workmen employed on the line, many of whom were located in spots far distant from a place of worship. The contractors were prohibited under heavy penalties, from any work being done on the Sabbath. They had also taken care to introduce a provision that the men should not be obliged to buy goods at the shops established by their employers (tally shops).

Belford at this time must have noticed an increase in the number of passenger coaches coming through the village. People could travel from Edinburgh to Berwick by train, then switch to coaches between Berwick and Newcastle. *The Railway Times* stated that there were nine or ten coaches running between Newcastle and Berwick, all of them full every day.

Belford Station
On the initial plans for the *Newcastle & Berwick Railway*, there was no location shown for Belford Station. Because of the almost level gradients deemed necessary, the line had to run to the east of Belford village. The nearest points to Belford where an existing public highway crossed the proposed line of the railway were at Crag Mill, where the Belford to Bamburgh road crossed (0.90 miles north east from Belford Market Cross), or at Mousen, a point on the Wooler to Waren Mill and Bamburgh road between Mousen and Outchester (2 miles south east from Belford Market Cross). Both locations were unsuitable for a station for a number of reasons:

- The Crag Mill site was constrained on the south side by the whinstone rock (difficult to cut through) and on the north side by wet open ground where the line of railway would have to be built up to cross on a large embankment. Also, the pleasure grounds of Belford Hall forced the Bamburgh to Belford road to ascend a very steep hill on the north side of Belford Hall estate, then making a ninety degree left turn onto the Great North Road to descend the equally steep North Bank to arrive at the Market Cross.

- The Mousen/Outchester location was no better. It was two miles from the village centre - not an easy walk! And carriage of passengers or goods to and from there would have incurred tolls charges on the Great North Road at the Belford Turnpike.

In August 1846, it was reported in the *Berwick & Kelso Warder, that the station is to be sited three quarters of a mile from the town near Crag Mill.* This made very little sense to the people of Belford. They were used to boarding transport on the Great North Road - on their doorstep, not going up and down hill and covering a mile to enable them to travel. They were not happy. They also thought that the steep downhill gradient on the road to the intended station at Crag Mill, and the fact that the railway line was to cross the road on a level crossing, would be dangerous for traffic. Also fearing for the loss of trade for Belford, *traffic of the west and south districts will be thrown almost entirely into the Mousen and Lucker stations,* at the end of August 1846, the people of Belford petitioned for a bridge rather than a level crossing.

> *The inhabitants of Belford and its vicinity who knowing the earnest desire of the Rev. John D. Clarke to promote the prosperity of the town, have got up a petition already numerously signed to be presented to him as Lord of the Manor, soliciting his best endeavours with a view to induce the Directors of the railway to throw a bridge over the crossing at Crag Mill and to place the Belford Station eastward of the tile works..... From Belford very little new road would be necessary and the station could be connected with Waren Mills by a road that might be made to join the old one, either near Outchester or near Crag Mill (a track was probably already in existence between Easington village and the tile works); and the proposed Mousen station might be dispensed with.*
>
> *We wish success to the petitioners and hope they may find that they have not been too late in looking after their interests.*
>
> Berwick & Kelso Warder 29th August 1846

This confirms that a station at Mousen had been proposed. In fact it appears that a form of 'station' had already been created at Mousen on the east side of the line, albeit for handling the materials coming from Waren. After storage there, the materials would be moved up and down the line by contractor's horse drawn

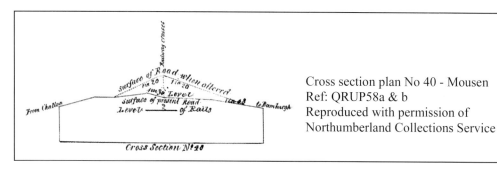

Cross section plan No 40 - Mousen
Ref: QRUP58a & b
Reproduced with permission of
Northumberland Collections Service

vehicles or locomotives, as and when they were needed. Our theory is that at this stage, August 1846, there were to be two stations, one at Crag Mill for passengers, and one at Mousen for goods. The Railway and contractor's plans showed that the intention was to provide a bridge at Mousen, with the road being raised 11 feet to go over the top of the railway. This would not present a problem as there would be access to and from a goods warehouse on the flat east side of the bridge.

It was probably envisaged that most goods would travel to and from the west (Wooler etc.) via the Mousen and Chatton roads, and not necessarily into Belford village. Later, at the time of the opening of the line, in July 1847, the *Berwick Advertiser* does refer to:

> *Mousen lane Station which is 50 miles 67 chains or upwards of 50 ¾ miles from Newcastle is placed where the highway crosses over the railway by a bridge of 30 feet span and leads to Waren Mills two miles eastward.*
>
> *Berwick Advertiser* July 17th 1847

Clearly there was something of note here, but there is no mention in any of the railway documents of a station or platform at Mousen lane. Most probably its identification was a mistake arising from the quantity of materials stored there. Tons of sleepers arrived at Waren during May, June and July before the opening, so it would have looked busy.

In November 1846, McKay & Blackstock won the contract to build the viaduct across the Tweed for £180,000. Hudson was desperate to get the line opened as soon as possible. This created a dilemma for McKay & Blackstock's No.4 Belford contract. Large numbers of masons were needed to build the Berwick bridge, yet none of the buildings around Belford, for which McKay & Blackstock were contracted to build to John & Benjamin Green's Elizabethan designs were even started! Indeed not even the site of Belford station was definite.

The road just south of Belford village, leading due east to the Brick Sheds and ultimately to the Tile Works, stopped short of the railway. It was decided that the *Newcastle & Berwick Railway* would extend the road from the Tile Works to a new station site, crossing the railway and continuing in a south easterly direction for 6/10ths of a mile to meet with the Mousen to Outchester road. This would be a private road, run by the railway, with a toll being paid to cross the proposed level crossing. The planned station was still one and a quarter miles from the village centre, but it was a flat route and toll free if travelling to the station from Belford.

On the 28th November 1846, the *Berwick & Kelso Warder* reported:

In the course of a few days the heavy embankment to the north of Cragmill
will be made up. Two powerful locomotives are at work drawing wagons
between Newham and a point as far north as Belford tile shades (sic), where,
we understand, it is now determined the Belford station will be situated.

The Belford people had won with their petition - but not for a bridge over the
railway at Crag Mill.

If the weather continues favourable, Messrs Blackstock & McKay expect that
in a month or six weeks their portion of the line will be ready to allow their
locomotives to pass from end to end, comprehending about 15 miles. The
work on Messrs Blackstock and McKay's contract is considered to be very
substantial, and their bridges are very much admired for their solidarity and
elegance.

Meanwhile, the contractors' line was being used for moving more than
materials, as is highlighted by an accident which took place at Fenham, on 30th
November. An accident occurred about 3 p.m. on Monday 30th November. John
Scullion, a 54 year old Irishman, broke his leg while working on the railway.
Messengers were sent to Belford and Lowick for medical assistance – but none
came, and the wound was not seen for two days. On Thursday, Scullion was
taken at first to the dispensary, and then to Berwick workhouse where, despite
having the wound dressed and the broken limb set, he died on Friday. Doctor
Henry Hunt of Belford was summoned to the Inquest to explain the delay in
Scullion receiving treatment. He stated he had been out on his rounds all day,
and his horse was fatigued. He was called to see a patient at Newham, and
decided to go there by the engine used for dragging the wagons on the railway.
On the return, however, the engine only went as far as Lucker, so he was
obliged to walk the rest of the way home, not arriving until 10 o'clock at night.

Belford and the Royal Border Bridge

Herapaths' *Journal & Railway Magazine* reported on 5th December 1846:

We understand that active operations for the construction of the bridge over
the Tweed will be commenced in about a fortnight, under the superintendence
of Mr. Mckay, one of the contractors. The Stone will be brought from a
quarry near Belford by the railway, and from 1,000 to 1,500 men will be
constantly employed upon the work until its completion.

So Belford was on the map in terms of the supply chain for the viaduct at
Berwick. Teams of horses were taking the stone from the quarry to the railway -
freight preceding passengers at Belford, but we do not know which quarry. The
year 1846 ended with great snowstorms in the area for two weeks, setting back
both the opening of the railway and the stone quarrying. The cold weather also
had its effects on the navvies. On 12th January, Thomas Bailey alias 'Scotty'
was convicted and fined £5 for poaching hares on the estate of Mr. Clark at

Belford. On the 23rd he was again convicted for poaching hares at Wandylaw near Ellingham. He refused to pay the fines and was committed to three months hard labour in Morpeth jail. He said he thought the farmers should present him with a present for killing so many - perhaps this was how the navvies survived in the harsh winter. The snow had stopped work and it was not until the end of January that quarrying seems to have been resumed.

On January 30th, 1847, the *Berwick and Kelso Warder* broke the news that:
Mr. McKay has now entered into an agreement with the landlord (Rev. J.D. Clark) and the farmer tenant concerned for the working of the Rogue's Road[1] Quarry on the Belford Estate from which part of the materials to be used in

The Rogue's Road Quarry – Brian Rogers

constructing the railway bridge over the Tweed to be obtained.
It is calculated that the quarrying and the conveying of the stone to the railway line will give employment in the neighbourhood to 100 men and 40 horses for more than two years. This must prove very advantageous to the town of Belford.
This was very good news for employment in Belford.
The *Warder* had a further report on the quarry on 24th April 1847:
Mr McKays men are now engaged in clearing out the Rogue's Road Quarry

---

[1] The Rogue's Road is the bridleway running from the Belford to Old Lyham road, across Newlands North Moor to Chatton Colliery Farm. The quarry was at the northern end.

preparing the excavation of stone for Berwick Bridge. The stone is of excellent quality (sandstone) *and blocks may be obtained of immense size if necessary.*

We believe that the stone travelled from the quarry passing Sionside, downhill into Belford then probably along the road to the tile sheds (avoiding a steep hill north and turnpike south) and on to a temporary road and siding at the current Belford station site. The distance from the quarry to the station site was just short of four miles and involved a drop in height of nearly 500 feet. Fortunately, the carts would be empty going back up the hill!

Then on 10th July 1847, McKay & Blackstock signed an agreement with Prideaux John Selby J.P. of Twizell House to obtain stones for the bridge across the river Tweed from a quarry on his land, at a shilling per cubic yard of stone. They built a wooden bridge across Waren Burn near Twizell saw mill. Knowing that damage would be done to the highways (they probably had experience from Rogue's Road Quarry), the contractors agreed to enter into an agreement with the surveyors of the highways to keep the roads in good repair.

The landowners were certainly benefitting from the arrival of the railway!

Partial opening of line

After much speculation, the line from Tweedmouth to Chathill including the whole of contract 4 through Belford was opened without any ceremony on Monday 29th March 1847. The line was still not open between Chathill and Morpeth, due to problems with bridges, so passengers had to transfer to a horse-drawn omnibus to complete the journey to Morpeth, where once again they could board a train to Newcastle. The *Berwick Advertiser* reported:

A train of carriages apparently borrowed from the Newcastle and Darlington line consisting of one first class, two second and one third class were ranged under the temporary station house (at Tweedmouth). Shortly after 8 o'clock one of the engines of Mr Stephenson's most improved construction was attached and at 10 minutes after 8 it darted off with its attendants. The number of passengers was small.

Not so at Belford, where:

at Belford station on Monday last, the day of opening of the Newcastle & Berwick Railway, 58 tickets were given out. Berwick & Kelso Warder 3rd April 1847

Which Belford station?

We think that passengers boarded the trains on the partial opening day (29th March 1847) and thereafter at Crag Mill, albeit there was no proper station building. The main Belford station as we know it today was not started until

May 1847, perhaps because masons were more urgently needed for the bridge at Berwick or for those between Chathill and Morpeth. Realising that the station would not be finished in time for the full opening, the contractors built a temporary wooden station at Crag Mill during July and August 1847.

On 1st July the remaining part of the line was opened between Morpeth and Chathill. There was no real ceremony other than some of the contractors and officials travelled the whole of the line from Newcastle to Berwick. The bridges across the Wansbeck, Blyth and Coquet were still not built in stone and were at this time single line, wooden bridges.

Notice of opening of the line throughout from Newcastle to Berwick on and after Thursday 1st July the line will be open throughout for passengers and goods traffic, trains will leave each terminus at the following times.

From Newcastle	From Tweedmouth	
Weekdays	Weekdays	As can be seen, there were
Morning: 7.30, 10.30	Morning: 6.30, 9.0, 12.0	only 6 trains each way on
Afternoon: 2.30, 6.40, 7.0, 11.30	Afternoon: 2.30, 6.0, 7.45	weekdays, plus three from
Sundays	Sundays	Newcastle and four from
Morning: 10.30	Morning: 12.0	Tweedmouth on Sundays.
Afternoon: 2.30, 11.30	Afternoon: 2.30, 6.0, 7.45	

The *Berwick Advertiser* of 17th July 1847 covered the whole of the line in great detail and mention was made of a station at Mousen.

Mousen lane Station which is 50 miles 67 chains or upwards of 50 ¾ miles from Newcastle is placed where the highway crosses over the railway by a bridge of 30 feet span and leads to Waren Mills two miles eastward.
Below Belford the line enters a deep cutting terminating at Mr. Clarks plantation, where a highway leading to Bamburgh crosses the line on a level (Crag Mill). At this part is Belford Station which is 52 miles 27 chains or about 52¼ miles from Newcastle. A little in advance there is an embankment 15 feet high.

The measured distance from Mousen Bridge to Crag Mill crossing is exactly 1.5 miles, the same distance quoted by the *Berwick Advertiser*, therefore there is additional proof that Belford Station when the line officially opened to through traffic on Thursday 1st July 1847 was at Crag Mill.

The opening of the full line brought an almost immediate change in the town's fortunes. Within five days, the Post Office had switched carriage of the mail from coaches to the railway. The *Berwick Advertiser* reported that *Monday 5th July was the last day for the Mail and Stage Coaches on the Great North Road between Berwick and Newcastle.* The Mail Coach was draped in the Union flag. The change reduced the time taken to carry mail between Berwick and Newcastle by four hours to two and three quarter hours. The sad end to the

Royal Mail coaching days was reflected in the advertisement in the *Newcastle Courant* on the 9th July and repeated on the front page of the *Berwick Advertiser* on the 10th July, only nine days after the railway opened from Newcastle to Tweedmouth. The Mr Macdonald referred to was the Post Master at Belford. The horses being put up for sale on the 13th were described for their power, yet nobody wanted them anymore; the predicted market for these superb horses was to pull cabs to and from the new stations. It was also a bitter blow for Belford businesses.

Meanwhile the two Belford Doctors (Davidson & Hunt) were still being kept busy, as reported in the Berwick papers on the 8th May 1847.

> NEWCASTLE-UPON-TYNE,
> **EIGHTY MAIL COACHES HORSES**
> FOR SALE,
> REMOVED TO NEWCASTLE-UPON-TYNE FOR CONVENIENCE.
> The last of the London and Edinburgh Royal Old Mail Coach now a matter of History.
> **MR SAMUEL DONKIN**
> Is intrusted by the several Proprietors of the Teams between Felton and Berwick,
> **TO SELL BY AUCTION,**
> Within the Spital of Newcastle, on Tuesday, 13th July Instant,
> THE annexed list of **MAIL COACH** and POST HORSES:—
> 35—The Stud of Mr Macdonald, Belford.
> 25—From the Stables of Mrs Wilson, Swan Inn, Alnwick.
> 10—The Property of Mr Watkins, Blue Bell, Belford.
> 10—Belonging to Mr Leckie, Smeafield, Belford; and a beautiful dark Grey Colt Pony, 5 Years old, and perfectly Quiet in Harness, the Property of Mr Leckie, will be put up for Sale.
> The nature of the gradients of many Portions of the great North Road between Felton and Berwick, taken in Connection with the Pace required of the Mail, imperatively called for a Combination of Blood, Power, and Action in the Horses. A single Inspection of the Studs for Sale will convince any Judge of the Merits of the Horses—that these animals have been selected under the eye of a master. Young, and in excellent working Condition, they are admirably adapted to those countless Vehicles now plying the thorough-fare, of our Cities and Towns; and which the swelling tide of Travellers setting in towards the great Trunk Lines of Railway must still further multiply.

> *On Saturday Michael O'Hare 25 a labourer from the County of Down aged 25 was coming to Belford from Embleton by one of Mr. McKays wagons, and leaping off near Belford new station-house, while the train was in motion the brake of the wagon caught him and threw him on the rails, when five wheels passed over his leg. The limb was so severely crushed as to render amputation necessary. The operation was performed by Mr. Thomas Davidson surgeon Belford. Dr's Cahill, Hunt (Belford) and Alexander were present during the operation.*

Days before the line was opened the *Berwick & Kelso Warder* of 3rd July 1847 gives a full account of a fatal accident at Belford:

> *As the up train which leaves Tweedmouth at half past 2pm was passing between Detchant and Middleton bridges, both in the parish of Belford on Saturday 26th June, Robert Nelson aged 36 a native of Chatton, since last Whitsunday last residing at Newlands with his brother, one of Mr. Dinnings hinds, met with his death in these circumstances.*
> *He was breaking stones on the railway between the two lines of rails. His back was turned to Berwick from which the train was coming. Though first warned by one of his fellow labourers to get out of danger, he did not desist from working saying, 'it was not time'.*

And though the whistle was duly sounded and the rest of the workmen had got
out of the way, Nelson continued to work till the train was within yards of
him, when suddenly raising himself up from his stooping position, he made a
step backward to the line on which the train was coming, when the engine
struck him and pitched him forward about 20 yards onto the other line of
rails, where he was found quite dead, bleeding at the mouth and nose.
The train was backed up as soon as possible and conveyed the body to
Belford station from which it was taken to Belford Church Watch-house to
await a Coroners inquest.
The deceased was an inoffensive, sober and illustrious man.
An inquest was held on the body at Belford on Monday before Thomas A.
Russell Esq. After hearing the evidence, the jury returned a verdict of
'accidental death' and were unanimously of the opinion that the engine driver
had done all in his power for Nelson's safety.

Belford Station

The mention of Belford new station-house in the accident report confirms that,
during May, work finally began on the present station building, platforms and
goods warehouse, over a month after the line was partially opened:

The platforms were of uniform length, 200 feet on both sides of the line, faced
with ashlar work and laid with strong lazenby flags.

Berwick & Kelso Warder 26th June 1847

Work on the station building took two years, from May 1847 to April 1849. It
was not straightforward. Where extra work had to be undertaken, certificates
detailing the work had to be submitted to the Company's headquarters in York.
Certificate 9, covering the period June and July 1847, details extra work in
relation to the station, including the new road from Belford Tile sheds across the
railway; the erection of water cranes and tanks; and the building of a cattle
dock, as well as alterations to the gradient at Crag Mill. A *York, Newcastle &*
Berwick Railway Inspectors' *Time Book* covering the dates July to December
1847, shows that, without these station facilities, the need to keep the engines
topped up with water was dealt with by the employment of two men at a cost of
19/6d. *pumping water* by hand pumps from the Newlands Burn into a storage
reservoir situated just south of the 'new' Belford station.

The initial foundations for the goods warehouse, put in at a cost of £354. 7s. 6d,
had to be abandoned.

First site fixed upon by the engineers and afterwards altered on account of
some roads, if it had stood where first intended, the Company would have had
to purchase a larger field - lengthen a large culvert - and alter the points and
a turnpike road.

Green's Ledger July 1847

At this stage, we are unable to locate the original site.

Work stopped from May until October, when a new site was found at the station complex and a similar amount of money was spent on the new foundations.
On 9th August 1847, the *Newcastle & Berwick Railway Company* (N&BR) was dissolved and amalgamated to become the *York, Newcastle & Berwick Railway Company* (YN&BR).

In McKay & Blackstock's additional work Certificate 10 (see next page), work continued on the cattle dock, plus a carriage dock was being built at Belford. This was for the gentry to be taken to the station in their own horse drawn carriage and then have the carriage loaded onto a flat bed wagon, so that the person could travel either staying in his own carriage or in the railway carriage. The horses could travel in special railway horseboxes, but generally livery would be available at the destination. The points, sidings, sleepers and the ballast were being laid at the various stations including Belford and Crag Mill stations, more proof of two stations. The road was still being laid to the station and a stone road to the cattle dock at Belford:

> *The Electric Telegraph is already in operation along the line from Newcastle to Morpeth and the telegraph posts are in place all the way to Tweedmouth for its continuation north.*   *Berwick & Kelso Warder* 26th June 1847

By September, the Belford station building was beginning to take shape; work included roofing, plastering, glazing and painting and making a covered shed for the southbound platform. The coal depots and sidings were being constructed. Certificate 11 shows that an additional rail was needed for the fencing at the side of the new road (probably to keep sheep off the road) to the station

Belford Goods Warehouse - Courtesy of Beamish Museum

and that the road got a top surface. Between September and November, the iron work contractors, Hawks, Crawshay & Sons of Newcastle worked on the station, the coal depot and a covered shed. In October, coal depot work continued and the new warehouse was begun. Even though the depots were not quite finished, coal began to arrive

Certificate No. 10   24th July to 28th August 1847

FENCING, GATES ETC.
Fencing new road from Belford Station £521. 3s. 7d.
Draining tiles and water cut at Belford Station £92. 12s. 0d.

EARTHWORK - INCLUDING LOWERING AND RAISING ROADS, SOILING SLOPES AND
ALL CONTINGENT EXPENSES.
Side cutting for cattle dock at the Crag Mill 140 cubic feet @ 1/- = £7.
Side cutting for the Belford Station 5760 cubic feet @ 1/3d = £360.

BRIDGES. BRICKWORK & MASONRY
Cattle Dock at Belford.
Foundation rubble 39½ cubic yards @ 8/3d = £16. 5s. 10d.
Walls blocking. 41 yards @ 15/- = £30. 15s. 0d.
Coping ashler. 408 yards @ 1/6d = £30. 12s. 0d.
Total £77. 12s. 10d.
Allowed formerly: £56. 1s. 3d.
Overspend of £21. 11s. 7d.

Carriage Dock at Belford
Foundation rubble 59 cubic yards @ 8/3d = £24. 6s. 9d.

Walls blocking 37 yards @ 15/- = £27. 15s. 0d.
Coping ashler 356 yards @ 1/6d = £26. 14s. 0d.
Total: £78. 15s. 9d. (No overspend!)

Water Cranes at Belford Station £15. 15s. 0d.

LAYING, BALLASTING & DRAINING PERMANENT WAY
"Turnouts as at Crag Mill, Belford, Lucker, Chat Hill & Christon Bank stations to docks and
coal depots".
Laying & Fixing turnouts, including crossings and points - Lineal yards - 870 @ 2/- per yard
= £87. 0s. 0d.

"Sidings at the above named stations".
Laying the way with sleepers. - Lineal yard. - 640 yards @ 1/6d per yard = £48. 0s. 0d.

"Ballast at the Crag Mill, Belford, Lucker, Chat Hill & Christon Bank stations"
Ballast laid down and spread - 1502 cubic yards @ 2/6 per cubic yard = £187. 15s. 0d.
Wrought iron pins - 60 cwt @ £1. 10s. = £90. 0s. 0d.
4000 oak compressed keys @ £6. 6s. 0d. per 1000 = £25. 4s. 0d.

METALLING OF ROADS
New road to Belford Station.
Metalling public road as per specification - 2000 square yards @ 1/9d per square yard
= £175. 0s. 0d.

Stoney road and approach to cattle dock at Christon Bank & Belford.
Metalling public road as per specification - 350 square yards @ 1/9d per square yard
= £30. 12s. 6d.

by rail on the 29th October 1847. The first colliery to supply Belford with coal was Togston Colliery near Amble when three wagons arrived, each carrying five tons of coal. The Inspectors' time book for the first two weeks in November showed three men being paid one day's work for digging holes and 'letting in' signal posts at Belford. This would coincide with the sidings and turnouts being installed. By January 1848, the buildings were being fitted out. Waite & Howard were paid £37. 7s. 8d. for a counter in the station, Curry & Gibson provided a stool and desk at £3. 3s. 6d. for the coal depot, and carpentry and glazing work was in hand for the warehouse.

Work now commenced on Belford office and weighbridge. The masonry work for this, at a cost of £72. 17s. 11d., was sub-contracted to James Dunlop, presumably as McKay & Blackstock's masons were still busy with the bridges elsewhere. This continued during April, with Robert Curry receiving £15 for carpentry and John Preston £4. 10s. 0d. for slating. John Gibson, one of Belford's general store and ironmongers was paid £2. 0s. 6d. for painting seats and lettering sign boards. Clearly the station was nearing completion. Work continued on the weighbridge in May and June, but by July efforts were concentrated on the station boundaries. On the 20th July, at a meeting of the *YN&B Railway* Committee of Management it was resolved:

> *That the offers of Messrs W. G. Armstrong and Co. (Newcastle) to supply and erect at the Morpeth and Belford Stations (one at each station) two steam engines for pumping water for £320 – and the offer of Thomas Richardson & Son (Castle Eden) to supply two tanks for the same for £205 be accepted.*

At last the manual pumping was to be replaced by a steam engine. This was housed below the new water tank and pumped water from Newlands Burn up into the large storage tank.

Belford Water Tower
Courtesy of Beamish Museum

In August, James Glaholm was paid £3. 9s. 0d. for lamp irons and fitting to pillars at the station. Further fittings followed in October - Waite & Howard were paid £31. 14s. 3d, for ticket cases, bookcase, seats and sign boards. The total costs for the buildings at Belford were:

	Contracts	Extras
Station House	£1358. 4s. 5d	£312. 14s. 3½d
Station Fittings	£82. 2s. 4d	
Total cost of Station £1753. 1s. 0½d		
Coal Depots, Office and Weighbridge	£967. 15s. 7d	
Platforms, shed, wall and gates	£1213. 13s. 3½d	
Goods Warehouse	£1846. 2s. 7d	£10. 17s. 3d
(additional foundations first contract)	£354. 7s. 0d	
Additional plate glass	£39. 15s. 0d	
Total cost of Warehouse £2251. 1s. 10d		
Metalling	£197. 4s. 7½d	
	£6059. 4s. 10d	£323. 11s. 6½d
Total £6382. 16s. 4½d		

In contrast, the cost for the temporary station at Crag Mill was £163. 9s. 10d. At last Belford station was finished.

Belford Station
North Eastern Railway Association, Ken Hoole Study Centre/John F. Mallon collection.

The table below compares the numbers of people travelling by train from
Belford during April and August 1848.

As will be seen Sunday was the most popular day for travel.

Date	Day of Week	Belford Passengers April 1848	Belford Passengers August 1848	Day of Week
1	Sat	Not available	49	Tues
2	Sun	Not available	26	Wed
3	Mon	31	39	Thurs
4	Tues	42	41	Fri
5	Wed	36	26	Sat
6	Thurs	37	70	Sun
7	Fri	23	65	Mon
8	Sat	34	76	Tues
9	Sun	55	41	Wed
10	Mon	24	22	Thurs
11	Tues	38	23	Fri
12	Wed	34	21	Sat
13	Thurs	26	83	Sun
14	Fri	25	55	Mon
15	Sat	34	59	Tues
16	Sun	58	44	Wed
17	Mon	25	29	Thurs
18	Tues	48	20	Fri
19	Wed	17	38	Sat
20	Thurs	9	71	Sun
21	Good Friday	31	34	Mon
22	Sat	18	73	Tues
23	Sun	60	39	Wed
24	Mon	29	40	Thurs
25	Tues	46	28	Fri
26	Wed	90	32	Sat
27	Thurs	62	61	Sun
28	Fri	25	21	Mon
29	Sat	36	51	Tues
30	Sun	37	47	Wed
31	Mon	-	28	Thurs

Coal Traffic into Belford

An ample supply of coal was, of course a necessity. This came from collieries across Northumberland. Coal flowed first from Togston Colliery (2/8d. per ton) in October 1847, then in November from Broomhill Colliery (2/6d per ton) next door. Killingworth, just north of Newcastle, (4/4d. per ton) began deliveries in December 1847. Then, in 1848, Netherton (3/5d. per ton) and Acklington Collieries (2/8d. per ton) provided supplies. Scremerston Colliery (near Berwick) delivered one load of coal (4 tons @ 1/9d. a ton) to Crag Mill on 5th February 1848, but then deliveries stopped. Perhaps this was just a trial, or poor coal?

Coal deliveries to Belford Station during 1848

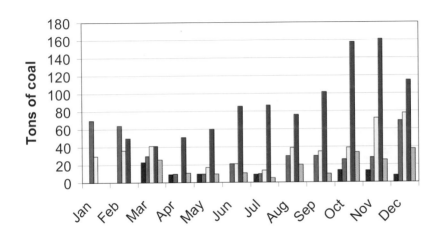

■ Acklington ■ Broomhill ☐ Killingworth ■ Netherton ■ Togston

Completion of the London Edinburgh line

On 1st September 1848 approval was given by the Commissioners of Railways to use a temporary bridge across the Tyne. Then, on Tuesday 10th October 1848, the temporary wooden bridge across the Tweed connecting the *North British Railway* with the *York, Newcastle and Berwick Railway* was completed. Captain Simmons, the Government Inspector, passed the bridge as suitable for goods trains that afternoon and passenger trains the following morning. So finally, on Wednesday 11th October 1848, the continuous line of railway between Edinburgh and London (passing Belford) was opened to passenger traffic, albeit using temporary wooden bridges. Sadly, George Stephenson died on 12th August, so he did not live to see his vision finished.

People

It is worth ending with a look at two of Belford's first railway officials. From a *York, Newcastle & Berwick Railway* Inspectors *Time Book* covering the dates July to December 1847, the *Watchman* at Belford Gate is shown as John Davidge. As we have seen, at this time this has to refer to Crag Mill. John Davidge was 35 years old, married with a three year old daughter. He was not a native of Northumberland, being born at Blandford in Dorset. His wife Mary (24) was born in Tweedmouth and, just to show how cosmopolitan this family was, his three year old daughter Mary had been born in Westminster, Middlesex!

The Highway (Railway Crossings) Act 1839 declared that the proprietors of any Railroad shall employ *good and proper persons* to attend to the opening and shutting of such Gates. The gates were to be kept shut across the road and opened by the crossing keeper whenever road vehicles approached and it was safe. *Section 9 of the Railway Regulation Act 1842* permitted the level crossing gates to be kept open for road traffic or rail traffic whichever was deemed safer. So John was considered *a good and proper person* and his job on the railway was to operate the level crossing gates. He would open and shut the gates to allow appropriate traffic to pass and would probably operate a signal in the form of flag, light or signal post, as some of the trains would stop at Crag Mill. On the 4th May 1847 James D. Smith was paid £38 for the supply of 4 small wooden boxes for the Level Crossing gate keepers, between Belford and Tweedmouth. John would occupy one of these, to keep out the weather whilst waiting for the trains. According to the Inspectors *Time Book* for the period July to December 1847, John worked every day (no rest day) and was paid 14 shillings per week or two shillings a day. The first train of the day would be from Tweedmouth arriving Belford about 7 a.m. and the last train would be from Newcastle arriving Belford about 1am. He did have plenty of 'free time' between trains and lived on the job, so that would be classed as compensation for the lack of a rest day!

Each passenger train (but not all freight trains) was allocated a number on the timetable and a time that it would be expected to arrive at Belford. Armed with a good issue watch, Davidge would shut the gates to road traffic ten minutes before the train was due to arrive, and open them once the train had gone. This is confirmed in the reporting of an accident at Scremerston Mill House crossing when an engine pulling soil wagons struck a cart on a crossing killing the cart driver. Blame was at first levelled at the man in charge of the crossing, but his defence was put,

> *He is required to shut the gate whenever it is within ten minutes of the arrival of a passenger train – the soil wagons are not regulated by time.*
>
> *Berwick Advertiser* 27th May 1848

Trains were despatched and no other train could follow within ten minutes. Drivers were warned of the time interval and told to be aware of the possibility that the train in front might be travelling slow. This was essential, as without electric telegraph, there was no means of communicating to the next station. Drivers had to be aware of the possibility of the train in front breaking down, an additional train to the timetable, or an unnumbered freight train, as in the case above.

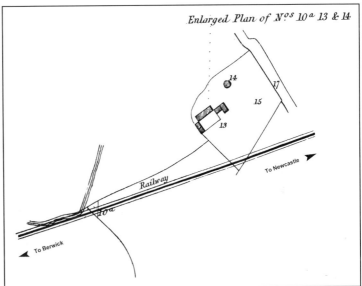

Crag Mill showing 'Windmill' (14) on GNBR deposited plans Ref: QRUP47a Reproduced with permission of Northumberland Collections Service

Where did John and his family live? On the deposited plans for the *Great North British Railway* in 1839, there is a detailed map of the area around Crag Mill, showing the land owned by the Clark family of Belford Estate. On the plan a circular mark at No.14 is labelled *windmill*. The buildings nearby are shown as *Homestead* and *dwelling*.

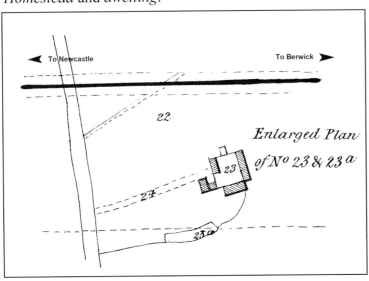

Crag Mill showing 'Windmill Cottages' - without Windmill Ref: QRUP58a Reproduced with permission of Northumberland Collections Service

On the deposited plans for the *Newcastle & Berwick Railway* some five years later, the windmill has gone. The buildings are shown as Dwelling house and farm homestead, with an occupation road 24 and at 23a, a garden! These buildings are within the perimeters of land needed for the railway on the deposited plans and became the property of the railway. In 1862 the then North Eastern Railway produced a report into all its housing. It shows that the railway owned four properties at Crag Mill and gives the occupiers of one of them as John Davidge. In the 1851 Census they are referred to as 'Windmill Cottages'. The properties were next to the crossing, an ideal house for the crossing keeper

'Windmill Cottages' at Crag Mill,
the Railway line is to the left of the cottage on the embankment
Courtesy of Michael Fordy

and possibly temporary station buildings for the issue of tickets before the main station was complete? The cottage at Crag Mill crossing today is nothing to do with this phase of the railway. It was built some years later.

The first Station Master at Belford was Benjamin Thompson, 35 years old and born in Morpeth. His wife, Dorothy, was also an incomer to Belford, 24 years old and born at Chester-le-Street. His eventual home would have been Belford Station, but it was not finished when the line opened. He may have resided at Crag Mill or in Belford and looked after the temporary station at Crag Mill. His role was to look after the station, goods warehouse and coal sales, and ensure discipline was kept at all times to enable the safe and timely passage of all trains. White's *Directory* of 1847 confirms Benjamin Thompson as the station master.

In Conclusion

At the end of 1848, just over a year since the line was opened and only twelve years since a railway for Belford was first mooted, what changes had the railway brought to Belford?

To begin with, there was an immediate population explosion during late 1845 and early 1846 with the navvies lodging in the village, but long term, very little change. The Census of 1841 gives the population as 1157, with an addition of only 69 to the 1851 total of 1226. The railway provided short term employment for local people in terms of building the railway and quarrying. The shop and Inn keepers would have seen increased trade, selling goods to the navvies. This period also brought additional crime, death and serious injury and an increased workload for the Belford Doctors.

Once the building was over, and with the loss of the long distance and Royal Mail coaches, Belford people would have soon realised that the railway had brought about a decline in the importance of the Great North Road through the village, and with it loss of trade and status.

There were physical changes on the eastern side of the village with the division of fields, new buildings, bridges, embankments, cuttings and the diversion of water courses to benefit the line of railway, but no physical change to Belford itself. The new road beyond the tile works passing the station and linking into the Waren to Chatton road, provided a more direct route from Belford to Waren and Bamburgh, but also would lead to a decline in coastal shipping to and from Waren, once the railway network expanded further.

The railway brought a loss of convenience in terms of direct communications. The mail was handed over direct to the post office before the railway, but now,

> *Mr. Watkins of the Blue Bell Inn has contracted for the conveyance of the mails between the station and the town, and has got a very neat and commodious omnibus for the railway passengers.*
> Berwick & Kelso Warder 10th July 1847

The problem of transferring the mail and passengers to and from the station had been overcome by the provision of a no doubt well used, horse-drawn bus service. There was also more work for carters transferring goods to and from the large goods warehouse to Belford and all points west. With the building of cattle docks at the station, farmers could move cattle in good condition direct to Newcastle market, rather than walk them there, with the consequent loss of weight and condition. The direct line between various collieries and the coal depot at the station eventually brought about cheaper and better coal for cooking and heating, but also resulted in the decline in open cast or shallow mined local coal, and the consequent loss of jobs. Passengers now had a huge choice of rail destinations. An Act of Parliament stipulated that the railway company must provide one train every day that stopped at all stations with fares not to exceed 1d. per mile – the *Parliamentary Trains*. This really did bring rail travel to the masses.

Life in Belford at the end of 1848 had changed forever. The market place was no longer the sole focal point of the town. The railway station was one and a quarter miles away and there was constant activity there, in terms of passengers and goods. The two were joined by omnibus for passengers and mail, and carts for goods, but passing trade from the Great North Road was in serious decline.

The immediate sale of the post horses once the railway arrived showed the sudden change. In 1825 the news of George Stephenson and the *Stockton and Darlington Railway* was probably viewed with wonder and amazement in Belford, but by 1848 their opinion may have changed. After all, it was Stephenson's route for the railway that, because of his desire to please the shareholders ahead of communities, and his blinkered view of levels, left Belford people so close and yet so far from a railway station. With all the uncertainty of the various routes and the problems siting the station, it really was a case of Belford gets a railway – just!

Sources:
Herapath's *Journal and Railway Magazine*
Jackson, Christine E., *Prideaux John Selby - A Gentleman naturalist* Spredden Press 1992
Skeat, W. O., *George Stephenson The Engineer & His letters* The Institution of Mechanical Engineers 1973
Tomlinson, W. W., *The North Eastern Railway - its rise and development* Andrew Reid & Co. Ltd., Newcastle upon Tyne 1914
The National Archives (TNA) - Kew
Northumberland Collections Service, Woodhorn
The Ken Hoole Study Centre, Darlington
The *Railway Times*
The *Berwick Advertiser*
The *Berwick & Kelso Warder*

THE QUARRIES OF BELFORD PARISH
by Tony Lee

The Geology of the Area

We are told that the Cheviot hills were formed by volcanic action millions of years ago, and that sand and mud flows created deposits in the surrounding area which was covered by the sea. This has been a major influence on the geology of the Belford area, and on the local quarrying enterprises over many years. The hard volcanic whinstone, resulting from these eruptions, may have intruded through the sedimentary deposits. It is mainly limited to the north of an east-west line through the village. The whin sill tends to cap the summits, while the valleys comprise shale and sandstone. There are, however, outcrops of limestone on the higher ground, and also of coal on Belford moor where the signs of its excavation from Bell Pits can still be found. To the south of the village, sandstone and limestone predominate.

Evidence of Quarries

A number of small disused sandstone or limestone quarries can be found south of the village on Newlands Moor and, just outside the parish, Rayheugh Moor; Quarry Wood near Rosebrough farm; Lucker South farm; Newham; Bellshill; and Twizell. A remarkable number of small worked-out quarries are shown on the current Ordnance Survey map around Linkey Law.

On Belford moor, south of the road to Old Lyham, on the 'right of way' to Newlands North Moor, is Rogues Road sandstone quarry. It gets its name from its position on the route of an old hill track, shown on some early maps, which may have been used by smugglers bringing in cheap liquor from Scotland.

More intriguing is a reference, in the County History by Bateson (1893), to a quarry north of Whinny Hill, west of the village. It is claimed that *till fifty years ago* this produced limestone that was then burned in a kiln in nearby Blagdon Dene. In fact there are two quarries shown in the Dene, north of Sionside farm, on the 1733 map produced for Abraham Dixon III (1689-1746), the then owner of the Belford estate. The same map shows a 'limestone quarry' near Craggy Hall farm, where there is still a well preserved limekiln.

The 1733 map also shows a 'slait' (sic) quarry at the foot of Whinny Hill. This, together with the lime production, must have been an important source of

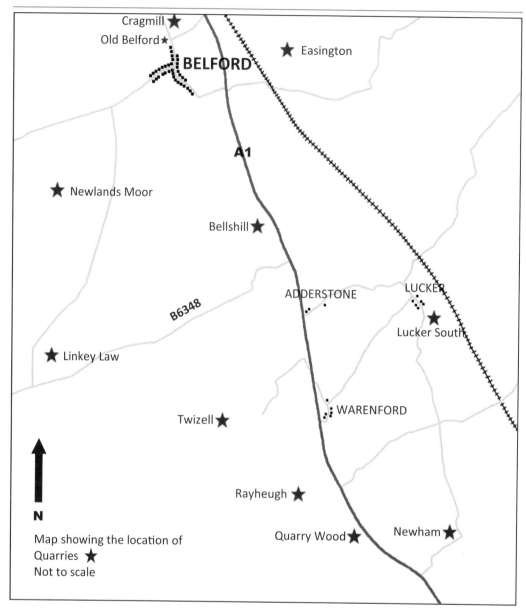

Cragmill ★
Old Belford ★
★ BELFORD
★ Easington
A1
★ Newlands Moor
Bellshill ★
ADDERSTONE
LUCKER
B6348
★ Lucker South
★ Linkey Law
Twizell ★
WARENFORD
N
Rayheugh ★
Map showing the location of
Quarries ★
Not to scale
Quarry Wood ★   Newham ★

building materials when Abraham Dixon IV was improving the village. The 1897 Ordnance Survey map still shows a small area of rough ground and some suggestion of a quarry, in the angle between the Chatton road and Whinny Hill, but there is now no trace. An elderly resident recalls that this old quarry was still in use as the village tip in the 1930s.

In his book *Contractor Leather*, David Leather did not include much information about Middleton (the summer home of the Leathers) but, in an unpublished supplement, he refers to Swinhoe Crags on the Estate, and the fact that, below them, his ancestor and hydraulic engineer John T. Leather (1804-1885) converted an old pond *in a former quarry* into two ornamental lakes by raising a dam. These can readily be reached by a right of way from Swinhoe farm. It is still possible to find the four inch pipe, installed in 1883, which fed the Estate houses lower down. Another pond, that was formerly a small sandstone quarry, can be found east of Middleton cottages on the old A1, on the lane to Low Middleton farm.

Turning towards the eastern boundary of the parish, there seems little doubt that a quarry existed many years ago, some 400 metres to the east of Waren Mill. It is now totally covered by well-grown trees, in an area of woodland called 'Sea Lands' on the current Ordnance Survey map. Remains can still be seen of a wooden jetty, that ran out, off Kiln Point, into Budle Bay, used for the export of stone (and possibly grain from the Mill). This, however, necessitated a wagon way for almost 800 metres along the foreshore, on the line of the present coast road. It also means that then, small vessels could find sufficient depth of water at the head of the Bay - an impossibility these days.

More speculative is the site of another old quarry at Spindlestone, referred to by Tomlinson (1888), when discussing the legend of the *Laidley Worm*. He states that *the hole and trough ..... were on the north side of the South Hill but they have been destroyed within recent years by the opening out of a quarry.* An old map in the *County History* (page 175) indicates a well in that position, now disappeared. The Ordnance Survey map 2000 shows a pond at this site, which has since dried out and been replaced by an area of rushes. A little to the south-west of South Hill appears to be the remains of a small quarry, largely filled in, that may have supplied stone to the nearby lime kiln.

Old Belford Quarry
Old Belford Quarry lay off North Bank to the west, and could date back to the late 18th century, when Abraham Dixon IV was doing so much to improve the village. The earliest map on which a small quarry there seems to be indicated, is that by John Dobson, who surveyed the Belford estate for William Clark in 1820. The Ordnance Survey map of 1851 shows what is described as 'old quarry', an indication perhaps that it had been disused for some time. Whellan's *Directory* of 1855 says that the village *abounds in coal, limestone and building stone*, though there is no mention of quarrymen among the listed inhabitants. Kelly's Directories of 1858 and 1879 do not refer to quarrying in any way.

In the *Berwick Advertiser* of 17th December 1886, however, there is a lengthy report on the re-opening of *Belford Whinstone Quarries*, by James McLaren and John Thompson, in February 1885, under a lease from the owner of the Estate,

Old Belford Quarry painted by Rev. Hull c.1930
Courtesy of Audrey Petrie

G. D. Atkinson-Clark. It is claimed that between 10,000 and 12,000 tons of whinstone were removed - *a figure which will be largely outstripped this year* (1886) - and that 60 men were employed. McLaren and Thompson were listed as *whinstone merchants* in Bulmer's 1887 Directory. An examination of the 1891 Census, shows James McLaren, aged 32, as a *Quarry master and innkeeper* living in High Street, but no sign of John Thompson in the district. A David McGregor, aged 37 and residing in Church Street, is described as a *Quarry master and Contractor*, possibly replacing Thompson.

The inn held by McLaren in 1890 was the *Lamb* in West Street, but the following year he moved to the *Black Bull* in the High Street, staying for three years. Strangely, the licence at the *Lamb* was transferred to James McLaren in 1890 by a John Thompson. It is therefore possible that, before Thompson left the village prior to the 1891 Census, both *quarrymasters* may have been innkeepers. This Census shows only 20 local men employed as *sett makers, stonebreakers* or *quarrymen*, which is a far cry from the 60 men recorded as working in the quarry by the *Berwick Advertiser* in 1886. The apparent change in management, and the fall in the number of employees, suggest that activity in the quarry must have declined. Indeed, this is confirmed in an entry in the National School log book dated 1ˢᵗ May 1891:

> Owing to the slackness of work in the Belford Whinstone Quarries several children have left the school, their parents having had to remove to fresh fields of labour.

In 1915, Mark Appleby Ltd. (incorporated in 1913) leased the quarry from G. D. Atkinson-Clark. The plan, with the new lease, shows the quarry as developed by McLaren and Thompson, with its blacksmith's shop and powder store. The lease was originally for ten years, with annual option to renew at £20 yearly rental, subject only to Landlords' Property tax! An additional rent of £5 per acre was to be applied to land adjoining the existing quarry. Furthermore there was a Royalty of 6d. (2½p) per ton of whinstone for 'setts' and 4d. per ton for rubble. The quarry was sold to the lessee for a total of £1798. 8s. 5d. in the 1923 Sale, (approximately £54,000 in today's money). Previously, it was thought that Mark Appleby Ltd. had bought the quarry for £900, but an examination of the company ledgers shows a total payment of £1798. 8s. 5d. made in two parts: firstly *To quarry and plantation at Belford £922. 0s. 0d.* and a second item: *To completion of Belford quarry purchase £876. 8s. 5d.*, both dated 8ᵗʰ February 1923, this being the date of the sale. In the Sale catalogue, there is a reference to a *downhill run to the railway station*. This was to a siding at Cragmill station on the main line, close to the present level crossing on the Easington road. This station was certainly in use for passengers as far back as 1862, and a siding is shown on the 1860 Ordnance Survey map. This served a 'coal depot' which may also have handled stone consignments. It seems to have closed for passenger use in 1877, but the siding remained in operation.

Mark Appleby (1885 - 1976) was already operating quarries at:
- Embleton, leased in 1898;
- Newton by the Sea from 1910; and
- north of the road into Craster village, leased in 1909.

It has not been established how long Applebys worked the Belford quarry after its purchase in 1923. The surviving Appleby accounts at the Northumberland Archives do not indicate when quarrying ceased and there seems some confusion as to which quarry various entries relate. (Old Belford, or Easington). At some unknown date, possibly after the Second World War, they appear to have sold the quarry to Sydney Armstrong, Matthew Arris and two others. It is thought that the local building firm, Tully's, bought the land surrounding the quarry from Armstrong and Co. An application for planning permission to develop the area had failed, but Tully's built several houses on the adjoining Cragside Avenue after 1953. In 1958, Arris, who had evidently retained the quarry itself, applied unsuccessfully to use it as a winter park for caravans. Two bungalows were later built in the quarry. Mark Appleby Ltd, who owned other quarries in the south of the county, ceased trading in 1975, continuing as a small property company until dissolved in 1986.

Even to this day the old quarry is called *McLarens* by some of the older inhabitants of the village, despite the later development at Cragmill by an entirely different family of McLarens.

Cragmill Quarry

The author has been favoured with the opportunity of studying the surviving Balance Sheets and Minute Books of the McLaren business. Unfortunately there are significant breaks in these papers and consequently this account cannot be comprehensive. It is inevitably limited to the period before the take-over of the company in 1985.

The story of this quarry which is still in operation, though not under the original owners, is bound up with another McLaren family. Three McLaren brothers

Early days at Cragmill Quarry
Courtesy of Peter Brown

emigrated to Canada in the early 20th Century but returned to Belford to purchase Chesters farm from George Scott, part of which became the site of their new quarry. The first Balance Sheet, for the year ending September 1924, shows Robert Wood McLaren (1873 - 1937), George Joseph McLaren (1882 - 1965) and William McLaren (1884 - 1964) as equal partners. Between them, in 1924 , they contributed £7,150 towards the £11,192 purchase price, the balance being met by a Bank overdraft.

In 1928, a fourth brother, J. Roland McLaren (1879 - 1950) joined the partnership, having previously quarried for some years at Craster, in company with H. G. Prowde. They also developed the harbour there with some success, erecting a silo on the east breakwater which was fed from the quarry by an overhead ropeway; the concrete base remains to this day. The 1914-18 War, however, brought a severe downturn in business and that quarry was abandoned in 1923.

Roland contributed less capital than the three founding brothers but the four partners signed off the 1928 accounts as seen here.

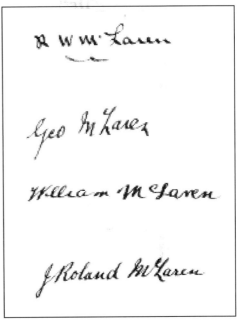

The four partners ranked equally for a significant trading loss in the four months ending January 1932, despite the profitable disposal of plant from the Craster quarry which the Belford company had taken over in 1931. At this point Roland McLaren left the partnership. An examination of the balance sheet at this time does not throw much light on his departure. The year to

Courtesy of Peter Brown

September 1931 ended with a small loss of £697 after depreciation of assets to the tune of £1,714. However, in the four months to 31st January 1932, when the break-up occurred, there was a trading loss of £3,681 before charging depreciation of £5,217 (mainly on Sentinel steam wagons) leaving a total deficit of £9,399 to be divided equally between the four partners. Though the depreciation factor exacerbated the loss, it seems that the poor results of the previous year, to September 1931, persisted into 1932 as there was only a small profit of £634 for the eight months to September 1932, (after a very low depreciation figure of £311). There was a reference to *a loss on disputed contract: J. R. McLaren Junr.* amounting to £401. Roland McLaren was to go on to develop another quarry - old Brada between Waren Mill and Glororum, trading under the name of Rolmac, before selling out to Amalgamated Roadstone.

In 1933 the partnership (now without Roland) was on an even keel again with a profit of £2,826 despite a serious machinery fire. Robert McLaren died in 1937 and his executors maintained capital in the partnership until the company was incorporated as McLaren & Co. (Belford) Ltd in 1938. The book value of the partnership assets conveyed to the new company in 1938 were as follows:

Offices in Hume Street, Newcastle	1000.00
Chesters farm and quarry, Belford	6000.00
*Divet Hill farm and quarry	2500.00
Houses in High Street, Belford	100.00
Houses in Knowe Head, Tweedmouth	100.00
Land at Craster	50.00
	£ 9750.00

*Divet Hill was a quarry near Great Bavington, 13 miles west of Morpeth. Plant, machinery, wagons and book debts were valued at £7,753 after deducting liabilities (principally bank overdraft, trade debts and taxation) of £2,1752.

In March 1939, it was agreed to purchase the Belford Hall estate, including the Home farm, for £9,636 from the executors of R. T. Hodgson deceased. Bricksheds farm was also bought in 1939, and Woodside and Woodend farms the following year. These two farms are 2 miles (3 km) west of Lowick, and their sale was discussed later by the directors, in November 1948.

After the traumatic events of 1932, profitability had risen until 1939 (as indeed had the wages bill) but dropped back to between £1,500 and £2,500 during the years of the Second World War. Belford Hall was requisitioned by the military authorities and occupied by troops. The annual rent received was scarcely generous at £110! The many and varied public works carried out by the company included, in June 1939, a contract with Tynemouth for the *construction of air raid precaution trenches*. There was *contract work at Cramlington aerodrome*. This had been a base for 36 Squadron R.A.F in the First World War, and for civilian use in the inter-war years; no record has been found of any military operations in the last War. It was possibly used as a satellite airfield, being midway between an active field at Tranwell (Morpeth) and Woolsington, which was later to become Newcastle Airport. A lease of Bellshill limestone quarry was signed in March 1943 and for some 20 years stone was taken to Cragmill for crushing. A lime spreading service for local farms was also introduced.

Business was inevitably at a low level during the war years and the available Minutes suggest that official meetings between the two directors, George and William McLaren, were fairly infrequent until new contracts were available after 1945.

Immediate post war activities included demolition of pill boxes and repairs to Beadnell harbour; road renewal at Cragside, near Rothbury, and at Bamburgh Castle; new sewers at Blagdon; and road works at Bedlington Colliery. These called for increased wagon capacity. By 1948, the property assets, enhanced by the acquisitions of farms, quarries, Belford Hall and six houses, had a book value of £39,000.

It seems that the surge in business in the immediate post-war euphoria was rather short lived. In the spring of 1951, the Chairman suggested that the quarries needed more turnover before a satisfactory trading result could be shown. On the subject of securing new business, the view was expressed that *we let the business come to us instead of looking for it*, and that a degree of publicity should be sought. In July the same year, the downward trend was expected to justify *every possible economy*.

In January 1951, the five foremen listed below, with their wages, had been given a rise of 10/- (50p) per week:

F. W. Purvis	£6. 10. 0d	+ free house and overtime.
J. Trotter	£6. 10. 0d	+ overtime.
J. Romaines	£6. 0. 0d	+ overtime.
W. Weightman	£6. 0. 0d	+ overtime.
W. Gibson	£5. 15. 0d	+ overtime.

A directors' meeting held in February 1951 considered a weekly wages' scale for a shorthand typist and the following was agreed:

16½ years to 17 years	£2. 15. 0d (£2.75)
17 " 17½ "	£3. 0. 0d
17½ " 18 "	£3. 5. 0d (£3.25)
18 " 18½ "	£3. 10. 0d
18½ " 19 "	£3. 15. 0d (£3.75)
19 " 19½ "	£4. 0. 0d
19½ " 20 "	£4. 10. 0d

It was pointed out that, by city standards, this was a very low wage for a shorthand typist. The Chairman, Mr. George McLaren, said that the scale could be adjusted later if necessary.

It was around this time (1951) that a decision was reached to build four semi-detached houses on quarry land, extending the east end of Clark Place southwards. This extension was named McLaren Terrace. The Company also had a significant County council contract. Cragmill delivered by wagon over 10,000 tons of gravel to Northumberland County Council undertakings, in the year ending March 1951. Crushed gravel was quoted at 17/- (85p) per ton (c.1018 kg) delivered.

The company was expanding through the later 1950s as the following letter to Robert Dunlop, dated 23rd March 1957, illustrates:

> *McLaren Co. (Belford) Ltd hereby instruct Mr. Robert*
> *Dunlop that he is charged with securing in relation to*
> *their quarries situated as follows:*
> *Cragmill quarry, Belford; Divet Hill quarry; Capheaton;*
> *Bridge End Gravel works, Wooler; Bellshill quarry,*
> *Belford; Kyloe quarry, Beal; and Cheswick Sand pits,*
> *Beal, the fulfilment of the responsibilities of the owner*
> *under the Mines and Quarries Act, 1954, and Orders and*
> *Regulations made thereafter.*
>
> *For and on behalf of*
> *McLaren & Co. (Belford) Ltd*
>
> *Directors: Geo. McLaren (Chairman)*
> *Wm. McLaren.*

In a Minute of 29th March 1957, the following quarry managers were appointed:

Mr. R. Dunlop, Overall Manager of all the company's Quarries
Mr. G. McLaren (Jnr), Manager, Belford; Bellshill; Kyloe; Beal and
    Cheswick Sandpit
R. Thomson, Deputy Manager Cheswick
F. W. Purvis, Deputy Manager Cragmill and Wooler
J. Romaines, Deputy Manager Bellshill and Kyloe
J. Robson, Manager Wooler Gravel Works
W. J. Weightman, Manager Divet Hill Quarry
H. Spears, Deputy Manager Divet Hill Quarry

On the introduction of a tax on capital gains in 1965, it was necessary to have a valuation of all the company's assets on 1st April that year:

SUMMARY OF VALUATION

of FARMS and OTHER PROPERTIES belonging to Messrs McLaren & Co.
(Belford) Ltd., Belford, Northumberland, Made and Taken by A Veitch O. B. E.
F.I. A (Scot.) Est. of Berwick Auction Mart Co. Ltd., 23 Castlegate, Berwick-on-
Tweed, as at 1st April 1965.

BELFORD HOME FARM	£46,300	0	0
PLANTATION FARM	36,750	0	0
THE CHESTERS FARM	37,700	0	0
THE BRICKSHEDS FARM	25,675	0	0
TIMBER	3,200	0	0
PROPERTY AT MCLAREN TERRACE, BELFORD	13,235	0	0
PROPERTY AT NORTH BANK, BELFORD	4,430	0	0
PROPERTY AT DINNINGSIDE, BELFORD	4,500	0	0
PROPERTY AT HIGH STREET, BELFORD	3,150	0	0
NO. 1 INGRAM ROAD, BAMBURGH	2,300	0	0
PROPERTY AT BOWSDEN, BERWICK ON TWEED	3,000	0	0
BELFORD MANSE AND KENNELS	1,900	0	0
78, OSBORNE AVENUE, NEWCASTLE UPON TYNE	2,000	0	0
PROPERTY AT TYNELY, CHATHILL	6,160	0	0
BLACKHILL COLLIERY	1,900	0	0
FACTORY AT HUME STREET, NEWCASTLE UPON TYNE	29,000	0	0
LAND AT CRASTER, NORTHUMBERLAND	230	0	0
	£221,430	0	0

Signed: A L Veitch
O.B.E F.I.A(Scot.) Est.

Courtesy of Peter Brown

Towards the end of 1966 sand from the pit at Cheswick was used to start the production of ready mixed concrete. Plantation farm had been purchased in 1962 and West Road and South Meadows farms were bought in 1968. A substantial £93,000 tender for work on the A1 at West Mains (Beal cross roads) was accepted in January 1968. Of similar value, was a contract on the A1 at Warenford. In that year the total expenditure on capital equipment (excluding the farms) was over £50,000.

In 1970 four new, detached houses were built on the road up to Belford Hall which became known as McLaren Drive. The weekly rent was to be £4.10.0d plus rates.

In 1978, the company paid Amalgamated Roadstone £15,450 for surplus stone at the old Brada quarry, previously operated by Roland McLaren. There was also a considerable expenditure on new equipment - October 1979 brought the purchase of three new wagons - a Truckmixer (£33,308), a Foden tipper (£30,573) and a Foden 8 Wheeler (£33,844). By January 1981, however, the Minutes refer to a recession in trade. It was agreed to resist working more than a 40-hour week where practicable.

In this year, Belford Hall was sold for £5,250 to a Mr. & Mrs. Stanley McKale who hoped to convert the building into a hotel. The surrounding farmland (Home Farm) was not included in the sale.

McLaren Farms had been hived off as a separate entity in June 1966. After the construction of the Belford by-pass in 1983, it was then sold, in 1985, for some £6 million, at the time of the take-over of the quarry business by Ready Mixed Concrete Ltd.. The quarry was later taken over by Cemex (U.K) Ltd. Cemex still owns the remaining farmland up to the lane to Chesters farmhouse and has permission to extract whinstone, until 2042, according to the Northumberland County Council Minerals Local Plan of 2000. This includes the following reference to Cragmill:

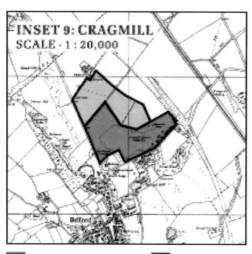

INSET 9: CRAGMILL
SCALE - 1 : 20,000

Existing Site   Preferred Area

Courtesy of Northumberland County Council
Northumberland Minerals Local Plan March 2000

Cragmill extension

5.77 Permitted reserves within Cragmill Quarry will become exhausted towards the end of the plan period. An area of land containing up to 6 million tonnes of reserves has been identified as a potential extension area. The area identified would mean that working would move further away from the village of Belford.

5.78 The quarry currently operates under a planning permission granted in 1948. the conditions controlling operations are inadequate by today's standards. There are no conditions governing the frequency, times and level of blasting and this has been a cause of concern for the residents of Belford. Similarly, there are no adequate conditions requiring restoration of the quarry. However, the

Environment Act, 1995, now enables the County Council to review old mineral permissions and agree new sets of planning conditions to control operations.

5.79   The issues which any planning application in this area should address include:

a)   Transport

Whinstone is currently transported by road along the A1, and a small amount (3% of total output) is transported to south-east England by ship from Berwick Harbour. Proposals for an extension should examine the potential for rail transport of the mineral to reduce the numbers of lorries on the public road network.

b)   Visual impact

A detailed visual appraisal would be required to assess the impact of the proposals, in particular from the A1, the C58 north of Belford and the North Northumberland Coast AONB.

c)   Impact on residential properties

The proposed extension would bring mineral extraction closer to Middleton Lodge and The Chesters. Proposals should include measures to reduce the impact of mineral working to an acceptable level.

d)   Nature Conservation

There is an SNCI adjacent to the preferred area. Any scheme should ensure the protection of features of value.

Easington Quarry

Easington Quarry lies north east of the old Belford railway station and, according to the County Council Minerals Local Plan (2000), which calls it Belford Quarry, there has been a quarry on this site *since about 1900*. However, the earliest firm record found is the Lease granted by G. D. Atkinson-Clark to Mark Appleby Ltd in 1915. This ran for 21 years at an annual rent of £180 rising to £200 if the Lease of the old Belford quarry, which as we have seen was also held by Appleby, should cease. Additional rent of £11 or £12 was payable on acreage not yet taken in hand. Royalties were the same as on old Belford quarry production. This Lease includes a map showing a "tramway" from Belford station and there is a reference in the accounts to *Surveyor's costs re: proposed railway*. No proper siding was constructed, however, until 1919. In the Appleby papers there are entries in September of that year, relating to charges of £2622. 5s. 8d. (approximately £55620, in today's money) from C. M. Skinner & Co. for *railway and sidings*, and from the North Eastern Railway of £180. 0s. 8d. (approximately £3,819 today) for *sidings, etc.* Additionally, between 1916 and 1919, there were freight charges from the Railway Company. Recent Ordnance Survey maps (which all refer to *Easington quarry*) show a short branch line running to the quarry from Belford station. The track for most of this standard gauge line is still in place and, though much overgrown, could be brought back into use. William Appleby was Quarry Manager at Easington in 1920 and lived at *Windy Gyle* (now reconstructed as *Cragside*) in West Street, Belford. In 1925, this was bought by the company.

Mark Appleby Ltd. purchased the 'Easington Estate' from G. D. Atkinson-Clark in 1922 (before the sale of the Belford Estate in the following year) for £14,703 (£311,900 today). Comparison with the figure of only £1,798 for the old Belford quarry a year later, suggests that the *Easington Estate* was much more substantial and may have included agricultural land.

It has been suggested that the Easington Estate, *on which the railway station was built*, was bought for £13,500 by Captain Landells R.N. whose executors later sold it for £18,500 to an unknown party who, in turn, profitably sold it to *Mr. Clark of Belford Hall* for £20,000. Whether the boundaries remained the same during this period is open to question. The information in this paragraph is contained in a hand-written note in the County Archives (reference ZH8) that frustratingly omits dates, but would seem to relate to the early part of the 19th Century. William Landells or Landless, one of Collingwood's Lieutenants at the Battle of Trafalgar, purchased Easington in 1808, and retained it until his death in 1826, when it was sold again.

In the 1960s, the quarry was sold by the Applebys to Slaters, and later taken over by Tilcon Ltd. in whose ownership it still remains. Despite an extension to planning permission in 1995, a recession in the construction industry and the loss of a major ballast contract with the railway company, caused the suspension of operations. Part of the quarry has been flooded for some years, the rest has been levelled. Permission to extract whinstone is still available until 2015 but, in the meantime, Tilcon has, in conjunction with the Northumberland Wildlife Trust, produced a Biodiversity Plan to protect the sensitive area around the quarry.

Postscript:
We have seen how the names of Mark Appleby and the four McLaren brothers dominate the story of the major local quarries. It seems quite appropriate to find that all five are buried in the Spitalford cemetery at Embleton.

Acknowledgements:

Northumberland County Council.

Particular thanks are due to Peter Brown and William McLaren for allowing access to the surviving papers of McLaren & Co. (Belford) Ltd. and to Roger Jermy for his input.

Sources:

Bateman E. *A history of Northumberland, Volume 1* Andrew Reid, Sons & Co. Newcastle 1893

Chorlton M. *Airfields of North East England* Countryside Books 2005

Leather D. *Contractor Leather* The Leather Family History Soc. 2005

Linsley, Stafford *Ports and Harbours of Northumberland* Tempus 2005

Northumberland County Council *Minerals Local Plan, 2000*

Robson D. A. *A guide to the Geology of Northumberland and the Borders* Natural History Society of Northumberland, Durham and Newcastle upon Tyne 1965

Tomlinson W. W. *Comprehensive Guide to the County of Northumberland 1888*. Re-published Davis Books 1985

The *Berwick Advertiser*

Berwick Records Office

Companies House, Cardiff

Land Registry, Durham

National Railway Museum, York

National School log book (1891) Belford

Northumberland Collections Service, Woodhorn

Northumberland Wildlife Trust Ltd

1891 Census

Numerous old Ordnance Survey and privately commissioned maps

8

LEST WE FORGET

The impact of the First World War on the Belford area and its people
by Ian Main & Jane Bowen

This research began in an attempt to identify the men recorded on the Belford War Memorial and how they died. In the event much more information was found, although two of the dead have remained elusive – William Gray and James Hogg (for whom there are several contenders). It does not claim to be a definitive account of the Belford men in World War I. In the main, the accounts of those who survived are drawn from the pages of the Berwick Advertiser, and while some families clearly were happy to share the triumphs and disasters of their husbands and sons, others were not, so omissions simply reflect a lack of available information.

On the 28th of June 1914, the Austrian Archduke, Franz Ferdinand, was assassinated in Sarajevo, by a Serbian nationalist – Gavrilo Princip. There were major diplomatic repercussions. Austria looked to her allies, Germany and Italy, and Serbia turned to Russia, who then called on her alliances with France and Britain. A month later, all diplomatic manoeuvring was at an end. Austria declared war on Serbia on the 26th of July; on the 30th of July, Russia mobilized to support Serbia; Germany declared war first on Russia, on the 1st of August and then on France on the 3rd; when Germany then invaded Belgium as a way of bypassing the French defences, Britain declared war on Germany on the 4th of August.

In North Northumberland, the reality of war was felt first by those men already serving as territorial volunteers in the 7th Northumberland Fusiliers. Overnight, they exchanged weekly parades and exercises and a summer camp, for full time military service. They were called up immediately and sent to Alnwick for further military training. Among those who went then were brothers James and Herbert Clark from Belford Station, Robert Clark from Ross Farm, John William Falla, George Graham, brothers Richard and William Hall, all from the High Street, John Fife from Twizell Mill and James Hogg from Newham.

Generally, in Belford, at the beginning of August, people were more interested in the approaching Belford Show and sports for which, in July, the Rural District Council voted as usual to lend their tents. Three weeks later, however, the Show and sports were abandoned, *due to the European crisis*. At the same time, in a recognition that war might impact more directly on life, ambulance classes were arranged in the village. The two village doctors, Dr. James McDonald and Dr. Phillipson, agreed to run the courses in the Ferguson Memorial Hall on Wednesday and Friday evenings.

As elsewhere in the country, however, young men who, a month previously, had seen little likelihood of living their lives any differently from their fathers and grandfathers, and to whom a journey of even 50 miles was a major enterprise, suddenly saw an opportunity to see the world, and have an adventure. They were anxious to grab it before, as the papers foretold, the war would be over by Christmas. Their opportunity came on the 10th of September, when a recruiting meeting was held in the West Street Hall (now the Community Club). Mr. Maurice Coates, the land agent for the Middleton Hall Estate, chaired the meeting and introduced the two speakers, Captain Sitwell of Barmoor Castle, the recruiting officer for North Northumberland, and Captain Wilkins D.S.O., RN. Sitwell described the British situation as a *Fight for Life*, and spoke of the urgent need for men - the Northumberland Fusilier Territorials needed a further 400 men to bring them up to strength. Those present were encouraged to *do their duty to their King and Country, and assist the nation to come out 'Top Dog'*. Following the meeting some twenty men enlisted. Four days later they joined the other Territorials at Alnwick. There they found themselves training

Alnwick Camp

on Alnwick Moor and Pasture and doing daily physical exercise on the Duke's School playing field. The Duke allowed them to use the public baths in Clayport Street, and they received lessons in French from Lady Margaret Percy, his daughter.

At the outbreak of war, a number of Belford men were already enlisted in the regular army, and others, who had seen military service, were classed as reservists. There were also a few who had very specific and urgently needed skills. In August 1914, the destination of all these men was not Alnwick, but

France. A particular need was for men to care for the army's horses, and both Ralph Greshon and his brother Thomas, sons of Mr. Greshon of Buckton, were assigned to the Advanced Remounts to prepare the necessary facilities and organise suitable supplies, followed shortly after by Harry Dunn, the postman's son from West Street. The Remounts assembled at York, taking over the Cattle Market and the Fishergate Schools, and, together with 869 horses, took the train for Southampton on the 19th of August. From there they sailed to Le Havre, arriving on the 21st. There they found marshy ground unsuitable for the horses, a lack of fencing and insufficient water troughs. At the end of the month, a move to the racecourse at Nantes ensured somewhat better facilities, but with the Sanitary Authorities insisting that the men camped four and a half miles away from the racecourse, and only 60 men to care for the now nearly 1000 horses, life was not easy. On the 14th of September there were two successive stampedes into the town involving some 230 horses, the second in pitch darkness. Fifteen horses were killed or had to be destroyed, 121 needed veterinary attention and a further 54 were missing. After that it was agreed to let the men camp alongside the racecourse. Moving horses from the Nantes base to the front also proved problematic:

Capt. Fair with 300 horses for Le Mans was entraining & had got 146 in when the remainder stampeded, frightened by the persistent blowing of the railway engine; this also occurred in pitch darkness.

Problems persisted, more and more horses were arriving, often in poor condition after bad sea crossings, but the men were not reinforced. Eventually, in an attempt to deal with the problems which arose at night, the Commander bought up all the hurricane lamps in Nantes. Sometime in that first month the Greshon brothers must have accompanied horses from the Base Camp to the Front.

A Remounts Depot

The Greshons' brother, Robert, was a regular, serving in India with the Royal Field Artillery at the outbreak of war, and accompanied the first contingents of Indian soldiers to France, as did Joseph Langford, originally from West Street, serving with the Second Battalion Northumberland Fusiliers. Another vital service was the Royal Army Medical Corps, and George Davison from Buckton went out with the 6th Field Ambulance Brigade on the 5th of August.

The 1st Northumberland Battalion was part of the British Expeditionary Force to France, and in it were two men with Belford connections - John Scrowther of West Street and Christopher Leather, youngest son of the late Frederick Leather of Middleton Hall, and brother to the then owner, Major Gerard T. Leather. Both John and Christopher had originally seen service in the Boer war, and now rejoined the Army. The Battalion assembled at Cambridge Barracks, Portsmouth, before taking two special trains to Southampton on the 13th of August. There they and their transport wagons embarked on the *S.S. Norman*, while the horses were shipped separately on the *S.S. Italian Prince*. The *Norman* sailed at 3pm, docking at Le Havre twelve hours later. It took another two hours to get the battalion and its equipment disembarked, and then there was a problem. The ship with the horses had not arrived, so a platoon was left at the docks to see to the wagons, while the rest of the battalion marched five and a half miles to the rest camp. It was so hot that 82 men fell out on the march, and when they arrived it was to discover that the camp was not ready and there was no water for the men to wash with. The camp was at the top of a long steep hill, and the transport wagons which finally set off at 3 p.m, became stuck behind motorised vehicles which broke down on the hill. The last of the wagons finally arrived at Midnight. The following day was one of continuous heavy rain. At 5 p.m, the Battalion was ordered back to Le Havre to get the train at 3 a.m the following morning. By now the transport wagons had sunk into the mud, the horses could not pull them out, and the soldiers had to manhandle them on to the road. The return journey was no easier – with tired horses and muddy roads it was only a matter of time until something went wrong. Both water carts overturned, completely blocking the road, and delaying the Battalion for one and a half hours. All in all, it was not an auspicious beginning. Eventually, they got the train east from Le Havre to Landrecies, arriving just before midnight. After the previous two days it must have been a relief to find themselves welcomed with open arms by the French who showered them with fruit, flowers and cigarettes.

On the 23rd of August, the British attacked the advancing German Army at Mons, but a breakdown in communication between the French and British commanders resulted in the British beginning a slow retreat which continued until the 3rd of September. Regrouping, the two armies now faced the Germans

Action on the
Western Front

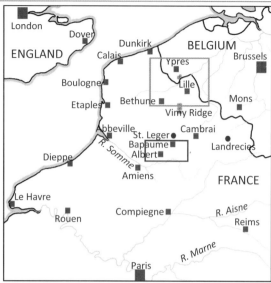

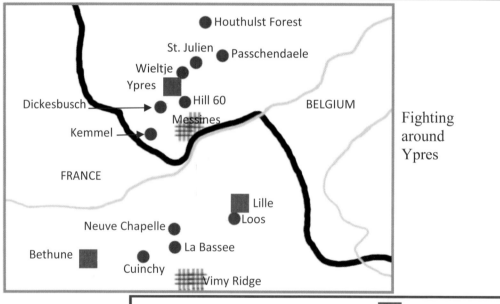

Fighting
around
Ypres

Fighting on
the Somme

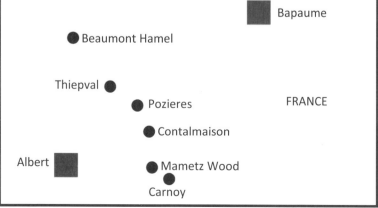

across the river Marne. On the 9th of September, the Northumberlands succeeded in crossing the Marne, taking 600 prisoners the following day. Pushing north east, they crossed the River Aisne on the 13th. The next day they moved further north in support of the Royal Scots, only to find themselves exposed and under enemy fire. The losses were heavy, and in this action, John Scrowther was taken prisoner, remaining in enemy hands until the end of the war. The Battalion was relieved on the 22nd of September, and for much of the next month was more involved in manoeuvres rather than direct fighting. By now the fighting was concentrating in and around the town of Ypres. On the 25th of October, the 1st Northumberlands were ordered to relieve the Lincolnshires at Neuve Chapelle, south of Ypres, on the following day. The change-over took place almost without incident in the early hours of the morning, but, by the afternoon, the Northumberlands came under heavy enemy attack, and although their line was not broken, it was pushed back. Two days later the Germans launched a major assault, retaking the village. In this Battle, the Northumberlands lost three of their officers, including Lieutenant Christopher Leather.   The 1st Battalion of the Black Watch also fought in the Battle, defending the Menin Road, east of Ypres. Among the heavy losses they sustained, was Thomas Nelson, formerly of Belford, killed on the 28th of October.

Another Belford area man to see action in this early stage of the war was John Dick from Brownieside, who served with the King's Own Scottish Borderers. They reached France on the 15th of September, and also fought at Mons and the Marne. At the beginning of October, they were sent north west, arriving at Bethune on the 11th, and were immediately involved in the offensive to take La Bassee. Like the Northumberlands, however, they came under strong German counter attack, and for three days were involved in very bitter fighting. Over sixty men and officers were killed or wounded. John Dick, however, held his nerve and was recommended for an award for his bravery at the Battle of Cuinchy for *assisting wounded to a place of safety under a heavy fire*[1].

The last of the Belford men to serve in France in 1914, was another reservist, T. W. Johnson, the Belford postman. He rejoined his regiment, the 16th Lancers, part of the Second Cavalry Division, and sailed for France on the 7th of September. Once there, like the Northumberlands, he was involved in the fighting at the River Aisne.

Back home, the Territorials and the new volunteers continued their training - the Territorials being posted to Gosforth, in preparation for taking responsibility for coastal defence in the area. It was while they were there that, sadly, the first Belford fatality of the war took place.   On the 14th of October, 'C' Company

---

[1] The Berwick Advertiser states that he was awarded the Distinguished Conduct Medal, but it has not proved possible to corroborate that.

was under orders to move to Earsdon, a march which required them to cross the railway line at Benton Square Station. The troops were warned to take particular care of the 'live' rail, but in the event, one of the soldiers, William Cameron had to re-cross the rails and stumbled on the live wire, being immediately electrocuted. William, the son of George Cameron, had been educated at the National School and was training as an apprentice joiner in Alnwick at the outbreak of war. He was buried with full military honours:

> *'C' Company provided a firing party and under-bearers... the coffin was draped with the Union Jack, with the deceased's accoutrements on top, and it was placed on a gun carriage provided by the 1st N.B.R.F.A. the Rev. C. M. Smith, Battalion Chaplain officiated.*

1915

In Belford and area, the new year began with Mrs. Leather Culley of Bamburgh arranging for presents to be given to all the children whose parents were on active service. The proximity of the war was also brought home with plans to station 400-600 soldiers at Bamburgh Castle and Armstrong Cottages. At the beginning of February, a concert in aid of the local Red Cross detachment took place in the West Street Hall. At the same time, the heavy losses experienced in France at the end of 1914, made more recruiting urgent. The *Berwick Advertiser* for 12th February carried an appeal for more volunteers from men who met the necessary criteria – aged between 19 and 38, physically fit and over 5ft. 3 inches in height. The only one of the Belford men to respond at that time was H. S. McDougall of Buckton, following in his brother John's footsteps. When there was a further appeal, early in March, emphasising that '*a man enlisting in the Battalion will serve with men entirely drawn from his own district and he will probably be among his own friends*', a further six men enlisted – Joseph Dingle of North Bank, David Elliott the School Board Officer, Robert Fairgreve of West Street, John Robert Gibson of Fenwick Steads, James Punton of Low Middleton and David Shiel of The Stables, Middleton Hall. In the event, not all served with the 7th Northumberlands - David Shiel was drafted to Horse Transports, James Punton, who enlisted in Newcastle, was assigned to the 2nd Battalion, and Robert Fairgreve became part of the Northern Cyclists.

The beginning of April saw a further recruiting drive, supported by a four day march through North Northumberland, leaving Alnwick on Easter Tuesday, accompanied by the Battalion Band, and continuing by way of Berwick, Beal, Belford and Bamburgh. It seems, however, to have yielded only one further recruit from the area and there is an account in the Berwick Advertiser of 23rd April, that, when he attempted to persuade others to come with him for the medical, no-one would go. This was probably Thomas Young, of West Street, the only Belford man recorded as enlisting in April 1915.

The war meantime had become concentrated around the city of Ypres and as spring developed, the tempo of fighting increased. In December 1914, the Germans had captured Hill 60, a man-made vantage point created from the spoil heaps formed when the railway line was built, and only one and a quarter miles from the city centre. Whoever controlled this, could observe all the troop movements to the south and east of the city. An unsuccessful attempt to regain this had been made by the British in February 1915. In March a second attempt was begun. Now, the aim was to tunnel under the German lines and mine them. It was a horrific task – before the tunnels could be properly begun, the soldiers found themselves disinterring the French who had been killed in the action of the previous December. Then the ground itself, waterlogged clay and sand, was ill suited for the task. Nevertheless, slowly, tunnels were dug, and mines laid. On the 17th of April, the mines were detonated, destroying the German trenches, and blowing part of Hill 60 apart. What remained once more came under allied control. In the aftermath of this action, however, the second of the

Hill 60

Leather brothers, Captain Edward Wilberforce Leather, serving with the 2nd Battalion, Yorkshire Regiment, was killed on the 18th of April.

Meanwhile, the men who had enlisted at the beginning of the war, were now deemed fit for active service. On the 20th of April, the 7th Northumberlands sailed from Folkestone for Boulogne, arriving at 2 a.m. on the 21st. They arrived at a particularly critical time. Over the winter months, the opposing armies had concentrated their forces around the city of Ypres, On the 22nd of April, the Germans launched their first ever gas attack on the allied troops –at 5p.m., 160 tons of chlorine were blown on to the French positions by a gentle north-east wind. The soldiers who encountered it either fled or were killed, and a gap of more than four miles was opened in the allied lines. With no time to become acclimatised to actual fighting conditions, the 7th Northumberlands found themselves drafted in to help plug that gap in a line to the right of the Canadian forces. On the 26th, at 1.40 p.m. they were ordered to support the attack on the village of St. Julien.

As soon as the Battalion moved off it came under very heavy artillery fire,
and in reaching the St. Julien - Weiltje road also came under heavy machine

gun fire. The Battalion moved up into the firing line to reinforce the 4th and 6th Battalions NF , the men advancing at the double in extended order. Advances were made by rushes, but no good fire position could be obtained, as it was seen that a trench to our front was occupied by the Seaforth Highlanders. The Battalion suffered heavy casualties until it gained the shelter of this trench. 3.30 a message was receive that the GOC[1] Brigade had been killed, and that the Battalion was to await further orders.

When these orders arrived the Battalion retired to the village of Weiltje.
Lance Sergeant William Hall, son of Richard Hall of the High Street, Belford, described the battle experience in a letter home which was published in the *Berwick Advertiser* of 7th May.

Well, we have been in action since Saturday night until this morning, and are now going to a rest-camp. It was like hell on Sunday – shrapnel, Jack Johnson's[2], coal boxes[2], snipers, and everything you can mention. I am proud to say that the Battalion did well, they went at it like old hands; so I can safely say the 'Terriers' have justified their existence....what a row the shells make passing over the trenches, but we just dig ourselves in and sleep when we are off duty. It is wonderful how you get used to them....We saw a German aeroplane brought down behind our trenches yesterday, and the crew made prisoners. They are daring. The airmen, they come over the trench, send a smoke-ball out, and then 'J.J.,' starts, but Thomas is holed by then. I have lived like a 'mowdy' these last four days underground, quite an experience.

In the overall battle for St. Julien, 1829 men and officers were killed. Only one of the Belford area men, Wilfred Wake, was killed. J McDougall of Buckton was blown up and had to be invalided home as was J.W. Falla, who lost a leg. Among others who received lesser wounds were Andrew Dumma, (Belford Moor), George A. Graham (High Street), Richard Pringle (Kyloe) and John White (Crag Mill). Sergeant Joe Purvis wrote home, describing the experiences of the less severely wounded:

I take the chance now. I am in hospital at present....they weren't long in getting me, were they? We landed in for quite a heap of trouble not many days after we got out. It was awful I promised to write you some time after I left England, so having plenty of spare time on my hands. We are all under canvas here, and it is situated in a fine district. The weather too is splendid, so that we are all A1......Mr. Davidson's son of Beal farm, is one of the doctors here.

In early May, the Battalion was in billets, recovering from the first experience of being under enemy fire, but from the 13th, the men were again deployed in and

---

[1] Brigadier General Riddle

[2] Types of German shell

around Ypres, mainly in a support role. On the 26th, they joined the 1st Battalion Rifle Brigade, defending the canal bank north of Ypres. The action there continued until the 2nd of June, and on the 1st, James Clark, who had worked at Robinson's cycle shop in the High Street and was the son of the foreman porter at the station, was killed in a shell explosion. Following this action, again the Battalion spent time in bivouacs or support trenches, and it was in this period that the wounded nineteen year-old Thomas Cuthbertson from Bamburgh Castle Hotel, Seahouses, died in the Wimereux General hospital at Boulogne.

In the middle of June, the Northumberlands were deployed to the Hooge defences, east of Ypres, in preparation for a proposed attack on the enemy. It did not go well. On arrival at the line, they discovered that Bull Farm, part of the defence line, had been mined by the Germans, and they had to move fifty yards south, to avoid being caught in the possible explosion. The following day, the 16th of June, they were ordered to assist the attack *if a favourable opportunity should occur*. On reconnoitring the ground, however, they discovered that in the 300 yards of open ground to be covered in the attack, there were three lines of uncut barbed wire! Even remaining in the defences, the men came under very heavy shell fire, and among the dead was William Carr from Ellingham School. For the remainder of June and July, the Battalion moved between bivouacs, support trenches and front line trenches, before going into billets at Armentières on the 24th of July.

The summer provided a good opportunity to redeploy the forces generally, and another Battalion on the move was the 2nd King's Own Scottish Borderers, with whom the shepherd from Elwick, Corporal Robert Gray, had enlisted. It went from the Ypres Salient to the Somme, near Carnoy. The official history of the regiment's war time service, records that for the next twelve months the Battalion was almost entirely deployed in garrison duties in the trenches there. It was particularly unlucky then, that just a week after their arrival, Robert was killed by a sniper's bullet. As luck would have it, the news of Robert's death reached his parents on the very morning that their son John left to join up.

The next major attempt to break the stalemate of the Western Front, came in September, with plans for a joint Franco-British attack on the German lines south of Ypres, in the vicinity of the town of Loos. This was very much a French initiative, with the British, who were still short of both men and munitions, finding themselves required to play a major attacking role over unsuitable ground. Their sole advantage was that the British too had now developed poison gas. The attack was scheduled to begin at 6.30 a.m. on the 25th of September, with the release of the gas. In the event it was a mixed blessing. While in some areas, it did force a German retreat, in others an uncertain wind blew it back on the attacking forces. Although there was a good initial breakthrough, with Loos itself being captured from the Germans, the lack of available reserve forces meant that this success could not be immediately followed up. By the end of the day, a sixth of the British forces, 15,470 men, were dead or wounded. The following day the Germans had regrouped and strengthened their forces far more successfully than the British, and although a number of further attacks were launched in the days that followed, there were no more gains. The 2nd Northumberlands were held in reserve until the 30[th,] when they relieved the Yorks and Lancashire Regiment in the trenches. The following morning, however, they were the subject of a surprise attack, when, unobserved, German soldiers crept along an old communication trench, and seized a hundred yards of the main trench with a surprise bomb attack. There followed three days of heavy action as the Germans continued to maintain a foothold in the British trenches and used it to launch a series of violent bombing raids. When the Battalion was relieved by the King's Own Royal Lancaster Regiment on the 3rd of October, there were three Officers and 23 men killed, 11 officers and 115 men wounded and 100 men missing believed killed. Among these last was Private James Punton of Low Middleton, a noted competitive cyclist in pre war days, believed killed on the 1st of October. The brothers, George and William Wilson, shepherd sons of James Wilson of Golden Hill (between Lucker and Bamburgh) were both wounded, as was Walter Smith, serving with the Seaforths in the thick of the battle. Sadly he did not recover from his wounds and died on the 10th of November. When the action ended on the 13th of October the cost of the Battle of Loos to the British was the lives of 61,280 soldiers.

Back at home, the news of the growing numbers of casualties was beginning to have an impact on the population as a whole. When, on the 16th of June, accompanied by stirring music from the Territorials' band, a further recruiting meeting was held at the West Street Hall, there was a much more positive response - twenty men enlisted on the night, making, it was said, a total of 80 men now representing the area. Other reservists, such as Mr. Attridge, the Master of the Workhouse, whose call-up had been deferred because of their civilian responsibilities, now found themselves under arms. As more news of the fighting filtered home, however, enthusiasm for enlisting became rarer. A further recruiting meeting held by the Tyneside Scottish in the West Street Hall in November 1915, attracted no recruits at all. At the same time, attitudes began to change towards those who had not volunteered. A hint of this can be seen in the letter William Wilson, who had lost his jaw in the battle, wrote home from hospital.

I often wonder if any of my old mates round about Lucker and Bradford who
have not yet made up their minds to come out here and do their little bit ever

think of the hardships that their own chums have gone through, where more
would have made it much lighter many a time, and perhaps would have had
the net much round about those unmerciful Huns by this time.

To go or not to go, however, was for many not a simple choice. For farm
workers in tied cottages, much depended on the attitude of the landlord. It was
one thing to be prepared to risk life and limb for one's country, it was another
to risk making one's wife, children or elderly parents homeless. Small family
businesses, too, often depended for their success on the strength and energy of
the younger generation. Nevertheless there was a growing sense that some, who
were well able to fight, were refusing to go. James Wilson of Golden Hill,
father of George, William and a third soldier son, Robert, did not mince his
words in a letter to the *Advertiser* on the 12th of November.

Now I know of several farmers in this locality with two and three sons of
military age, all at home, and no-one from these families to represent them in
the army. Well I maintain that if there are any one individual who has
benefited by this awful war, I say it is the farmers, and as everyone knows,
they are very badly represented amongst the ploughmen and shepherds at the
front. I should be pleased to see some of those selfish lads taking their share,
or as I should say, casting in their lot along with the horsemen, ploughmen
and shepherd etc., who have sacrificed their all, even their own lives, by
keeping the wolf at bay from those timid creatures.

The problem however was a national one, and in October 1915, the first steps
were taken towards introducing conscription.   Lord Derby introduced his
National Register of all unmarried men between the ages of 18 and 41, who
were obliged to register and await call up. Across the land, local tribunals were
created to adjudicate on whether or not men could be exempted from military
service. The first reference to the formation of such a tribunal in Belford is in
the *Advertiser* of 5th November when the membership is given as Mr. A. F.
Nicholl, Adderstone Grange; Colonel Marshall, Anton's Hill; Mr. James Clark,
Belford; Mr. G. D. Atkinson-Clark, Belford Hall; Rev. W. A. McGonigle,
Ellingham; Mr. J. Davidson, Seahouses; and Mr. T. A. Hogg, Detchant.

Concern for the welfare of those already serving was another recurring theme.
As the first soldiers returned home on leave, they heightened awareness of the
troops' medical needs. In July, the Young Women's Christian Association, who
met regularly in the Ferguson Hall, held a collection to raise funds for a motor
ambulance for the Expeditionary Force, and raised £6. 17s. 6d. In October a
house-to-house collection for the Red Cross raised over £13. Mrs Scott, of
Newton House, Christon Bank, launched an appeal for comforts for the troops.

The garments most required are flannel shirts, undervests, pants, socks, mufflers, jerseys, and mitts or gloves. The socks should be of thick wool, and the mufflers and mitts must be khaki in colour....If cigarettes, chocolates, soap etc., are enclosed in the parcels, it is particularly requested that they are not sewn up in the socks.

A later letter from her husband in the *Advertiser*, however, suggests that this appeal had only limited success. Perhaps, then as now, there was a feeling that the army should see its soldiers were properly equipped, or perhaps the Northumbrians preferred to keep their charity more local. The *Advertiser* for 29th October refers to a parcel sent by the Local Comforts Fund, organised by Mr. Brand, the Bank Manager, and Mr. Clothier, the head of the Presbyterian School. In December, Christmas parcels were sent to the local men at the front. Each parcel contained a towel, mitts, socks, a bread loaf, shortbread, chocolate, ham and tablet tea.

The year ended with the arrival of a Company of the Northern Cyclists Battalion to take up billets in Belford. They were divided between the Ferguson Hall and the ballroom of the Blue Bell – while their cooking was done at the Old Black Bull Hotel on the High Street, midway between the two.

Gallipoli

While the allied armies were becoming increasingly bogged down on the Western Front in 1915, Winston Churchill, then first Lord of the Admiralty, came up with a scheme to open up a second theatre of war at the Dardanelles, the narrow straits which controlled the entrance to the Black Sea. The passage

Landing Beach at Gallipoli

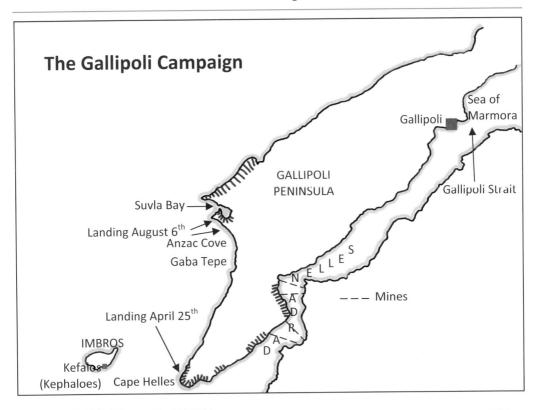

The Gallipoli Campaign

Sea of Marmora

Gallipoli

Gallipoli Strait

GALLIPOLI PENINSULA

Suvla Bay

Landing August 6th

Anzac Cove

Gaba Tepe

N E L L E S

D A R D A N E L L E S

– – – Mines

Landing April 25th

IMBROS

Kefalos (Kephaloes)

Cape Helles

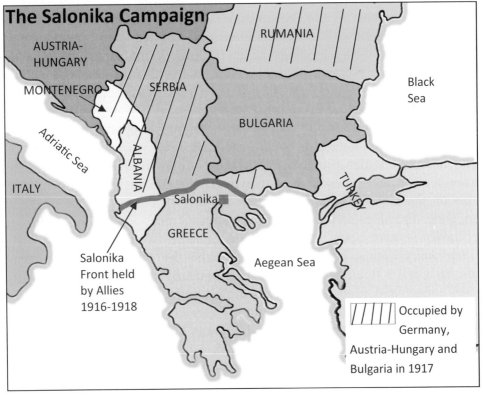

The Salonika Campaign

AUSTRIA-HUNGARY

RUMANIA

MONTENEGRO

SERBIA

Black Sea

Adriatic Sea

ALBANIA

BULGARIA

ITALY

TURKEY

Salonika

GREECE

Aegean Sea

Salonika Front held by Allies 1916-1918

Occupied by Germany, Austria-Hungary and Bulgaria in 1917

was controlled by Turkey, one of Germany's allies, thus preventing supplies reaching southern Russia. The Russians too were coming under increasing pressure from both German and Turkish attacks. The capture of the Dardanelles would damage Turkey, strengthen Russia and hopefully prove a distraction for Germany. Plans were made for a combined naval and military attack, strongly supported by Australian and New Zealand forces.

An initial attempt by the navy in March 1915 to put the Turkish guns out of action failed when the battleships fell victim to undetected mines. The plans for army landings were hindered by the lack of adequate maps. When, on 25th April, the first British troops were landed on the Gallipoli peninsula at Cape Helles, they were mown down by Turkish gunfire before they could get across the beach. They were followed by the ANZAC forces at Gaba Tepe, later called Anzac Cove. Although some of both forces succeeded in climbing the cliffs and getting off the beaches, they were unable to make any further progress against the Turkish army, and, as on the Western Front, there was stalemate.

In August, 1915 it was decided to reinforce the troops with a new landing at Suvla Bay. The plan was for the existing men to create a diversionary action, making renewed attacks on the cliffs above Cape Helles, while fresh troops were landed further north on the peninsula. The existing British and ANZAC troops did their best and some succeeded in gaining the heights above the beachhead. The cost in life, however, was horrific. In one attack 4,000 men were lost, and in another 435 of the 450 men of the Australian Light Horse were killed. The Suvla Bay landings achieved little. Commanded by an elderly general who had never seen battle service and with inexperienced volunteer troops, the odds were stacked against them. Although the landing was carried out successfully, a lack of effective leadership meant that no further action was taken for two days, in which time the Turks had ample opportunity to reinforce their lines. Yet another stalemate. Sickness, too, was taking its toll, with dysentery a particular problem. With the coming of the winter weather in November, the decision was taken to evacuate the troops. The main withdrawal began on the 13th of December, and by the 9th of January the last of the men were gone. The allies had lost some 252 thousand men. Five of the Belford men are known to have been involved in this debacle. William Turnbull and his brother Joseph, sons of the Turnbulls who for many years had run the Stationer's and a Butcher's in Belford, had enlisted in the Royal Field Artillery on 28th June, and found themselves almost immediately shipped out to the Dardanelles. They landed there on the 8th October. Three weeks later, on the 22nd, in the area of Anzac Cove, William was hit and killed by a stray shell, while his brother was beside him. Joseph Langford, a regular with the 2nd Northumbrian Fusiliers was sent out to the Dardanelles after the Battle of Loos.

He was wounded three times at Gallipoli, and evacuated to Egypt to recover. John Gilhome of Mousen had enlisted in the Royal Naval Reserves in 1915, and after training was also sent to the Dardanelles. The newspaper account states that *the nature of the duties he had to perform there being too much for him, he became ill and was sent to hospital in Malta, and after a while over to Gosport in England, from whence he was discharged as being unfit for Naval duties.*

John Harvey (Elwick) went out with the 6th East Yorkshires in 1915, but caught pneumonia the following winter and died at Keppaloes Hospital on the Island of Imbros on 23rd January 1916. Another casualty was a Bamburgh lad, Phillip Hall, who had emigrated to Australia in 1912, but almost as soon as war was declared, had enlisted in the 16th Battalion, the Australian Imperial Force, and arrived at Gallipoli with the other ANZAC troops. He must have been badly wounded in the initial landings, as he died from his injuries in hospital in Alexandria on the 16th of May.

1916

At the beginning of the new year, the 7th Northumberlands were fighting just south of Ypres, spending four days in the trenches and four in reserve. On February 3rd they once more took up support positions near Dickesbusch. Ironically, it was then that Richard Pringle of Lowick was killed. The events leading up to his death were described in a letter sent to his parents by his commanding officer, and published in the *Advertiser* of 18th February.

Dear Sir,

I am told that you are the father of Private Pringle of 'C' Company, 7th Northumberland Fusiliers and I am writing as the grenade officer of this regiment, to send you my sympathy and condolences on the sad tragedy that happened yesterday afternoon. You know of course that your son was one of the Battalion bomb-throwers, and that he was of great service to his regiment as a bomb-thrower. It is not a duty that everyone is fitted to take up, only the best and the most resolute of the regiment being chosen as bombers. He was detailed yesterday afternoon to go to the Brigade bomb store and prepare some bombs for use. While working there the store was shelled by the Germans and although he was behind a barricade at the time, your lad was struck by the last shell fired. He died almost at once, and I hope painlessly. A little later I went to see what had happened and it occurred to me that you might like to have a button off your lad's tunic that he was wearing at the time. I am sending it to you now. Pray accept my sympathy for your loss. We too have lost a life that we could ill spare.

Yours sincerely

Francis Buckley.

This was the beginning of a spell of bad luck for the Belford area contingent. The Scotsman, David McNichol was killed the following day, and a week later, Sergeant Harry Hill from Belford Station was one of five men killed near Sanctuary Wood, just after the 7th Battalion moved into the trenches

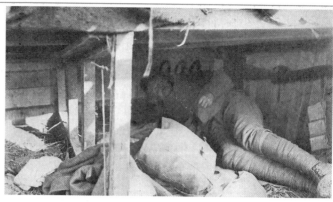

Trench dugout

there on the 12th of February. He had just checked out the condition of the trenches, reporting to his commanding officer *There are plenty of dugouts for the men here, Sir!* when he was killed by the blast from a shell exploding nearby. Other Belford casualties were Corporal Herbert Clark of Belford Station, Private George Graham from the High Street and Sergeant Ford from Twizell, all wounded during February. The third of the Leather brothers, Major Ernest Leather, was killed on the 10th of February in a separate action near Armentieres.

From February until the end of June, the 7th Battalion remained in reserve in the same area, providing support and relief as required. Although, on occasions, they came under heavy shell fire in the trenches, there were no major battles. George Morton, Belford's long serving postman, became seriously ill in April, possibly as a result of the *constant snow and frost* recorded in the War Diary for March, and had to be invalided home. Three of the Belford lads were wounded up to the end of May – John Jeffrey, previously of the Black Bull, Joseph Dingle from North Bank, James Wealleans, the gardener from Newlands. On the 25th of May, Ernest Currins (High Street) was killed by a trench mortar, only a week after he had returned from home leave. In writing to his parents, his Captain described him as *a sterling soldier,...one of their best range finders, and a handy man at anything connected with Machine guns.*

When the Battalion returned to the trenches on the 5th of June after a period in reserve, Robert White of Fenham was among the wounded. As the month progressed and it became increasingly clear to the Germans that the Allies were planning a new attack, tensions and the level of enemy fire increased. On 30th June, John Harvey from Smeafield Station was killed by a piece of shell alongside two officers. That this was not yet part of a full scale battle can be presumed from the account of his burial contained in a letter to his parents from the regimental chaplain:

His body was laid to rest on Saturday evening and a number of the officers and men, including Colonel Jackson, were present at the graveside. In addition to the burial service we had the hymn 'Now the labourer's task is o'er'....The Laiterie Cemetery, where he lies, is beautifully kept, and the

Battlefield graveyard

graves are planted with flowers. His own grave has been marked with a permanent wooded cross with a suitable inscription, which has been erected by the battalion.

If the first part of the year had been comparatively quiet, all this was about to change. In February 1916, the Germans had launched a major attack on the French city of Verdun, in the hope that they could force France out of the war before the British troops were fully reinforced from home. The French defended bravely, but it was clear that if they were to continue to hold the city, another assault was needed to distract the Germans. The decision was taken to launch a major attack on the German positions on the Somme at the beginning of July. The plan was to destroy the German positions and artillery by 5 days massive bombardment, before launching the attack at 7.30 a.m. on 1st July. In the event, there were two serious drawbacks to the plan - the long bombardment gave the Germans good warning of the impending attack, and they had already constructed very deep bunkers which survived the artillery onslaught. Throughout the first month of the attack, the 7th Northumberlands remained mainly in reserve, but the Tyneside Scottish Regiments, which also contained men who had begun their lives in Belford, stationed at Albert, were at the very centre of the attack, their objective being to capture La Boiselle, and continue along the ridge to Pozières. The plan was for the men, spaced at 2 pace-intervals, to attack in lines, the second line following when the first had advanced 150 yards, with the third and fourth following after similar intervals. The war diary of the 4th Battalion Tyneside Scottish records what happened:

Each line immediately it advanced to and over the front line came under a very heavy fire from the German Artillery and Machine Guns firing from the direction of Obillers and La Boiselle. Heavy casualties were at once incurred; many men of our first line even being hit whilst getting over the parapet. Each Company was played into No Man's Land by its piper who continued to play until either killed or wounded. Each line advanced without the least hesitation, and through and across No Man's Land. The Battalion suffered very heavily indeed in all ranks, the losses principally to the Machine Gun fire......

The German First Line was taken and the 2 (sic) *line was also reached, but owing to the heavy casualties it was impossible to hold on to these lines. A party of our men hung on for a time on to a portion of their front line trench, a little to the north of the Albert – Bapaume road. The Germans, however, launched a very strong counter attack against this party who fought gallantly but owing to being greatly outnumbered were obliged to fall back and take cover in No Man's Land where they lay all day and waited, ready to go forward again with the next attacking force. As dusk came in and as no further attack was to be made that day, these men under cover of darkness made their way back into our lines in an exhausted condition through the want of food and water and remained there until the following morning......Our stretcher bearers were conspicuous by their daring in bringing in wounded men in daylight under fire. The dressing station and the trenches near were soon congested with casualties, and only by continually and very exhausting work by Capt. J. W. Muirhead, our M.O. and his staff were they able to gradually relieve this pressure which was not until the following day.*

July 2: at 9 o'clock in the morning after all the men in the Battalion had been collected, they were formed up..... for a roll call to be taken and only about 100 men answered their names. During the course of the day about 20 men turned up.

Only two officers survived to attend the roll call.

In the first forty-eight hours of the attack, four men with Belford origins were killed, J. S. Jobson, T. H. Logan and A. A. Richardson, all with the Tyneside Scottish, and John Watson with the Royal Garrison Artillery. The final count for the whole of the first day of the Battle of the Somme was 19,240 dead, 35,493 wounded, 2,152 missing and 585 captured. Despite these tremendous losses, the attempt to push the Germans back went on, though gains continued to be small, and at great cost. On the 14th, Mametz Wood was taken after a bitter struggle. Among the dead on this occasion were Lance Corporal Joseph Langford, back to the Western Front after recovering from his Gallipoli wounds, and John Jeffrey, formerly of the Black Bull. Jeffrey died, having volunteered to go to a listening post, while the trench was under heavy bombardment.

The struggle continued through the fine summer weather, when the discomfort of the soldiers was increased by the heat, flies, maggots and rats who flourished on the shattered flesh which littered the battlefields. August was a quieter month as the army generals struggled to come to terms with the disaster which had befallen them. A new attack was planned for the 15th of September. Before then, however, yet more sad news was to reach Belford. Among the Northern Cyclists who had been stationed in Belford at the end of 1915 was James Forrest a young painter and decorator from Gateshead. He had met and fallen in love with Blanche Amos, whose mother ran a general store in the High Street. The pair had been married in St. Mary's Church on 19 June 1916. Every attempt had been made to make it a special day.

As the happy couple left the Church, a number of soldiers (comrades of the bridegroom) fell into line on each side of the path and formed an arch with crossed bayonets, through which they had to pass, and a little further on another soldier with a civilian companion compelled the smiling pair to go through the old fashioned custom of jumping the petting stool, the latter being prettily bedecked with flowers. On reaching the street another surprise awaited the bridal party, for here a band of soldiers were awaiting at the party's motor car, and this they towed to the door of the bride's home.

The couple had time for little more that a honeymoon in Scotland, before James was posted to France, attached to the Machine Gun Section of the Northumberland Fusiliers. On September 4, at Contalmaison, near Albert, he was killed.

On September the 13th, a new general order was issued, encouraging the soldiers to make even greater efforts in the coming attack. It also contained a reference to the arrival of a new weapon. This was the tank, which had been developed at home, in secret, since 1915. There were now two tank companies (60 vehicles) stationed at Abbeville, near the mouth of the Somme. It was with their support that the next offensive was launched on the 15th of the month. The 7th Northumberlands, stationed near Mametz Wood, were among the first regiments to see them in action. Things began well:

At 6.10 a.m. two of our tanks came up from behind. And crossed the assembly trenches at 6.18 a.m. the enemy saw them and at once sent up many red rockets. The enemy's artillery, however, were slow in responding. At 6.20 a.m. our first two lines got away and advanced in splendid order under our barrage. They rushed the first objective with few casualties.... consolidation started at once. Large numbers of German dead and wounded were found in this trench, but very few unwounded prisoners were taken.

But shortly after 7.00 a.m. things were starting to unravel. When the second advance began, the Germans, who still controlled the wood to the right, opened with a barrage of machine gun fire, resulting in some parts of the line losing contact with the main advance. Then the advancing lines came within range of their own artillery fire. Nevertheless, they successfully captured a German

Battery, before they were relieved by the 151st Infantry Brigade. The Territorials had done well, but at a cost, 4 officers and 40 men were killed, 11 officers and 219 men wounded and 74 reported missing, most of whom were never accounted for. Eight of the Belford area men lost their lives in the action, Thomas Anderson (Easington Grange), Robert Hall (West Street), Robert Hunter (West Street), John McDonald (formerly of Ross), James Nesbit, Arthur Sample, and brothers George and William Taylor (Low Middleton). Edward Tait (North Bank) was shot in the shoulder; William Ford (Twizell) was shot in the leg; Joseph Dingle was again wounded, this time in the arm; George Dunlop (the School House, Belford) a stretcher bearer, was also wounded, while his brother, William, was buried alive in the trenches.

As the autumn rains came and the battlefield increasingly resembled a quagmire, the battle gradually ground to a halt, but it was to claim more Belford lives before it was finally declared to be over on the 18th of November. John White from Cragmill died on the 3rd of October, fighting alongside the officer whose orderly he was. Both John and the officer were killed by the same shell. Alexander Rutherford (Low Middleton) serving with the 9th Royal Scots, Machine Gun Section, was badly wounded on the 9th of November, and died in hospital on the 15th. A final push against the German positions at Beaumont Hamel and Bapaume was ordered for the 14th of November. The 7th Northumberlands were at the eastern end of the advance, with orders to capture the high ground overlooking Butte de Warlencourt. Again a good beginning, with the soldiers taking target trenches in the first two hours of the attack, ended in their being trapped by a successful German counter attack. Among the lives lost were those of Lance Corporal John William Athey (Station Cottages, Belford), killed when a shell hit his dugout, Lance Corporal John Gray (Elwick), the second of the Gray sons to die in the war; Corporal George Gilbert Shiell (Middleton Hall), William Taylor (Middleton Farm) and William Anderson (Easington Grange) - the second Anderson son to be killed. Edward Tait, barely recovered from his shoulder wound of September, received shrapnel in his jaw, and John Johnson of West Street was invalided home as a result of his wounds to his thigh, arm and fingers. At the end of the action, one additional line of trenches had been captured by the Northumberlands at Bapaume, and, to the west, Beaumont Hamel was taken. Sometime during this action, Private John Fife, serving with the Northumberlands, volunteered to carry a dispatch for help, when his Company got into difficulties. For his bravery on that occasion, he was awarded the Military Medal.

The overall Battle of the Somme had cost some 600,000 casualties, and only 120 square miles had been captured. Verdun, however, had been saved, and over the winter, the Germans withdrew to a new line of defence.

If the people of Belford had ever doubted the seriousness of the war, 1916 was when it really hit home. Twenty three more men enlisted or were called up to serve in the forces. J. W. Falla returned home with his artificial leg *and can get about wonderfully with the aid of two sticks*. Others were less lucky. Twenty nine men from the area had been lost in battle. Even other events which attracted the attention of the local paper brought the reality of war home:

> *On Monday a party of thirteen wounded soldiers ...passed through Belford on their way to take part in hay-making at Chillingham Castle. They were from Convalescent Camps, and the change from the latter places to a hay-making field will be a great change to them, but not so great as from the thundering of the guns and clashing of the bayonets in the fighting fields of Flanders...*
> Berwick Advertiser 4th August 1916.

As the year ended, the only celebrations noted were festive dinners organised for the Northern Cyclists. On the 28th of December they were treated to a Dinner provided by public subscription, in the Blue Bell Assembly Rooms, which was followed by a sing-song given by the soldiers themselves. On January 2, they were provided with a second festive supper by Mrs. and Miss Freeman of Bellshill house.

1917

The first war death of the new year came at the end of February, when G. W. Young of the Royal Naval Reserve died of pneumonia in the Naval Barracks Hospital, Portsmouth, within a month of enlisting. Before joining up he had been a traveller for his uncle, John Laing, the grocer, and had also played a prominent part in village life, so his death came as a great shock to the area.

Although the 7th Northumberlands did spend some time in the trenches in the early months of the year, wintry conditions prevented serious fighting, and, with the coming of the thaw in February, mud was a greater problem than enemy bullets or shells. Two of the Belford lads are recorded as being wounded in March, J. Hunter (West Horton) and J Elliott (the Tollgate). During this period the Regiment moved north from the Somme to Arras in preparation for a new offensive. Things looked more hopeful from the British point of view. They had far more munitions and tanks than at the start of the previous year. Six new divisions of men were shipped out between January and March 1917. The plan was for the British and Canadian forces to attack across a thirty mile front from Vimy Ridge to Cambrai, while the French attacked from the south. The assault began on the 9th of April, and met with some immediate success, the Canadians successfully took Vimy Ridge, and under General Allenby the British forces succeeded in pushing the Germans back up to five miles in some areas. Bad weather, however, created problems for the tanks, with the result that some of the infantry forces overtook them, and then found themselves in their own firing line. On 12th April, in the midst of a snowstorm, Allenby threw a cavalry charge into the mix. It was a total disaster. Allan Lloyd's book *The War in the Trenches*, quotes a description of it by one of the soldiers there:

It may have been a fine sight, but it was a wicked waste of men and horses, for the enemy immediately opened on them a hurricane of every kind of missile. If the cavalry advanced through us at a trot or canter, they came back at a gallop, including dismounted men and riderless horses....

They left numbers of dead and wounded among us, but the horses seemed to have suffered most, and for a while after we put bullets into poor brutes that were aimlessly limping about on three legs, or careering madly in their agony like one I saw with the whole of its muzzle blown away.

This further disaster resulted in Haig ordering a halt to the main advance, although some fighting continued until the end of the month at the north of the front. On 17th April, the 7th Northumberlands distinguished themselves with the recapture of Wancourt Tower, the only point on the ridge from which the enemy could see both north and south, and also succeeded in gaining information on the German trench positions. In the actions at Arras, four Belford lads were wounded, John Aitchison (Easington), Norman Fisher (Mousen), John Moffat (Easington Grange) and Andrew Tully – Tully serving with the Durham Light Infantry was wounded on the 9/10th of April during the successful capture of one of the German front line trenches. Alfred Wyllie (Kettleburn), serving with the Royal Scots was killed, and Robert Wilson, the third of James Wilson's sons, died of the wounds he had sustained in the action.

In the weeks that followed, there was a mutiny in the French Army, so, for the first time, Field Marshal Haig had an opportunity to plan an independent attack against the Germans. He chose to concentrate his efforts in Flanders, close to his own supply lines from Britain, and where he hoped a break-through would allow him to take back the Belgian Ports and attack the German lines from the north. For more than a year, from over a mile distance, special troops of the Australian, British, Canadian and New Zealand forces had been tunnelling towards the German lines. When the lines were reached, mines were laid between 50 and 100 feet below the enemy in 21 different tunnels. On 7th June, at 3.10 a.m., the mines were detonated. The shock, as of an earthquake, was felt even in England, the largest non-nuclear explosion ever contrived. The Messines Ridge was taken and the front line moved significantly further east. For once there was some good news to be reported back home. The 7th Northumberlands were not directly involved in this action, so there were fewer casualties, John Graham (High Street) got a bullet wound in his foot, but James Thompson (Spindleston) died in the lead up to this action in May, and Gunner

Eddie Hall (High Street) was killed by a shell explosion in its aftermath, on the 23rd of June. This news reached his parents the day after they had received confirmation that his eldest brother Robert, missing since September 1916, was now presumed dead!

May brought the village a number of distractions from bad war news. There was the celebration of the Reverend John Millar's twenty five years' service as minister of the Presbyterian Church. Not only was Rev. Millar presented with a 'case of treasury notes', but Mrs. Millar was given a piano. There was also the very pleasing news that Edward Fenwick (the Kennels, Middleton) had been awarded the Military Medal for *conspicuous bravery in repairing telephone wires under heavy shell and machine gun fire.* Then on Whit Monday, the Northern Cyclists held a 'Grand Military Sports' on the cricket field, an event which attracted many spectators.

In July 1917, Annie Fairgrieve of West Street joined the Women's Army Auxiliary Corps and after a short spell of training, sailed with 19 others for France on 15 August. She arrived at the WAAC headquarters in Abbeville the following day, where she was assigned to work as an orderly at 20/- per week. Annie is one of only four women from Belford who are named as serving overseas during the First World War. Gladys Currins (High Street), joined the WAAC in 1917 and served in France, but no details have survived of the work she did, while two of the Harvey girls (Smeafield Farm) nursed in France.

About the same time, young Willie McDonald, youngest son of Dr. James McDonald received a birthday letter from his big brother John, fighting in France. After asking how things were at home, John provided a little insight in to trench life in the summer of 1917:

> *You will miss the car this fine weather, but you will always find some way to fill time. Is your cattie still to the fore and have you felled any more jackies? How about the two rats in the stable? You should see them out here playing hide and seek in the dugouts. We have good sport chasing them, but now I have a sort of fellow feeling for them, as we usually spend most of the day in holes in the ground. You should see the men creeping into their foxholes. This life would suit you I think without a lie. We never take our clothes off so that saves you the trouble of putting them on again. Besides we only wash when we can get water, so you would have some nearly as bad as yourself* (the next few words are unclear due to crease where the letter is folded) *you would not be conspicuous. Well we are moving up the line tonight again, so excuse more. Lets hear how you are fettling now and again and get Mary to write too.*
>
> *With love and kisses to all from your loving brother John*

Bad news   reached the village at the end of July, when it was learned that
William Clothier, the popular headmaster of the Presbyterian School, who had
been called up in October 1916, had been   killed on the 23rd/24th of July 1917
near Ypres. His loss was widely felt, both in terms of his influence on the young
folk he had taught, but also because he had contributed to the life of the village
as a whole, and, before his own call up, had been one of the organisers of the
Comfort Parcels for the troops.

At the end of September, there was a move within Belford to try and re-
establish some semblance of pre-war normality. The last weekend in the month
had been when the Belford Feast was held. It was not thought appropriate to
hold this, nor was there much point in trying to have the adult races which had
been the feature of the Monday after the Feast. It was decided, however, to
organise the traditional children's sports on the Tuesday, to the considerable
enjoyment of both the young people and their parents.

Meanwhile, in France the successes at Messines Ridge, had been overtaken by
the horror of Passchendaele.   Haig had insisted on pushing forward into
Flanders over land which had originally been reclaimed from the sea. Torrential
rain and the military strategy of bombarding the ground before an attack to take
out enemy artillery, had the effect of turning the whole battlefield into a
quagmire. The troops and the tanks became literally bogged down, with many
men and horses drowning in the mud:
  We fell into mud and writhed out like wasps crawling in rotten plums.

Passchendaele

The first of the Belford casualties was Rifleman J. W. Renton (Hazelrigg Mill), killed on August 3rd. At the end of August, a change of General brought a pause in the fighting while the situation was reassessed, but it, and the rain began again at the end of September. Captain Harold Brunskill was killed on the 29th. He had been the officer commanding the Northern Cyclists in Belford, and had been very successful in ensuring that his men contributed to Belford while they were stationed there. Indeed he had only gone out to the Front early in August. Again it was a loss felt by the whole village. In early October, Ernest Falla (North Bank), John Gibson (Fenwick Steads) and James Lee (West Street) were killed. Heavier losses came towards the end of the month. The 7th Northumberlands moved to the front line on the 24th. The main attack was scheduled for the 26th.

It proved to be an attack across a swamp against a strong line of unbroken pill-boxes, and the rain came down unceasingly. As a result the brigade lost over 1,000 casualties without being able to retain any of the ground they gained. As to the battalion, all the officers (save one) and over 100 men of those who took part in the assault were killed.

Among those who died with the Northumberlands were George Matthewson (Chesterhill) and Samuel Sanderson (Chillingham Barns). John McDougall, (Buckton) serving with the Durham Light Infantry was also killed, as was William Hall, brother of Phillip, formerly of Bamburgh, but now fighting with the Australians. The Northumberlands were relieved at midnight, and moved back to camp, only to be bombed there by an enemy aircraft. Captain Robert Neville M.C., who, prior to the outbreak of war, had been Instructor to the Belford Volunteer Company was killed, as was John Fife M.M. (Twizell Mill). Passchendaele itself was finally taken by the Canadians on the 6th of November, and the Battle declared over on the 15th of November although fighting continued throughout the month. The action saw two Belford men gaining the Military Cross. The news of Second Lieutenant William Hall's (High Street) award originally appeared in the Advertiser for 16th November, although it was not formally gazetted until 17th May 1918.

For conspicuous gallantry and devotion to duty. He displayed great courage in hand-to-hand fighting in an attack, personally killing many of the enemy, and led his platoon to their objective. Throughout many hours' fighting he rendered his battalion valuable service.

At the very end of the month, John R. McDonald, the second son of Dr. James McDonald, of the Villa, found himself fighting with the Border Regiment at Houlthulst Forest at the north of the Battle Line.

During a raid on the enemy line he attacked a post, accounted for eleven of the enemy, and brought back a prisoner, obtaining valuable information. He

showed marked courage,
coolness and initiative.
London Gazette Military Cross Citation
22.4.1918.

He was wounded on 25th November. It seems likely that the event described happened on that day. Overall cost of the campaign had been horrendous. It was not just the loss of life, but the great damage done to the morale of the soldiers fighting there, and the feeling on the part of many that the mistakes of the early years of the war were simply being repeated.

Houlthulst Forest

The Battle of Cambrai, launched by the British on 20th of November, was the first sign that an alternative approach to fighting might bring success. For the first time, the tanks were to be used as the main fighting machine rather than an adjunct to infantry attacks. It was immensely successful – across a six mile front, the army had advanced three to four miles against the strongest part of the German line; two Divisions of the German army were destroyed and thousands of prisoners taken together with much artillery. Church bells across England were rung to celebrate the victory. Again, however, it proved difficult to sustain the momentum. The tanks were not yet totally reliable and required much maintenance, and after so many reversals, the battalions were over-cautious. On the 30th, the Germans launched a counter attack which succeeded in taking ground to the south of the Cambrai line, but the British had held on to most of their gains when the fighting came to an end on December 3rd. If Cambrai had not been a complete success, nevertheless it had convinced the sceptics that tanks were the way forward. We know of two Belford men involved in this Battle, Reginald Rogers (Post Office) fighting with the Naval Volunteer Reserve and Sapper Percy Young (Ross Farm).

December was spent by the Northumberlands providing working parties for the light railways at St. Jean, before going into billets at Ypres. They returned to the front line at Passchendaele on the 28th, and were successful in repelling a German patrol and taking its officer prisoner.

1918

As in previous years, the winter weather did not lend itself to fighting, and in

January and February the 7th Northumberland Fusiliers were transported round Flanders, mainly deployed in working parties of various types. At the beginning of March, as a result of all the losses suffered, the Battalion was reorganised, and the original 'C' Company, the Belford Company, was broken up, which must have been hard for some of the men. At home, advantage was taken of Edward Fenwick's 14 days leave from France to recognise his achievement in gaining the Military Medal. A collection was organised in the area, and, on January 3rd, a presentation was held in the Assembly rooms of the Blue Bell during which he was presented with a gold watch by Mr. Coates of Middleton. The formal ceremony was followed by music and songs.

Over the winter, the situation in Europe changed dramatically. In 1917, following the Revolution, Russia had made peace with Germany, thus releasing more German and Austrian forces to fight on the Western Front and against Italy. At the outbreak of war Italy had been neutral, but had come in on the Allied side in 1915, fighting a series of eleven battles against the Austrians along the line of the Isonzo river. On October 24th 1917, however, the Austrians won a decisive victory at Caporetto, and it looked as if the Italian war effort would collapse. British and French troops were rushed to Italy to halt the Austrian advance. Among those who went were William Morton (West Street), Jack Bryson (Spindlestone), D. B. Clarke (West Mains Lodge, Beal) and the recently commissioned Second Lieutenant William Hall M.C. For three of them it did not prove a fortunate posting. In February 1918, Clark, with others, was sent to claim part of a trench when it was blown in by a shell, killing one of the group and wounding the others; he received a hole through his left leg about four inches above the ankle. About six months after arriving, in May 1918, Hall's horse stumbled on rough ground and William broke his leg, effectively ending the war for him, as he was invalided home. Bryson received gun shot wounds to the right leg and knee and was hospitalised late in October 1918.

When, on 21st March, fighting began in earnest again on the Western Front, it was the Germans who launched a major counter attack, pushing the allied lines back and getting to within 40 miles of Paris. The German advance continued until June. Robert Bertram (Elford) and Edmund Henry (Plantation Farm) were captured in March, and John Dick, fighting with the King's Own Scottish Borderers, in April/May was both badly wounded and captured, probably during fighting at Kemmel village. William Hood (Outchester), Joseph Hall (West Hall), and William Hogg, fighting with the 15th Battalion Durham Light Infantry, were killed in March, George Dunlop (School House), Ted Brown (Chillingham) and William Smith (West Kyloe) in April, and on the 30th May Tom Rogers (The Neuk) was captured, dying of his wounds a month later in a Bavarian Field Hospital. A significant number of the Belford area lads suffered in the fighting: James Dickinson (Old Lyham), Joseph Marsh (High Street) and William Rutherford (Low Middleton) were gassed; William Brown (Beal Farm), Robert Clark (Ross Farm), Joseph Ross (High Street) and Thomas Young (West Street) were invalided home, while lesser injuries were sustained by James Elliott (Tollgate), John Graham (High Street), 'Tot' Morton (West Street), William Purvis (Fenham-le-Moor), Andrew and Robert Robson (Fenwick Steads), Joseph Ross and Thomas Ryan (West Street).

It was not all bad news for the Belford Area, however. April brought word that Andrew Younger, Beal Farm, had been awarded the Military Medal for bravery in the field. For the first time, significant numbers of soldiers were returning to the village on home leave. On 31st May, John R McDonald received his Military Cross from King George V, during his visit to Leeds. On 17th June, William Dunlop, who after being buried alive in the trenches in 1916, was transferred to take charge of vital road construction work, was awarded a Meritorious Service Medal. Other events, too, provided pleasant distractions – the Northern Cyclists organised a concert party in the West Street Hall in March, and in August, the Lancashire Volunteer Regiment, stationed in

Troops involved in road construction work

the village, both organised a concert and laid on a social evening, providing free entertainment and supper for the villagers as a 'thank you' for the kindness and hospitality they had received.

By the end of June, the German attack was exhausted. On the other hand, the allies were now being strengthened by the ever increasing numbers of American soldiers arriving in Europe, following the U.S.A.'s declaration of war on Germany in April 1917. The French began a successful counter offensive on the south of the line, on 18th July, supported by the U.S. 1st and 2nd Divisions. On 8th August the British, Canadian and Australian forces launched a successful attack to the east of Amiens pushing the German line back 8 to 9 miles. A second push east of Arras began on 21st August with the allies recapturing the places over which they had fought so bitterly earlier in the war – Albert, Thiepval, Mametz Wood and Bapaume.   In this fighting, Thomas Hunter

(Bricksheds) was killed at Ypres, and John Taylor (Whitelee) at St. Leger; Driver John T. Moffat (Easington Grange) was wounded. As the British army pushed forward, the 7th Northumberlands were assigned the key task of repairing the roads and bridges in their wake, to ensure that reinforcements and supplies could get through. This too had its dangers, not least from unexploded mines. Andrew Dumma, John Johnson and Edward Fenwick were all wounded, Edward Fenwick losing both his feet. The following month brought the death of Robert Younger, fighting with the South Staffordshires, John Thompson (Bradford) fighting with the East Yorkshires, and James Thompson (Hoppen) – the second Thompson son to die, the gassing of Robert Cuthbert (High Street), the wounding of W. G. Haddon (North Lodge) and Andrew Tully, and the capture of Robert Dunlop (Waren Mill).

At the end of September, the allies made a united assault on the entire German line; although this was successful with the British army creating a six mile break in the German defences, it was not without its costs. October brought a significant amount of bad news to the village. Andrew English (Plantation Farm) was killed as was George Hope (Outchester) fighting near Landrecies, and William Hall (Lowick). Hall, who had only gone out to France in September, was seriously wounded in action exactly a month later, receiving injuries to his face, arms and legs. He was invalided home and died of his wounds in Southampton hospital on 29th October. Reginald Rogers (Post Office) also died from wounds received in action on 9th October, fighting near Bapaume. His mother, the telegraphist at the post office, had the dreadful experience of taking down the telegram announcing her son's death. John Mather (Bridge Farm Beal) was admitted to the military hospital in Rouen in October, and died there on 2nd November. Other wounded were W. G. Haddon (North Lodge) for a second time, and John Grey, Belford Station.

At the same time as the allies were pushing the Germans back on the Western Front, a push north from Salonika in Greece, drove Germany's ally, Bulgaria out of the war, adding to the pressure on Germany. The British troops had been sent first to Salonika in October 1915 to help the Serbs who were being attacked by the Bulgarians. By the time the forces arrived, however, the Serbs were already beaten. Nevertheless it was decided to maintain a British force on Greek soil. In 1916, the army was mainly involved in securing its own position through the building of a series of defences. In 1917, however, having been reinforced by additional international units, they began a successful counter offensive against the Bulgarians. The final attack began in July 1918 and in September Bulgaria surrendered unconditionally. Although much less famous than the war on the Western Front, it was nevertheless an important field of action and one in which several Belford men served with honour. J. Bertram

Ruins near the harbour at Salonika

(Elford) and James Crammond (Kyloe Cottage, Beal) went out with the Royal Engineers. Bertram returned, but tragically, Crammond caught pneumonia in November 1918, and died there two and a half weeks after the Armistice was declared. George Turnbull (Sandyfords) sailed for Salonika in August 1916 as part of the Machine Gun Corps, and remained there for the remainder of the war, being recommended for, and awarded a Military Medal for bravery in the autumn of 1917.

Another theatre of war which is often ignored is that of Egypt. Officially Egypt remained part of the Turkish Ottoman Empire, and Turkey had entered the war on Germany's side. Since the late nineteenth century, however, Britain had had a strong presence in Egypt, and was determined to use it as a base from which to attack Turkey. She declared Egypt a British Protectorate in 1914. It was used as a base for attacks against Turkey, but the British army also was involved in fighting Muslim nationalists who objected to European interference in the Middle East. A number of the Belford men served in Egypt between 1915 and 1918. They included David Elliott, the School Board Officer, Ralph Greshon (Buckton), Joseph Langford (West Street) and David McDonald, Dr. James's eldest son.

The former gamekeeper, Andrew Tully, twice decorated with the Military Medal for bravery by the British, and once with the Medaille Militaire by the French, seems to have had the distinction of being the last Belford man to be wounded before the Armistice, being injured in the hand, just before hostilities ceased on 11th November.

Threatened by mutiny and running out of supplies at home, the Germans had opened negotiations for an end to fighting at the end of September 1918, but it was not until the 11th hour of the 11th day of the 11th month of 1918, that the Armistice was declared. For the men who had survived the fighting, that it was all over was a strange sensation. The feeling is well expressed in some notes from the 9th Battalion Northumberland Fusiliers quoted in *The St. George's Gazette* 30 November 1918:

It is the finish. The last situation wire has sped along the cables of the world and the wording thereof is good to hear 'Final objectives gained'.....
And it is very hard to realise. It is like the sounding of the 'Full Time' whistle when one pauses uncertainly for a moment before turning to leave the field. But nevertheless it is true. We shall never again stand in the chilly, misty dawn waiting for the flash across the skies – the long rumbling roar –the sudden barking crash as the barrage opens. A final hitch to our equipment, a slithering scramble up and out – and another wave of FUSILIERS making forward to "take over" from the Boche. Nor again shall we know the old familiar scenes in the after hours when the gunners have slackened off and the German panic lights have ceased to amuse, when little parties of prisoners trickle along the roads and stretcher bearers wend a slow way back among new shell holes, where the risk of cordite still lurks.
So does it all pass into the land of yesterday, beyond our sight, our hearing, but never beyond our memory.
But to my mind it was all very neatly summed up by Geordie when he said to a pal, 'Aa aalways telt thoo we'd be gettin' a bit rest afore lang'.

At home in Belford, the end of the war was greeted not with great celebrations, the cost had been too high for that, but Thanksgiving Services were held both in St. Mary's Parish Church and in the Presbyterian Church.

In the weeks and months that followed, gradually the men from the village returned home. One of the first to return permanently was Joe Scrowther, who had been a German prisoner since September 1914. He brought with him grim tales of the early days after his capture when he had been glad to make a meal of potato peelings and a fish's head, and had been threatened with death simply for being a 'Tommy', although he said that conditions had improved after that. Another prisoner to return was Edmund Henry, who had been made to work as a platelayer on the railway until his health failed; he too had stories of dreadful food – cooked cabbage and mangolds, ground barley made into porridge and cooked hedgehog. The end of the war did not mean the end of the war deaths – on 13th February 1919, Thomas Collins (West Street) died from illness contracted on the Western Front in early 1918.

In 1919, on the anniversary of the outbreak of the war, there were celebrations nationally, and Belford was no exception. There was a series of events on the

Belford Peace Celebrations 19th July 1919
Courtesy of Sue Dyer

19th of July, which included local girls dressing up in the national costumes of all the allies. It was decided to hold a dinner for the returned soldiers on August 1st.

PEACE CELEBRATIONS.

The Inhabitants of Belford and District
request the honour of

Mr J. L. McDonald

company at a Dinner to be given at the Malt-
ings, Belford, on Aug. 1st, 1919, at 7.30 p.m.

The favour of your reply on enclosed card by the 22nd inst., is requested.

Courtesy of Alison McDonald

This was followed on the 16th of August by a grand Sports Day, organised by the Comrades of the Great War. The event was described in the following week's *Berwick Advertiser*.

> *The weather being delightful, and that coupled with the fact that many of the competitors were expected to be lads who had lived for periods of various duration in hourly danger of meeting death on the battlefield was the means of attracting a very large, representative and interested company to the field. In fact a number approximating one thousand paid for admittance at the gate. There were very large entries for the most important events, such as the Handicap Race, Tug-of-War, Pillow Fight, Stepping the Chain, etc. Each item was most keenly contested and evoked a great deal of enthusiasm. It would be unfair; in fact it is impossible to say which event was the most popular.*

> *The Ashington Brass Band was in attendance and enhanced the enjoyment of the afternoon's proceedings, which were throughout most eminently successful. About £44 was taken at the gate. In the evening a dance was held in the Malting, and was largely attended, somewhere about 175 couples having paid for admission. The music was supplied by Miss Ella Clark, Mr E. Duncan, and the Messrs Bell. The hour of midnight was drawing near when the merry party broke up and wended its way homeward, some of it not a little wearied with the excess of pleasure and excitement.*

One of the main concerns for the village, however, was how to commemorate the men who had lost their lives in the war. Colonel Gerard Leather of Middleton Hall, who had himself served as a Staff Officer in France, had lost three brothers in the war and seen a fourth wounded, took the lead in ensuring that a fit memorial was created. In January 1919, a Committee was formed to carry the matter forward, and while a number of projects, including a cottage hospital and a scholarship, were considered, it was agreed to create a memorial hall or institute. In support of this the squire gave to the committee the West Street Hall and such adjoining land as was necessary for the memorial. The committee then put their minds to fund raising so that the hall could be enlarged and adapted for the holding of meetings, entertainments etc. It was decided to seek subscriptions, but also to organise a series of fund raising events. The first of these was a Whist Drive and Dance held in March, where the musicians, the Scott brothers of Amerside Law gave their services free, and refreshments and prizes were also donated.

The War Memorial itself was designed by Mr. S. H. Lawson of the Newcastle Architects, Simpson and Lawson and was executed by William Tully. It was formally unveiled on the 22nd of March 1922. It was attended by the relatives of the fallen, given places to the right of the memorial, and a procession which included the schoolchildren, cubs and scouts, the officiating clergy, the choir, representatives of the Nursing Association, the Red Cross, the Parish and District Council and the British Legion paraded to West Street from the Ferguson Hall. Joseph Ross acted as marshal for the procession, and William Hall M.C. and Captain Ferguson D.S.O. flanked the memorial itself. The dedication service began at 3.00 p.m. with the hymn, 'O God our help in ages past'. Dr. James McDonald, three of whose sons had fought in the war, unveiled the memorial, which until then had been covered with a Union Jack, and proceeded to read the names of the dead. After a prayer of dedication, there was an address by Colonel Leather. This was followed by buglers from the Northumberland Fusiliers sounding the Last Post. After Reverend Millar had given the benediction and the National Anthem sung, friends and relatives laid wreaths at the Memorial.

It seems fitting to conclude this chapter on Belford and the Great War, with the concluding remarks of Colonel Leather's address:

My friends, it has been our endeavour to the best of our means to perpetuate the names of these fifty-four brave men, so that in the words you have heard read[1], they may not become as though they had never been. May generations yet unborn view these bronze tablets with pride, as a proof of the noble share that this little corner of Northumberland took in the Great War. May this spot be always treated as holy ground, because though their bodies lie scattered over the battlefields of the world and in the depths of the sea, nevertheless in spirit they lie buried under this Cenotaph. Let us therefore treat this place as holy, and may the Memorial Hall behind become the centre of all that is best in our social daily lives, then indeed these men will not have died in vain, and 'THEIR NAME LIVETH FOR EVERMORE'.

---

[1] A reference to the reading from Ecclesiasticus 44, 1-15

Appendix 1

Belford has two memorials to the fallen of the First World War, the main War Memorial in West Street, and a brass plaque inside the United Reform church in Nursery Lane. The names they bear are as follows:

War Memorial

First Plaque
MAJOR ERNEST A. LEATHER
CAP$^{T.}$ EDWARD W. LEATHER
LIEUT. CHRISTOPHER LEATHER
SERG$^{T.}$ ERNEST FALLA
SERG$^{T.}$ HARRY HILL
CORP$^{L.}$ THOMAS CUTHBERTSON
CORP$^{L.}$ JOHN FIFE
CORP$^{L.}$ J. R. GIBSON
CORP$^{L.}$ JOHN GRAY
CORP$^{L.}$ JOSEPH E. LANGFORD
CORP$^{L.}$ ALEX. R. RUTHERFORD
CORP$^{L.}$ GEORGE SHIELL
CORP$^{L.}$ WILLIAM TAYLOR
CORP$^{L.}$ JOHN TAYLOR

Second Plaque
L-C$^{P.L.}$ GEO. A. MATTHEWSON
BOMB$^{D.R.}$ RICHARD PRINGLE
P$^{T.E.}$ THOMAS J. ANDERSON
P$^{T.E.}$ W$^{M.}$ MABON ANDERSON
P$^{T.E.}$ WILLIAM CAMERON
P$^{T.E.}$ JAMES CLARK
P$^{T.E.}$ THOMAS COLLINS
P$^{T.E.}$ ERNEST W. CURRINS
P$^{T.E.}$ GEORGE DUNLOP
P$^{T.E.}$ ANDREW ENGLISH
P$^{T.E.}$ JAMES FORREST
P$^{T.E.}$ WILLIAM GRAY
P$^{T.E.}$ ROBERT GRAY
P$^{T.E.}$ JOHN WHITE

Third Plaque
P$^{T.E.}$ ROBERT HALL
P$^{T.E.}$ JOHN HARVEY
P$^{T.E.}$ JOHN HARVEY
P$^{T.E.}$ WILLIAM HALL
P$^{T.E.}$ JAMES HOGG
P$^{T.E.}$ WILLIAM HOGG
P$^{T.E.}$ WILLIAM HOOD
P$^{T.E.}$ GEORGE L. HOPE
P$^{T.E.}$ THOMAS HUNTER
P$^{T.E.}$ ROBERT HUNTER
P$^{T.E.}$ JAMES LEE
P$^{T.E.}$ JAMES M^{C}DOUGALL
P$^{T.E.}$ DAVID M^{C}NICHOL
BOMB$^{D.R.}$ W$^{M.}$ H. CLOTHIER

Fourth Plaque
P$^{T.E.}$ JAMES PUNTON
P$^{T.E.}$ JOHN THO$^{S.}$ ROGERS
P$^{T.E.}$ WILLIAM SMITH
P$^{T.E.}$ GEORGE TAYLOR
P$^{T.E.}$ JOHN THOMPSON
P$^{T.E.}$ JAMES WEALLEANS
P$^{T.E.}$ ROBERT WILSON
P$^{T.E.}$ ALFRED WYLIE
P$^{T.E.}$ R.E. YOUNGER
G$^{N.R.}$ JAMES EDMUND HALL
G$^{N.R.}$ WILLIAM TURNBULL
D$^{V.R.}$ JAMES CRAMMOND
R. D. ROGERS, R.N.
GEORGE W. YOUNG, R.N.

United Reform Church Memorial

HARRY HILL	WILLIAM H. CLOTHIER	WILLIAM HOOD
WILLIAM ANDERSON	ROBERT HUNTER	JOHN J.W. THOMPSON
THOMAS J. ANDERSON	GEORGE MATTHEWSON	THOMAS HUNTER
ALEX$^{R.}$ RUTHERFORD	JOHN M^{C}DOUGALL	GEORGE L. HOPE
GEORGE W. YOUNG	JAMES LEE	ALFRED WYLIE
JOHN THOMPSON	JOHN TAYLOR	WILLIAM HALL

The Tyne Cot Memorial on which are recorded the names of:- Ernest Falla, John R. Gibson, George A. Matthewson and John McDougall.

Memorial to the 149th Infantry Brigade, which included the 4th, 5th, 6th and 7th Northumberland Fusiliers, at St. Jean on the outskirts of Ypres.

The Menin Gate at Ypres on which are recorded the names of:- James Clark, James Hogg, Edward W. Leather, David McNichol and John W. Renton.

Acknowledgements:

For help received, particular thanks are due to the following individuals and organisations: Tony Brown; Florent Denaghel; Sue Dyer; Alison McDonald; George McDonald; George Nairn; Audrey Petrie; and the late Hilda Shields.
Lesley Frater and the Staff of the Northumberland Fusiliers' Museum, Alnwick
The Staff of the K.O.S.B. Museum Berwick-upon-Tweed
The Staff of the National Archives, Kew
The Staff of Newcastle Central Library, Newcastle upon Tyne

Sources:

Buckley, F. *The War History of the 7th Northumberland Fusiliers* T. Grierson 1919

Evans, Martin Marix *Over the Top* Arctura Publishing 2002

Flower, Newman, ed. *The History of the Great War* The Waverley Book Company Limited n.d.

Gibson, Stair *K.O.S.B. in the Great War* Thomas Nelson 1930

Gilbert, Martin *Atlas of the First World War* Routledge 1994

Lloyd Allan *The War in the Trenches* Book Club Associates 1976

Neillands, Robin *Attrition* Robson Books 2001

Reports from the *Berwick Advertiser* and *Berwick Journal* 1914 -1922;

Citations in the *London Gazette.*

The *St. George's Gazette*.

Regimental War Diaries for:
   The Base Remount Depot;
   1st Battalion Coldstream Guards;
   2nd and 7th Battalions Northumberland Fusiliers;
   4th Battalion Tyneside Scottish;
   15th Battalion Durham Light Infantry;
   10th Battalion East Yorkshire Regiment; and
   Women's Army Auxiliary Corps, Abbeville Area.

9

THE EVACUATION STORY
by Valerie Glass

Operation Pied Piper

The evacuation of people living in Britain's cities to 'safer' areas at the beginning of the Second World War was the biggest mass movement of people in British history. It took just over 4 days, involved over 3 million people, mainly children, and, for many, was short-lived as they returned home within months. Yet the impact of being uprooted from their family at an early age, and transported to a new and strange rural environment, had a powerful effect and one that many surviving former evacuees are able to recall clearly to this day.

This chapter is an attempt to recount some of the memories and experiences of children who were evacuated to Belford 70 years ago. It has been compiled from personal accounts written in response to requests made in 2008/09 for information, and from documentary evidence such as School Log Books and local and national regulations for the evacuation process. An account written in 1995 by the daughter of the Headteacher of a school in Newcastle is also included. In some cases, personal memories differ in small details from the official School Log Books but, for the most part, they are surprisingly consistent after a gap of up to 70 years.

The Log Books and other documents put the evacuation to Belford into context, but it is the accounts from evacuees themselves which provide fascinating details of their experiences. The strength of these memories belies the relatively short time the children must have actually spent in Belford, in most cases only a few months or even weeks. John Wake, whose father had already been recalled to the RAF, came in the first group, accompanied by his mother as a helper. His stay lasted from September 1939 until Christmas 1940, longer than most, but the details of his stay are as clear and vivid as ever. His emotional attachment to Belford resulted in regular return visits after the war up to recent times. He could remember clearly how they were told about the evacuation:

> On Tuesday 29th August 1939 we were given letters for our parents saying that the Chillingham Road School would close and that all the children would be taken into the country. This letter enclosed the familiar luggage label which had our names age etc. and a list of items which should be packed, change of clothes and sandwiches for us to eat when we arrived at our destination.

But what sort of preparations had gone into these arrangements? The Government had been anticipating this turn of events for some time and the authorities were well-briefed. With the threat of war between Germany and England becoming a real possibility, plans for evacuation were made during the summer of 1938. Sir John Anderson, who was placed in charge of the scheme, decided to divide the country into three zones:

- Evacuation (people living in urban districts where heavy bombing raids could be expected);
- Neutral (areas that would neither send nor take evacuees);
- Reception (rural areas where evacuees would be sent).

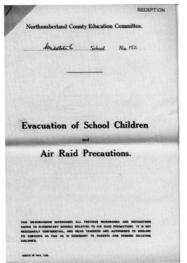

Newcastle-upon-Tyne became an Evacuation Zone and Northumberland, including Belford, a Reception Zone. Efforts were made by the government to forewarn the general public of the need for these arrangements. In Northumberland, for example, Headteachers were issued with memoranda during 1938 which were stated to be *not necessarily confidential and Head Teachers are authorised to disclose contents as far as it is necessary to parents and persons billeting children.* Headteachers were also attending briefing sessions regarding air-raid precautions and evacuation.

On 24th April 1939, Thomas S. Braund, who had been appointed Headteacher five years earlier, recorded in the Log Book of Chillingham Road Boys School, Heaton, Newcastle-upon-Tyne:

Standard VIA and VIB were combined to leave the Headmaster free to attend to urgent matters relating to the evacuation of schoolchildren and requisitions.

Meanwhile, Mr Graham, Head of Belford School, received a letter from

Chillingham Road School, Newcastle

Belford Rural District Council, dated 29th April 1939, stating that the evacuation process in that area would last 2 days, involving 200 persons each day and that, in order to assist the Billeting Officers, he and his staff should meet the train arriving at 12.32 p.m.. He noted in the Log Book on 10th July 1939:

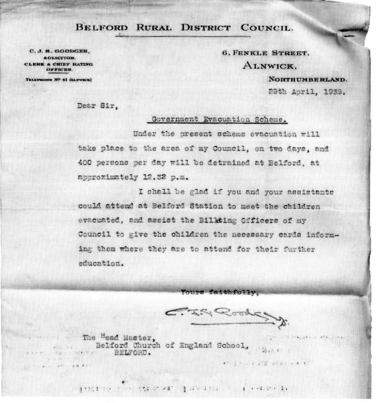

Belford R.D.C. letter to Mr Graham

I shall be absent from school for part of the afternoon in order to attend a meeting of Billeting Officers in connection with Evacuation of School children.

The likelihood of war escalated dramatically during the summer of 1939. A document dated 16th August 1939, drawn up by the L.N.E.R., detailed the transport arrangements for children in the North East Group of evacuation areas. In the case of Belford, up to 400 children were to be received from Chillingham Road School in Heaton, Newcastle-upon-Tyne, accompanied by teachers and some parents acting as helpers. On 28th August 1939 an entry in the Chillingham Road Log Book recorded:

No registers marked. School assembled at 8.30 am for an Evacuation Rehearsal and was later dismissed.

Normal routine was followed the next day and on 31st August:

School dismissed at 3.30 pm to prepare for evacuation.

The final entry reads:

1 September 1939: School evacuated to the following places - Belford, Bamburgh, Seahouses, Norham.

During the war Newcastle Local Education Authority required Head teachers to keep a separate wartime Log Book.
Operation Pied Piper was about to begin!

Almost all of the personal accounts described the journey from Heaton to Belford. Barbara Kennedy (née Braund) was the daughter of the Head of Chillingham Road and came with her parents to Belford, instead of accompanying her classmates to a school in Cumberland. She had clear recollections of her departure from Manors station on that Friday morning and her arrival at Belford:

> *We were shepherded into the cattle mart buildings where the Billeting Officer set to work to house all the children. We were each given a carrier bag of rations which among other things contained a tin of corned beef and a bar of chocolate...eventually a kind gentleman took us in his car. As we went up the sweeping front drive I remember wondering what we had come to - the large grey stone house with its pillared porch looked very imposing, quite different from our neat little semi-detached with small front garden! It was explained to us the Croft had been the dower house to Belford Hall but was now owned by a Mr and Mrs Purves.....*

The experience of being taken to the cattle market is one recalled by several respondents. John Wake spoke of the journey:

> *On Thursday 31st August the whole school assembled at 9 am and we were sorted into groups, infants and senior boys were sent to Belford and the junior classes were sent to Norham. There were exceptions, juniors who had younger brothers or sisters were sent to Belford. As soon as the sorting had been done we were walked in line to Heaton station, and boarded a special train, front carriages Norham, and the remainder for Belford.*
>
> *Those of us for Belford arrived about midday, and were then walked to the Auction mart where we were chosen by the local people who had volunteered to take part in the scheme. Because my mother was with us, no one could accommodate us, and we were eventually taken home by Miss Newbould, who was in charge of the billeting arrangements. ....For me this was a lovely place. The Newbould house was just off the North Bank, with a wood next to it and the old quarry on the opposite side, wonderful places for a small boy to explore, and the crags just at the top of the hill were a real bonus.*

John Williamson was aged 10 when he was evacuated.

> *I remember being taken from Belford station to the cattle market. We were allocated to families. My brother and I were taken in by a Mrs Young who ran the local grocers, Youngs. It was opposite the Blue Bell pub. We were very*

well looked after. It wasn't as dramatic for us as it seems to have been for some other children. You read all sorts of stories but for us everything was very well organised. I don't remember being excited or scared. It was just something that happened. We accepted it.

Evening Chronicle 22 July 2009

Nancy Houstin was only four years old at the time, and came with older sister Jean and her mother:

I remember that we assembled in the school yard where we were lined up and given a brown paper carrier bag containing various items. The only thing I remember about the contents was a chocolate bar. Did we also have an arm -band identifying us and also a label to hang round our necks? And of course we had our gas masks too.

It proved more difficult to secure billets for children accompanied by mothers and, probably for this reason, Nancy and her sister Jean were sent to Seahouses.

Not all of the children who came to Belford came from Chillingham Road School. William White was a pupil at West Jesmond Primary School. His school was due to be evacuated to Woodburn, near Bellingham:

My mother just didn't want her little treasure being cared for by alien hands in Woodburn, when he could be safely tucked up with his grandma in Seahouses.

Being a resourceful soul, she found out that Chillingham Road School was being evacuated to Belford, just a bus ride from Seahouses, so on the appointed day I was taken round there with my gas mask and little bundle of clothes and told to keep quiet while mother made me a bogus pupil of this school. I remember her quite clearly pointing to the list and asking the official why my name was not on it. 'Of course he goes to this school'', I remember her saying, reaching behind and putting her hand over my mouth, 'Why isn't his name on the list?'. The poor chap gave in to her strictures, put my name on the list and off I went with all the genuine pupils of the school, to the Central Station, where we were put on the train to Belford. We were given a carrier bag of provisions containing corned beef and a few other wartime delicacies to hand over as a sweetener to our host families.

Fortunately, the other children were too apprehensive about the whole operation to take much of an interest in my presence amongst them and anyway a railway journey was a rare and exciting event in those days, so their curiosity was diverted from the stranger in their midst.

On arrival at Belford, I remember we were herded into a shed, where no less apprehensive hosts were introduced to their evacuees, but I just ran up all

smiles to my Grandma and we were quickly ensconced on the bus to begin a
blissful sojourn in Seahouses.

After a short stay at Seahouses, William left when his father was transferred to
Leamington Spa but, in the latter part of the war, he returned to the area and
attended Belford School.

Doris Palmer travelled by bus with her mother as a pre-school evacuee so was
spared the experience of being picked out at the cattle mart:

I can remember getting on the bus at the Haymarket Bus Station, Newcastle-
on-Tyne. The bus was always a single Decker, and all the windows were
blacked out. I have always been a bad bus traveller, and the dark bus didn't
help. We used to get off beside the Blue Bell Hotel and hire a taxi to take us
up to Craggy.

Marion Austin (nee Hall) had an amusing story to tell!

I was eight years old and (my brother) Sid was thirteen. We left Chillingham
Road School on buses with many other children, and then we were out on a
train for hours going from one place to another & eventually reached Belford,
we were taken to the cattle market and many people were there to choose
the children they wanted to look after. While we were on the train my
brother got friendly with a boy called Walter Hall & decided to say he was our
brother. Consequently we were the last three children left because no-one
wanted three children! Two gentlemen then took us to a very large Victorian
House on the Main Road. There were two old ladies living there and were
told they had to take us in because they had plenty of room.

A villager remembered the arrival of the evacuees:

It was sometime in September 1939 when the evacuees arrived in Belford.
They travelled by special trains from Newcastle and I think they were
evacuated by school groups along with some of their teachers. We had two
sisters come to live with our family, they were about the same age as me (I
was six) and we became great friends. They were pupils from Chillingham
Road, Heaton. (JM)

Official railway documentation records that on Friday 1st September 1939, a day
later than John Wake remembered it, Train No. 121 left Heaton railway station
at 10.20 a.m. bound for Belford and Tweedmouth. A smaller number of pupils
from Chillingham Road School were to disembark at Tweedmouth, bound for
Norham. Head teachers had been instructed that mothers were not permitted on
the station platform. It is not difficult to imagine the distress of parents

reluctantly agreeing to safeguard the welfare of their children by sending them to what may as well have been seen as 'foreign parts'. Recognising this, a Nurse or Medical Officer was to be posted on the platform of each departure station. The train was due to arrive in Belford at 12.32 p.m. From there, the children would walk the mile into the village to be collected by residents willing to billet them.

The scale of evacuation was massive: 6350 children would leave from Heaton Station on each of the first two days of September. Although the practical arrangements for the physical movement of children had been drawn up with great care, much less attention was paid to preparing the families for the emotional impact of evacuation, and even less to preparing the receiving families. In many cases, the allocation of children seems to have been carried out on an ad-hoc basis, unimaginable in today's climate of child protection and accountability.

Settling In

At that time, Belford School was a relatively small one with approximately 160 pupils aged 5 to 14 years. School reopened after the Summer Holiday on 28th August 1939 and, on the 29th, notice was received that evacuation would take place the following day. It was planned that the school would close for at least three days during this process. In the event it did not re-open until 11th September. The Railway Documents predicted maximum number of 400 pupils did not materialise; the Belford School Log Book entry for Friday 1st September records:

85 scholars chiefly from Chillingham Road

No.	NAME	
10.	White	William G.
24	Wakenshaw	James
71	Watson	Stuart R.
86	Wakenshaw	Lilian M.
87	White	Hilda
103	Watson	Yvonne E.
104	Wilson	Jennie
148	Watson	June
149	White	Lilian
177	Wake	John
178	Wake	Pamela
185	Whitaker	William
192	Woodhall	Dorothy
196	White	Janetta A.
197	White	Margaret C.
209	White	James J.
246	Whittingham	Hilary
247	Whittingham	Garth.
263	Waddell	Norman
265	Watson	Ernest
269	Watson	Basil
275	Watson	William Alexander.
323	Walker	Rhoda
327	Walker	Lily.
362	Williamson	Patricia.
355	Watson	Stella
381	Wilson	Ann Shirley
396	Wright	Isobel
414	White	William H.
415	White	Rosemary
433	White	Hazel.
434.	Weallans	Margaret.
435.	Weallans	John.
458.	Weallans	Daphne.
484	Willis	Sarah Maureen
485	Willis	Isobel Beatrice

Section of Belford School admissions register showing the evacuees in red

Chillingham Road pupils on the steps of Belford Hall, Mr Braund on the top right
Courtesy of Barbara Kennedy

School arrived today and have been billeted in or near the village. Most of the scholars are senior boys.
Mr Braund brought with him seven teachers, two students and five helpers.

The following day Mr Graham recorded:
Mothers and young children arrived but there were four scholars of school age. I made an effort for permission to use the Ferguson Hall as a place for recreation but have not yet had a definite answer.
The request obviously fell on sympathetic ears as, instead of the Ferguson Hall (belonging to the local Presbyterian Church), the larger premises of Belford Hall were offered. This grand 18th century Palladian mansion had lain empty for almost 20 years. Village children had been used to playing in it, so it was probably not in a very good state, but it had the advantage of space, with landscaped grounds and a field, just right for the various activities Mr Braund had to organise when the children were not attending lessons.
I remember Leslie Ridley leaving the goalmouth rather quickly when a cow came across the field to see what was happening! We town folk hadn't much experience with large animals like that!.....We were allowed to shelter in the main room at the front if it was wet but the rest of the building was considered unsafe. I think it was owned by Mr McLaren who owned the local quarries. It was in poor repair - I think he had plans to repair it and convert it into flats. I was naughty one day and went off exploring upstairs and in the

back. It was dilapidated but nothing fell down on me! The first room opening off from the steps had large mirrors round the walls and the next room had red walls with white plaster work. I can also remember opening a door upstairs onto a precipitous flight of stairs which must have been the servants' stairs down to the kitchen area. I felt so sorry for the maids who must have had to toil up and down to those awful stairs with coal and hot and cold water. We can only have used the place for a short time - I don't remember going there after the weather became cold. (BK)

When we were not at school we spent time at Belford Hall where we had lessons outdoors or in a large room at the front of the hall some afternoons we were taken on walks into the surrounding area and had lessons in drawing plants, fences and dry stone walls.
On one of these we were invited to visit the Manse for buns and lemonade; however it was one of those days when wasps were on the warpath and many of us were stung much to the dismay of the minister and his wife. (JW)

There were plenty of happy memories of winter in Belford:
The winter was very cold and the snow lay on the road for weeks, with a snowplough every day, all it seemed to do was polish the road which was great for sliding on. Sledges were in great demand, and the bicycle and radio shop did a roaring trade, 3s6d each (17p) the slope used by the boys (I can't recall any girls taking part) was behind Miss Newbould's house and went right down to the burn, the art was to turn quickly at the bottom avoiding the trees and a ducking. (JW)

When the snow came I bought a sledge for sixpence and spent hours with most of the school and the local children too. I can't remember where we were but I have a mental picture still of a sloping field with a frozen stream at the bottom, somewhere at the top of the village. (BK)
Present day children in Belford still sledge on this slope!

The Headteacher quickly secured a supply of books, magazines and games from villagers. A further eight girls from Richard Gardner Secondary School, Tynemouth, arrived a few days later. A temporary timetable (double shift) for educating both the Belford and evacuee pupils was implemented, with Belford children attending in the mornings and evacuees in the afternoons, on a fortnightly rotation.
On Monday we started school and we shared the old village school with the local children - half-days only, one week in the mornings and the next in the

afternoons, alternate weeks, so we didn't get to know the locals much except in our billets. The old school was down a lane and over a stream, and I was thrilled to see a snipe wading at the edge of the water - a bird I had never seen. (BK)

With such a large influx of children to the village our little school-the Old School at the time- was bursting at the seams. The problem was resolved by the evacuees attending the school in the mornings and us local children attending in the afternoons, the system alternating the following week. You can imagine how popular that system was with us school children! (JM)

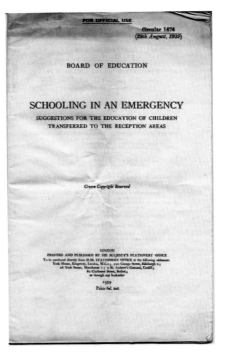

Mr Braund and Mr Graham collaborated on a scheme of work *based on local conditions and text books available.* The Chillingham Road pupils had been followed by several privately evacuated children, making an overall total of 150 at the school, of whom 95 were evacuees. The building in which the children were taught was a small Victorian one, so it was very cramped despite the double shift system. Over half of the Chillingham Road scholars were of senior age.

Barbara Kennedy was correct in her recollection of the time spent at Belford Hall not lasting long; regrettably the use of the Hall lasted only two weeks because it was needed by the military authorities. Permission, however, was obtained for the use of the field and the garden at the new school site which was being built at the top of West Street. Already the school had received visits from the H.M.I. and local authority advisers for P.E. and Horticulture. The latter promptly ordered tools to enable work to begin on the school garden. When these were delayed the boys, for it was deemed a boys-only activity, provided their own spades!

Both evacuees and soldiers seem to have been warmly received by villagers:
Another memory was of a convoy of soldiers who stopped in the road up to the Hall and who made their way through the trees to Mrs Purves's garden fence and she and Peggy and Hilda made them all cups of tea. I can see them

Bless my life! what's this I see?
If it isn't a little EVACUEE
Don't be afraid
when it's dark at night.
They simply can't put out my light.

now dashing out with a huge teapot! (BK)

One little five year old was evacuated to Belford all on her own, with only her gas mask - no change of clothes, no spare shoes, not even a cuddly toy. She was taken in by a lovely couple who cherished her as their own, bought her new clothes and toys and eventually adopted her. It is nice to think that some good came out of that experience. (BK)

The Headteacher, however, noted that, after a weekend when soldiers were billeted in the school, some of the library books went missing.

The evacuees wrote a play with the title *The Mystery of the Crags*. An original copy survives and even lists the names of the actors.

Some of the older evacuees wrote a play based on an invasion and the boys hiding in crevices to attack them. (JW)

We thought it was terrific and I thoroughly enjoyed the rehearsals even though I only had a small part. It was produced at the end of term at a Farewell Concert but unfortunately we had already been recalled by then and father had to go back before the rest of the

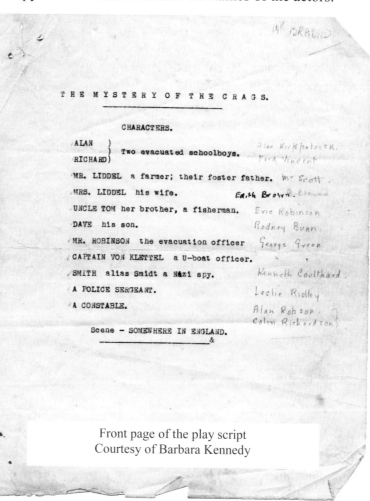

Front page of the play script
Courtesy of Barbara Kennedy

school to get things ready and, although he went to Belford on the bus for the day, I had a cold and wasn't allowed to go. My part in the play was taken at short notice by one of the local girls - Edith Brown. (BK)

Visits by the school medical officer and dentist were made during the first two months.

The school dentist came in a caravan which was parked in the playground. He was a nice young man and I didn't mind having three teeth filled by him. (BK)

Just four weeks into the new arrangements 14 evacuees had returned home, fear of air raids in Newcastle proving less daunting than remaining away from the family. By the end of October only 53 of the original number remained, and this had reduced to 40 at the end of November. Some of the teachers from Newcastle returned home as the children left. On 16th November the school received a visit from the Assistant Director of Education for Northumberland for the purpose of discussing *the difficulties under the emergency conditions and future organisation.* The reduced numbers meant that all the younger Belford pupils were able to return to full-time schooling in December. Holidays for the teachers were staggered so that some of the Newcastle staff were on duty to look after the evacuees during the school holidays, although most returned home temporarily for Christmas.

The first Air Raid Warning during school hours took place on 29th January 1940. The arrangements seemed to work well, with children living outside the village being sent home with those living within it. However, the children's first experience of a warning had already taken place earlier than they could possibly have expected:

On Sunday 3rd September we were all assembled at the school and walked to the church, where the vicar announced that war had been declared, we all met up again in the afternoon when there was an air raid warning, and were lined up along the side of the walled garden on North Bank, in hindsight not a good place. (JW)

George Green was one of three older boys billeted, like the Braund family, at The Croft. He often spoke of his time at Belford to his son, Ray:

We know this was a particularly happy time of

George Green, Norman Easton and Kenneth Coulthard in the Purves's garden
Courtesy of Barbara Kennedy

his life......He always told me he learned to drive here - in a wagon. The Purves family at The Croft were hauliers. I remember a photo of father with one or two other boys posing on a wagon with a big house behind, presumably, The Croft. Then the Army arrived in Belford and the Officers were billeted at The Croft so the evacuees were moved out and into the village. Father moved into a hairdressers. Apparently he had to brush the hair up off the floor. Whenever we drove through Belford when I was younger he always pointed out the arched entrance to Middleton Hall. His class had often walked here to sketch the arch.

George was not alone in remembering walks to Middleton:

Other activities included long walks and sketching. I well remember my drawing of the Gatehouse to Middleton Hall which came out rather well. At other times we learnt about wild flowers. (BK)

John Wake recalled:

I was involved in the concerts held regularly in the Memorial Hall (I could sing then) but then moved to the new hall.

One of the advantages of having troops in the village were film shows and ENSA concert parties in the Memorial Hall to which everyone was invited, an excellent alternative to travelling by bus to the cinema in Berwick.

Films at the Hall in West Street (now Belford Community Club) proved very popular:

During the war years films were shown at the Memorial Hall, on the north side of West Street in Belford. We remembered seeing Will Hay and George Formby, Charles Laughton in 'Mutiny on the Bounty' and a film called 'I Walked with a Zombie', which gave us sleepless nights! (WW)

The 'Memorial Hall' up West Street was turned into a cinema. This was Government policy to keep people at home and stop them raking about seeking amusement further afield. We went often and absorbed all the George Formbys, the Abbot and Costellos and Laurel and Hardys. Towards the end of the war we were told we must see the film taken when Belsen and another of the Nazi Death Camps were opened. This affected the crowds at the cinema that night to such an extent that no-one spoke when departing. (MB)

Evacuation was not such a happy experience for everyone. Margaret Burn (née Leybourne) who arrived in early 1940 remembered:

We went, with our mother, as evacuees in the spring of 1940, after repeated

German bombing on Tyneside and night after night in next door's shelter.
Then I was just 10, Douglas 7½, Alison 2½ and Christine just under 1½.
Mother and the babies were Grandma's evacuees and Douglas and I were
Auntie Margaret's up the North Bank. She ran the shop while Uncle Tommy
was in the forces. Many women in Belford had to get on with things on their
own.
Douglas and I went to Belford School for the summer term of that year. I
hated it. We were mocked for talking 'posh', the big boys were rough. I
watched with fascinated disbelief when one of them, while being caned,
wrenched the cane from the teacher - much smaller than he was. I learned
'Ducks' and 'The Highwayman' and have never forgotten them.

On 11th March 1940 the number of evacuees had decreased sufficiently for Mr
Braund to return to Newcastle, leaving the evacuees in the care of Miss Bailes.
The new wartime Log Book states:

14 March 1940: Chillingham Road Senior Boys School reopened at North
Heaton School working on a double shift.

Belford school held an Open Day for the evacuees on 16th March 1940 and
many of the parents travelled to it from Newcastle, being entertained to tea after
a concert. By the beginning of the Summer term, only 18 evacuees from
Chillingham Road remained, as well as eight from other schools. This period
became known as the 'phoney war' - the country had been geared up to expect
an early invasion which did not materialise. Those who remained were taught
in the existing school building, while the Belford pupils moved to the new
school on West Street in May 1940, together with pupils from the small
Middleton school which was closed.

Soldiers became a frequent sight in the village:

Late February/early March saw the local T.A. unit march out of the village to
join up with the 4th Battalion Northumberland Fusiliers in Alnwick {they
marched all the way}. They took part in the battles in front of Dunkirk and
suffered heavy casualties; one of the survivors was awarded the Military
Medal. In June or July there was a huge convoy of army vehicles passing
through the village following the German invasion of Norway, they were all
large saloons, many of them carried inscriptions 'Donated by the Government
of Canada' and took about 4 hours to pass through with some of them
refuelling at 'Nixon's' garage. (JW)

Military traffic and personnel abounded. The Duke of Cornwall's Light
Infantry(?) were stationed at Belford and I can see a few of us teenagers
(though that wasn't a word) sitting on Pringles' shop steps or round the

Market Cross talking and giggling with some of the lads, in 1944 on their way to the D Day landings. How many survived? (MB)

Nance Turnbull, Belford born and bred, remembered fondly the Royal Scots and the Seaforths playing *The Retreat* on Sundays at the market place during the war years. Margaret Rogers had many memories of life in Belford during the 1940s. Her family ran the Post Office and she remembered the counter being extra busy with soldiers and airmen:

Any registered mail and HVPs (High Value Packets) had to be carefully guarded as some contained money. Often they were hidden in the house bread bin rather than be kept in the safe! A signed receipt had to be obtained when delivering registered mail and the slip "gloyed" into its numbered place in a book. One flew away on a gusty day and the postman wrote in the space "Gone with the Wind".

One year after the evacuation, Belford had seen a number of changes. There was a new Headteacher at Belford, Mr Dowson, Mr Graham having left for a new appointment at Lynemouth Council School. Most of the evacuees had returned home and a new school with superior facilities had been opened. Although some evacuees remained until the end of the war, the Belford School Log Book makes few references to them. The new wartime Log Book for Chillingham Road School must have remained in Newcastle, as there are no entries at all written from the places of evacuation.

At Belford there is frequent mention of activities to support the war effort such as the collection of rose-hips, Scrap Metal and Rubber Drives, Warship Week, Fire Watching by staff, jam making for the school canteen using rhubarb brought in by the children and Salute the Soldier. After a visit in October 1942 from an official from the Ministry, Mrs Feeny, who wished to secure the co-operation of the school and the school children, it was decided to make a school metal and rubber dump:

There is no doubt about the enthusiasm with which the children have taken to the scrap metal drive. Start of school was delayed 10 minutes this morning while barrow loads of metal were wheeled up West Street.

Belford School Log Book

We used to scour the hedgerows collecting rosehips which we handed in to our various classrooms- great competition as to which class had the most- and then the school duly sent them off to be made into rosehip syrup, rich in Vitamin C, when oranges were difficult to find. (JM)

The Log Book refers to over 100 lbs. of gooseberry jam being made and 16½

61

16th Oct 1942. During the past fortnight the children and Junior Youth Service League gathered 16½ stone Rose Hips and 672 lbs Horse Chestnuts.

Extract from Belford School Log Book

stone of rose hips and 672 lbs. of horse chestnuts being collected in 1942!

Another campaign from school was for collecting wisps of sheep's wool that were found snagged on the fences and gorse bushes etc. although I have no idea what it was eventually used for when it was sent away.
One campaign, in particular, 'Salute the Soldier', in this case I vividly recall the excitement of riding in a Bren Gun Carrier- a small tank-like tracked vehicle! (JM)

Salute the Soldier was a National Savings Campaign which, in December 1944, resulted in Chillingham Road pupils back in Newcastle (by then the number on roll was about 500) investing a total of £1,025.

Locals missed their visits to the beach:
The beaches were closed to the public at this time and access was barred by large concrete blocks and festoons of barbed wire. Some of the beaches were rumoured to be mined and some - Ross, in particular - were used as artillery firing ranges. How we longed to go on the sands! (JM)

Boys over 12 were permitted time off from school to help in potato picking due to the shortage of adult labour. In July 1941, the children visited Middleton woods to fetch material to camouflage the walls of the school. We can assume the remaining evacuees took part in these efforts.

The Final Years
By January 1942, only five evacuees remained. After most of the Chillingham Road pupils returned to Newcastle with Mr Braund and staff, they endured months of regular air raids. His school was then evacuated to Windermere, but the Log Book provides no details of the numbers

Courtesy of Fiona Renner-Thompson

Private evacuees Jack and Ron Cameron gardening at Renner's farm involved. The school re-opened a few weeks later, and was forced to operate a double shift system as they had at Belford, because there were insufficient air raid shelters. Mr Braund was recalled from Windermere in April 1941, and again took charge at Chillingham Road. The school now became a mixed one for girls and boys.

The end of the war saw Belford School join in village celebrations. There was an extended holiday for *Victory in Europe,* and the children enjoyed massed country dancing in the afternoons - obviously a rare treat! A concert in aid of the *Welcome Home Fund* raised £50. The Belford pupils gave a performance of the play written by the evacuees, and sent photographs to Mr Braund and family back in Newcastle:

I was so pleased to think that our work had been used and that we had been remembered. (BK)

Regardless of the question of the rights and wrongs of evacuation, the experience was one that has not been forgotten by participants. Those who contributed their recollections spoke overwhelmingly of happy and amusing memories. Most have spoken of the positive aspects of living in a small village which must have seemed a very long way from Tyneside.

This scholar clearly enjoyed his stay and was reluctant to return home:

Much to my dismay we had to return to Newcastle at Christmas, I wanted to come back to Belford but my mother's deafness worsened and she was unable to do the shopping etc. on her own. Ironically having been evacuated to avoid the expected bombing at the beginning of the war, our house was bombed in April 1941. (JW)

And the enthusiasm in this writer's memories shines out:

There were two cottages at the front overlooking all the fields and it was lovely. There was a cottage next door, and two more at the back, which later on, were made into 1 cottage. We had to go down into a field where there was a well, to collect all the water we needed, and guess who got this job, when I was older. All the water had to be boiled. Our toilet, was one of two at the back of the cottages. These middens were emptied by men with a wagon. Behind the cottages there was a wood, and we collected all the firewood we needed, and we always left enough wood for the next occupier. We didn't live there permanently, but came back and forwards during the year. When it was hay-making time Tommy Riddell used to let me sit on the wagon, it was great fun. There were also many farm kittens, and I used to dress them up. There was also an old caravan to play in, and I can remember using it to play shops.

There was a wash-house which my mam and aunties used when we had company if needed. At the very back of the cottages there were crags, which I can remember climbing. Once at the top you could see Bamburgh and Seahouses. I also used to make and fly my home made kites. (DP)

For young children from industrial Newcastle, Belford must have seemed like a rural idyll! The village obviously left a deep impression upon her, and it comes as no surprise to learn that Doris spent her honeymoon at Craggy in 1956, returning regularly during the following years. Another who returned for a honeymoon at *The Blue Bell* in 1948 was George Green. How many more may have done so?

William White held happy memories of not only Belford and its school but of Mr Dowson, the Headteacher:

I went to school in Belford where at last I found some much needed stability in life and I flourished. I still have the Standard IV class prize from December 1944, signed by Mr Dowson, the then Headmaster. He was a very influential figure in my life because he was the first person to tell me that I had some academic abilities, 'If you work hard' he added, in headmasterly fashion. I think they had somehow got lost in all my wanderings up to then but he was clear about it and happily he was right. He was a great schoolmaster......He stimulated my interest in science, which I kept up at secondary school and university.

I also remember him giving me the cane for slacking, remarking afterwards: 'Yes, you're a bright lad, but your life won't be a bed of roses.' How right he was.

Marion Austin was clearly unhappy at leaving her mother at the age of 8 and made an abortive attempt to walk back to Newcastle after only two days stay, which she remembered later as *a few weeks*. She returned home to her mother and was later evacuated to Keswick where she had a happier experience. Her eventual return to Belford was reassuring:

I didn't go back to Belford until 35 years later with my husband. Found the big house I stayed in and noticed in the garden some kiddies' toys, a swing and bicycles and was thrilled to see it as a happy family home and enjoyed walking around this pretty village. And laid the Ghosts so to speak.

It is remarkable that so many vivid memories have survived from what was, in fact, a very short time in the space of a lifetime. Two generations later they still retain the flavour of what it was like to be a wartime evacuee. Some of these contributors were able, like John Wake, to pay regular visits back to Belford in the intervening years. A few eventually made their homes here. As Margaret Burn remarked: *Funny place, Belford, people come back to it.*

After the children left Belford, the war was to take many different turns before its conclusion. For some, there was tragedy when fathers did not return. For others there was the excitement of returning fathers and, in many cases, getting to know men who had left when they were quite young.

> *Attendance has been poor for a fortnight. Colds and jaundice prevalent. The demobilisation of fathers has had an effect on attendance as many are keeping their children from school while they visit their families or while they take a short holiday.*   Belford School Log Book December 1945

All these children were influenced in different ways by their sojourn in Belford, wherever their later lives took them.

Contributors:

My thanks go to the following people who took the time to contribute their memories: Marion Austin; Margaret Burn (MB); Ray Green, son of evacuee George Green; Nancy Houstin; Barbara Kennedy (BK); Jean Murphy* (JM); Doris Palmer (DP); Margaret Rogers*; Nance Turnbull*; the late John Wake (JW); William H. White (WW); John Williamson.
* Belford resident

Names of other Evacuees mentioned in Contributions:

Jack Cameron*; Ron Cameron*; Kenneth Coulthard*; Norman Easton*; George Green*; Walter Hall; Leslie Ridley.
* named in photographs.

Sources:

Hunter, Colin, *The Contribution of Belford to the 2nd World War* in Belford and District Local History Society *Aspects of Belford,* Blackhall Publishers, 2008

Pears, Brian, *Evacuation from Newcastle and Gateshead in 1939* on www.genuki.org

Chillingham Road School Log Books 1922-1949 and 1940-44 Tyne and Wear Archives

Belford School Log Book Belford First School

Northumberland Education Committee: Evacuation of School Children and Air Raid Precautions, May 1939